inside **TRIATHLON**

Training Diary

A weekly log
for tracking your
multisport fitness

Edited by
Joe Friel

Printed in the United States of America.

10 9 8 7 6 5

Distributed in the United States and Canada
by Publishers Group West.

International Standard Book Number: 1-931382-16-6

Library of Congress Cataloging-in-Publication Data
Inside triathlon training diary : a weekly log for tracking your multisport fitness / edited by Joe Friel.
    p. cm.
    ISBN 1-931382-16-6
    1. Triathlon—Training—Charts, diagrams, etc. I.
    Friel, Joe. II. Inside triathlon.

GV1060.73 .I58 2002
796.42'57—dc21

                                        2002029649

VeloPress
1830 North 55th Street
Boulder, Colorado 80301–2700 USA
303/440-0601 • Fax 303/444-6788
E-mail velopress@insideinc.com

To purchase additional copies of this book or other VeloPress books, call 800/234-8356 or visit us on the Web at velopress.com.

Cover design and interior design by Susie Alvarez Perry
Cover photo by Galen Nathanson

Contents

Tracking
Your Training
by Joe Friel

Some triathletes and duathletes are good at keeping a training diary, but others see it as a waste of time. That's a shame because a carefully maintained record of training is a great tool for improving racing. Without a diary you're forced to rely on memory, which all too often recalls only exaggerated versions of what happened months, weeks, or even days before.

There are several other good reasons to keep a diary. It can serve as a positive reinforcement and boost confidence before particularly challenging races. By looking back to workouts or other races that loomed large, but were mastered, you feel assured that you have what it takes. A diary also reveals whether or not fitness is improving by comparing recent measures such as time trials, interval results, or even resting heart rates against similar standards a year or more ago when you were in great shape. In the same way, you can thumb back through a diary to discover what has and hasn't worked before. This could be a peaking procedure from an especially good race, a way of dealing with an injury that once proved successful, or a pacing strategy that worked well.

Perhaps the main argument for using a diary is in the prevention of overtraining—a necessity for nearly every serious athlete. More on this later.

WHAT IS A TRAINING DIARY?

Record keeping works best in accomplishing the above if it's in the form of both a daily log and journal. Technically, a log is a record of basic data, usually numbers, that relate to progress like miles covered or heart rates, while a journal is a record of your thoughts

1

and experiences. Log information is objective while the journal portion is subjective. Both are important. By combining the two into a diary, the information you collect covers a broader spectrum of needs.

You may decide not to use all of the spaces provided in this diary—that's okay. Whatever you write down, make it only what's important and useful to you. Everything else just gets in the way when trying to analyze your training.

The "O" Word

The most common use of the diary is the avoidance of overtraining. When it seems that training isn't going well, and you aren't quite sure why, looking back through diary notes for the last few weeks may reveal a cause. Look for phrases used repeatedly such as "feel tired" or "no snap today" or "sluggish." These are sure signs that you're doing too much—overreaching. Also check the numbers for trends and patterns. You may find that every third day or so sleep quality is poor and fatigue is high. Such a pattern is telling you to allow more recovery time between the hard workouts. Another possible sign of doing too much is when heart rate data and workout ratings don't agree. For example, your heart rate is low, but the effort seems high. Such a review of the training diary helps you decide if it's time to take a long break, or just cut back for a couple of days.

Just Say "No" to Compulsion

Keeping a diary is helpful for making progress in triathlon and duathlon, but don't let it become a handicap to your training and racing. Athletes who believe they *must* achieve and record certain numbers in their training diary each week often lose focus of what swimming, biking, and running are all about—having fun! This diary is merely a tool to help you achieve your fitness goals, and a record of what you accomplish this year. Using a training diary as described here won't guarantee your success in races. It will, however, increase the likelihood. Happy training!

HOW TO PLAN YOUR SEASON

Multisport athletes are goal driven people. Show me a triathlete or duathlete who has no desire to swim, bike, and run stronger and faster, and I'll show you an athlete who is not long for the sport. Success is not possible in multisport without high motivation. Triathlon and duathlon are just too grueling to do it in an indifferent manner. Every athlete wants to improve, but a passion to excel is nothing without a passion to prepare to excel.

Preparation is where the most erstwhile of athletes fail. Most are willing to put in endless hours on the road or in the pool, but not a minute is devoted to planning. That's a shame, because planning is the first step in achieving any goal in life, including those accomplished in endurance sports. A goal without a plan is just a wish.

Most athletes could achieve their goals by making only one small change: writing down a plan for how to train throughout the year. Just as with a diary, training plans may comprise the most minute particulars or provide just a rough outline. Regardless of the detail, better racing will result from deciding in advance what you'll do in training and when.

The Annual Training Plan (see page 14) is a tool that will help you incorporate periodization into your training. Periodization is a way of training in which fitness is built from the most basic to the more complex aspects in stages or periods. The purpose of periodization is fast racing when it counts.

The following step-by-step description guides you through each part of the Annual Training Plan that follows. It may take you thirty minutes or so to design your personal plan—time well invested. It's best to write only in pencil as things are likely to change during the season.

Step 1: Annual Hours

How many hours did you train last year? Are you capable of doing more, or do you need to cut back this year due to time constraints? Would you like to race more competitively this year, or is this a year just to maintain your race level?

The answers to these questions will help you decide how many hours to train in the coming year. There is a relationship between how many hours or miles you covered in a year and how you race. If you're unsure of your hours from last year due to poor record keeping, now is a good time to start rectifying that problem so it won't be an issue again.

Here are suggested annual hours by race distance. These are not absolutes; in other words, you don't have to train at these hours to race competitively or even complete these race distances. Some athletes do more and still race poorly. Others do less and win frequently. Also listed are suggested annual hours for junior racers.

Race Distance	Annual Hours
Ironman	600–1200
Half Ironman	500–700
International	400–600
Sprint	300–500
Juniors	200–350

Step 2: Season Goals

What are three major racing accomplishments you'd like to achieve this year? Write them down on the Annual Plan. Keep it to three or less as having more is likely to complicate your training and racing.

Goals are best if they're realistic, specific, measurable, and performance-oriented.

An example of a goal that meets these criteria is:

Break 2:30 for an international distance race by August 1.

Also write your goals on the jacket flap so that you'll see them every time you open it. Goals are most effective when they're written down and frequently reviewed.

Step 3: Training Objectives

Training objectives are the aspects of fitness or the workout performances needed to achieve your season goals. Just as with the goals, objectives are best if realistic, specific, measurable, and performance-oriented. An example of a training objective that might support the above example of a season goal is:

Run a 10k race in less than 45 minutes by July 15.

Just as with the season goals, write these objectives on the diary flap so you'll see them often.

Step 4: Week #, Mon.

In this column write in the dates of each Monday in the year. For example, January 5 is 1/5.

Step 5: Races

List all of the races you *may* do this year in the "Races" column placing them in the proper weeks according to their dates. If unsure about a particular race, list it.

Step 6: Priority

Give a priority ranking to each of the races using the following guidelines.

A-Priority Races

These are the most important races—the ones that will determine success in the coming season. They are closely related to the Season Goals at the top of the page. You will peak and taper for each of these races. Limit these to no more than four A races in a year. Two in the same week counts as one A race. It's a good idea to "clump" two or more of these races together within a two- or three-week period. That way you can peak two or three times in a season. Trying to peak more times than this prevents you from coming into top form since there's not enough time between them to re-establish fitness.

B-Priority Races

These aren't as important as the A races, so there isn't any peaking and tapering. A few days of rest, however, precedes each of them. Assign a B priority to up to eight races, again counting two in the same week as one.

C-Priority Races

These least important races are ones that you may not even do. You'll "train through them," meaning they are treated the same as hard workouts. They are best used as tune-up races before A- and B-priority races. They also make good workouts and build experience in novices. There is no limit on the number of C races, but they can interfere with training, so choose them conservatively. Frequent racing without a break is a common cause of burnout and overtraining.

Step 7: Period

This where the periodization begins. You now divide the season into periods starting with your A races. A clumping of A-priority races is called a "Race" period and may last as long as six weeks or as short as one. The week or two before each Race period, write in "Peak." Preceding each of these Peaks is a six- to ten-week "Build" period. The first Build period of the year is preceded by an eight- to twelve-week "Base" period and before that a three- to four-week "Prep" period. It's a good idea to plan for some rest after each of the Race periods by plugging in a one- to six-week "Transition."

The suggested characteristics of each of these periods are as follows.

Prep

General adaptation to training with weights, crosstraining, and swim, bike, and run drills.

Base

Gradually establish the basic fitness elements of endurance, hill strength for running and biking, and leg and arm speed. Begin muscular endurance with training near lactate threshold.

Build

Develop greater anaerobic fitness with intervals while refining muscular endurance and hill strength. Maintain endurance and leg/arm speed. Work especially on improving personal racing limiters and achieving Training Objectives.

Peak

Reduce volume and allow for more recovery days between hard workouts that simulate racing, such as bricks, and refine needed skills.

Race

A period of focused racing with greatly reduced training.

Transition

An extended period of rest and recovery.

Step 8: Hours

Write in the approximate hours you will train each week, including weights and crosstraining, based on the Weekly Training Hours table (see page 16). The actual hours you work out each week will vary from this based on many circumstances such as weather or other unexpected complications. This is a guideline only. Feel free to change it to meet your exact needs.

Divide hours between the three sports in a way that reflects the nature of the event for which you're preparing and your racing limiters. For example, most triathlons are lopsided in favor of the bike leg while the swim is relatively short. Weekly bike and swim training times may reflect this, however, if swimming is weak for you but biking is strong, favoring the swim with a disproportionately high number of hours is often a wise decision. Most duathlons are fairly well balanced as far as duration of the combined race legs, but a weakness in one might cause you to favor it.

Step 9: Most Important Workouts

Each week list the key workout types following the period guidelines offered above in Step 7. You might list something such as "form drills," "three-hour ride," or "run intervals."

HOW TO USE THIS DIARY

A training diary is only as useful as you make it. If you record little or write in it inconsistently, a diary has little value. On the other hand, recording lots of needless data that you never look at again not only wastes time, but also makes it harder to analyze later. The key is to write down immediately following every workout what was important, and nothing more. The longer you wait, the greater the possibility you'll forget something or those feelings will erode.

To ensure that it's used, keep this diary in a place that you go to following every workout, such as near where workout gear is kept. That way you see it and are more likely to write in it right away. Your log is a constant reminder of your goals and progress. Filling it out after every workout will help to keep you on track throughout the season.

The following describes the various parts of the diary pages that make up most of this book. You may decide not to use some parts, or you may want to modify the information you record in other parts from what is suggested here. The most important point is that you keep an accurate record of training and racing for future reference. The bold headings listed here are the parts of each diary page.

WEEK BEGINNING: 3/17/03   **PLANNED WEEKLY HOURS:** 15:00

Week's goals (check off as achieved)

✓ Run 4 x 1 mile at 7:30 pace with 90 second recoveries

✓ Ride 6 x 1 mile hill repeats in various gears — easy to hard

✓ Conduct a 1500-meter time trial

Week Beginning

At the start of each week indicate Monday's date. These correspond with the "Week #, Mon." column of the Annual Training Plan.

6

Planned Weekly Hours

The approximate number of hours you plan to train this week are recorded here based on what you wrote on the Annual Training Plan in the "Hours" column. This is a rough guideline only. You may decide to change this a little one way or the other. The idea, however, is to remain consistent with your plan so that a high-volume week remains much the same, as does a low-volume recovery week. On the other hand, if you aren't feeling right late in the week, it's better to cut back than to risk overtraining or illness. When in doubt—cut it out.

Week's Goals

At the start of each week, write in three goals you want to accomplish that will help achieve your training objectives on the Annual Training Plan. For example, if one of your training objectives is "Run a 10k race in less than 45 minutes by July 15," then at some point in the season, after building the necessary fitness, this becomes a weekly goal. Prior to that, other weekly goals will build up to this: "Run 4 x 1 mile at 7:15 pace with 90-second recoveries." Check off your goals as you achieve them.

Monday ___/___/___

Write in Monday's date (also write in dates for the other days of the week).

Warning Signs (Sleep, Fatigue, etc.)

The purpose of this part of the diary is to help you listen to your body. Every day it gives you clues about what condition it is in. By closely monitoring some of the signals it sends out, you can head off overtraining, burnout, injury, and illness.

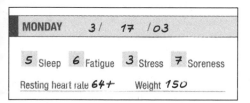

The first thing every morning rate your perceptions of the previous night's sleep, your fatigue level, psychological stress, and soreness. Use a scale of 1 to 7—with 1 being the best, most favorable rating, and 7 the worst, most unfavorable rating. Write the appropriate number in the circle preceding each signal.

Resting heart rate is taken while still in bed and recorded as above (+) or below (–) normal, based on a one-week average found when you were well rested. While a low resting heart rate is usually a good sign for fitness, it is not always so. Some scientific studies have found obviously overtrained athletes with low resting heart rates.

Ratings of 4 or greater on any of the above are considered as warnings that something isn't right. The more warnings, the more cautiously and conservatively you should train on that day.

Also record your body weight right after getting out of bed. Fluctuating weights relate to a diet that is out of harmony with needs, low hydration levels, emotional stress, and high training workloads. Consider a two-pound change in two days as a sign that something is wrong.

Workout #1 or #2: S B R O and Duration

At the start of the week, briefly summarize what you'll do in training each day and the intended duration of each workout. This will only take five to ten minutes and is time well spent when you consider how much time is put into daily training. The column on your Annual Training Plan called "Most Important Workouts" will help with this task.

Notice that there is only room for two workouts. Few multisport athletes, mostly pros, should ever train more than twice a day. A regular diet of three-a-day workouts is a good way to wind up overtrained for most.

Circle the S (swim), B (bike), R (run) or O (other) to indicate the type of workout. "Other" includes crosstraining such as cross-country skiing or weight lifting. Then schedule the general type of workout, such as endurance, intervals, or hills; or write in a specific workout:

Bike 4 x 10 minutes in zone 4 (3-minute recoveries).

Workout 1

S Ⓑ R   O *intervals*

Duration *1 hour*   Weather *hot + dry*

Route *Neva Loop*

You may even develop a code for specific workouts and record these in the back of the diary under "Notes." For easier access, write these codes on the inside of the flap.

In this part, also write in the planned duration of the workout in time or distance. These daily duration totals should be approximately equal to the "Planned Weekly Hours" recorded at the top of the first page.

Weather, Route, Distance, Time

As soon as you finish the workout, write in the details. This may include the major aspects of the weather like temperature, wind, snow, or rain. Later you may discover a pattern of weather-related problems, such as fading near the end of hot runs. It's also good to know when reviewing your log a year or more later what the conditions of the workout were. This may explain why you were so fast or so slow on a given day. Also describe the route. Most triathletes and duathletes have common bike and run routes with short names. You may want to note these in the "Routes and Best Times" section in the back of the diary (page 238). Write in the distance covered in the workout and the time, either elapsed workout time or time of day.

Time by Zone

Summarize the heart rate intensity of the workout in these boxes by indicating how many minutes were spent in each zone. If your monitor has memory you can easily indicate three zones ("above," "in," and "below" in heart rate monitor language). This is important information that will indicate if you're getting enough low intensity training early in the season, and if the weekly volume in the higher zones is adequate later on as a race period approaches. This section, when filled out following a race, gives a clearer

insight as to the intensities necessary to race thus providing guidance for the training intensities needed.

Workout Rating

Use this section in any way you prefer. You could, for example, "grade" the workout in terms of accomplishment. Another use is to indicate how hard the workout seemed, or even how you felt. The workout rating may serve as an additional signal that something is not going well if the perception of intensity doesn't agree with heart rate data, or if you see a pattern of feeling poorly. Then again, this section may serve as an encouraging reminder that everything is going well.

Notes

This is the journal part of the diary. Here record comments about the workout such as who you trained with, how you felt, interval heart rates and times, outside factors such as work that left you tired, soreness, noticed improvements, or results of self-tests. Later, as you go back over the diary trying to figure why you raced so well at some point, these comments will give life to the workout details logged above.

It's also a good idea to record any changes made to your bike in this part, such as moving the saddle or new pedals installed. A few days or weeks later some problem such as knee pain may appear, and knowing what changes were made and when helps in the detective work. Also note such changes on the Bike Measurement Chart near the back of the diary.

Racing

Summarize the important details of any race done this week including splits, finish time, and placement. Add a personal evaluation of how you did and what needs work. After the race also fill

RACE: *Boulder Peak*

	Distance	Time	Place (overall/division)
Swim	*1500M*	*25:14*	*210*
Tran 1	—	*1:42*	
Bike	*42K*	*1:18:16*	*340*
Tran 2	—	*0:53*	
Run	*10K*	*47:34*	*394*
Finish	—	*2:33:41*	*268/10*

Notes *Top 10!*

out the "Season Results" (page 237). It is a quick reference to see how you did last year in this same race and serves as a seasonal race resume that may come in handy when approaching sponsors. For the full details of any race, you can then turn to the appropriate day in your log.

	Time/dist.	Year to date
Swim	3:15/9000M	65:00
Bike	4:00/80mi	80:00
Run	3:00/22.5mi	62:00
Strength	1:00	23:00
XC Ski	————	10:00

Weekly   Year-to-date
total *11:15*   total *230:00*

Soreness *OK*

Notes *Back off next week*

Weekly Summary

Summarize the week by totaling weekly swim, bike, and run times and distances. There is also space to total time and distance for the "Year to Date." This will come in handy at the end of the season when you start planning for next year. Keeping it tallied weekly is easier than going back and adding it up later. "Strength Time" tracks time in the weight room. The blank rows are there for crosstraining activities such as cross-country skiing. Write in which activity was done and the totals.

Describe any "Soreness" encountered, no matter how slight, in case it recurs or gets worse. Knowing when it started may help determine a cause.

In the "Notes" section briefly summarize how the week went. Brief, to-the-point comments are more likely to help you later than overly detailed discussions. This is also a good place to give yourself a pat on the back—or a kick in the pants.

OTHER DIARY USES

A training diary is the best place to store all sorts of basic information about your training, equipment, race results, and other personal details. At some time in the future— next month, next year, or three years from now—something will come up that you need to remember. How did I do in this race last time? How much volume did I do in my best year? How was my last bike set up? How much intense training did I do last spring? This section will provide the answers quickly.

The pages at the back of this diary offer ample room to keep track of many details, and customize them to fit your exact needs and interests. Here are some possibilities.

Design-Your-Own-Graph Grids

When training information is graphed, trends are more easily seen. The grids provided here could, for example, display weekly training hours or distances by sport; the longest weekly workout; the volume of weekly high intensity training (a good predictor of performance); or daily heart rates, either waking, recovery, or post-workout. You can probably come up with other creative ways to use this section.

Here's an idea that combines both the duration of a workout with its intensity and is easily graphed to reveal how hard you're actually training. The purpose is to assign a "workload" value to a workout. One way of doing this is to multiply the number of minutes in a zone by the numeric name of the heart rate zone. For example, if ten minutes was spent in zone 4 on a given training session, the workload is 40 (10 x 4) for that portion of the workout. A session's total workload is the combined workloads for each of the five heart rate zones. While not a perfect system, this allows you to roughly determine what kind of stress is applied each day and to compare workouts between sports. Graphing cumulative workloads for a week on one of these grids gives a better idea of what your training is like than merely recording miles.

Bike Measurement Charts

Have you ever changed your saddle position and then tried to set it back to the original position only to find that it was never quite right again? Completing this diagram with your exact measurements will resolve this once and for all. It will also allow you to set up a new bike to your exact position without a lot of trial and error. Any time equipment is changed, having a position record can potentially save lots of time and frustration.

Routes and Best Times

If you're like most multisport athletes, you have established routes that you frequently run and ride. Sometimes at the end of a workout you realize that you went especially fast and try to remember what times were like on this same course before. Here is the place to note such times for later reference.

Another use for this section is as a record of self-tests. For example, pick out a flat five-mile course and ride it at a given heart rate, say 9–11 beats below your lactate threshold heart rate, in a standard gear. If you've done a good job of controlling variables such as warm-up, rest, diet, and weather, decreasing times are a sign that fitness is improving. The same procedure is possible on the running track for one or two miles. This is called an "aerobic time trial."

Monthly, all-out time trials on a standard course or track also serve as good indicators of progress when done regularly, especially before the race season begins.

Season Results

Keep a good record of your race results on the page provided at the back. This will come in handy when it's time to seek a sponsor or just remember how you did last year.

Race Day Checklist

Almost every athlete forgets to take something critical, like racing shoes or helmet, to a race at least once a year. Your memory just isn't good enough sometimes to recall all of the many items needed. The night before a race, gather your gear together and check it off (in pencil). That reduces the race day stress the next morning and allows your mind to relax and think about racing well instead of wondering if your sunglasses are packed.

Notes

It seems like everything was covered in the previous pages, but some little tidbit of information is sure to come up. For example, what products and therapies seem to work for you when a cold starts coming on? If you only get one or two colds each year, it's hard to remember. Write it here. How about the combination for your padlock at the health club? Ever forget that? Jot it down. You could also keep track of personal best lifts in the weight room, the phone numbers of training partners, or any number of other details. Write down anything that will free your mind to focus on racing faster.

Joe Friel has trained endurance athletes since 1980. Joe has authored *The Cyclist's Training Bible, Cycling Past 50, Precision Heart Rate Training* (co-author), *The Triathlete's Training Bible*, and *The Mountain Biker's Training Bible*. He holds a masters degree in exercise science, is a USA Triathlon and USA Cycling certified coach, and serves as the Co-Chairman of the USA Triathlon National Coaching Committee. His services are described in detail on his Web sites—www.ultrafit.com and www.trainingbible.com.

ANNUAL TRAINING PLAN

ANNUAL HOURS

Season Goals

_____

_____

_____

_____

_____

_____

_____

_____

_____

Training Objectives

_____

_____

_____

_____

_____

_____

_____

_____

_____

_____

Week #, Mon.	Race	Priority	Period	Hours	Swim	Bike	Run
01 /							
02 /							
03 /							
04 /							
05 /							
06 /							
07 /							
08 /							
09 /							
10 /							
11 /							
12 /							
13 /							
14 /							
15 /							
16 /							
17 /							
18 /							
19 /							

Most Important Workouts

Week #, Mon.	Race	Priority	Period	Hours	Most Important Workouts		
					Swim	Bike	Run
20 /							
21 /							
22 /							
23 /							
24 /							
25 /							
26 /							
27 /							
28 /							
29 /							
30 /							
31 /							
32 /							
33 /							
34 /							
35 /							
36 /							
37 /							
38 /							
39 /							
40 /							
41 /							
42 /							
43 /							
44 /							
45 /							
46 /							
47 /							
48 /							
49 /							
50 /							
51 /							
52 /							

WEEKLY TRAINING HOURS

Period	Week	200	250	300	350	400	450	500	550	600	650
Prep	All	3.5	4.0	5.0	6.0	7.0	7.5	8.5	9.0	10.0	11.0
Base 1	1	4.0	5.0	6.0	7.0	8.0	9.0	10.0	11.0	12.0	12.5
	2	5.0	6.0	7.0	8.5	9.5	10.5	12.0	13.0	14.5	15.5
	3	5.5	6.5	8.0	9.5	10.5	12.0	13.5	14.5	16.0	17.5
	4	3.0	3.5	4.0	5.0	5.5	6.5	7.0	8.0	8.5	9.0
Base 2	1	4.0	5.5	6.5	7.5	8.5	9.5	10.5	12.5	12.5	13.0
	2	5.0	6.5	7.5	9.0	10.0	11.5	12.5	14.0	15.0	16.5
	3	5.5	7.0	8.5	10.0	11.0	12.5	14.0	15.5	17.0	18.0
	4	3.0	3.5	4.5	5.0	5.5	6.5	7.0	8.0	8.5	9.0
Base 3	1	4.5	5.5	7.0	8.0	9.0	10.0	11.0	12.5	13.5	14.5
	2	5.0	6.5	8.0	9.5	10.5	12.0	13.5	14.5	16.0	17.0
	3	6.0	7.5	9.0	10.5	11.5	13.0	15.0	16.5	18.0	19.0
	4	3.0	3.5	4.5	5.0	5.5	6.5	7.0	8.0	8.5	9.0
Build 1	1	5.0	6.5	8.0	9.0	10.0	11.5	12.5	14.0	15.5	16.0
	2	5.0	6.5	8.0	9.0	10.0	11.5	12.5	14.0	15.5	16.0
	3	5.0	6.5	8.0	9.0	10.0	11.5	12.5	14.0	15.5	16.0
	4	3.0	3.5	4.5	5.0	5.5	6.5	7.0	8.0	8.5	9.0
Build 2	1	5.0	6.0	7.0	8.5	9.5	10.5	12.0	13.0	14.5	15.5
	2	5.0	6.0	7.0	8.5	9.5	10.5	12.0	13.0	14.5	15.5
	3	5.0	6.0	7.0	8.5	9.5	10.5	12.0	13.0	14.5	15.5
	4	3.0	3.5	4.5	5.0	5.5	6.5	7.0	8.0	8.5	9.0
Peak	1	4.0	5.5	6.5	7.5	8.5	9.5	10.5	11.5	13.0	13.5
	2	3.5	4.0	5.0	6.0	6.5	7.5	8.5	9.5	10.0	11.0
Race	All	3.0	3.5	4.5	5.0	5.5	6.5	7.0	8.0	8.5	9.0
Trans.	All	3.0	3.5	4.5	5.0	5.5	6.5	7.0	8.0	8.5	9.0

700	750	800	850	900	950	1000	1050	1100	1150	1200
12.0	12.5	13.5	14.5	15.0	16.0	17.0	17.5	18.5	19.5	20.0
14.0	14.5	15.5	16.5	17.5	18.5	19.5	20.5	21.5	22.5	23.5
16.5	18.0	19.0	20.0	21.5	22.5	24.0	25.0	26.0	27.5	28.5
18.5	20.0	21.5	22.5	24.0	25.5	26.5	28.0	29.5	30.5	32.0
10.0	10.5	11.5	12.0	12.5	13.5	14.0	14.5	15.5	16.0	17.0
14.5	16.0	17.0	18.0	19.0	20.0	21.0	22.0	23.0	24.0	25.0
17.5	19.0	20.0	21.5	22.5	24.0	25.0	26.6	27.5	29.0	30.0
19.5	21.0	22.5	24.0	25.0	26.5	28.0	29.5	31.0	32.0	33.5
10.0	10.5	11.5	12.0	12.5	13.5	14.0	15.0	15.5	16.0	17.0
15.5	17.0	18.0	19.0	20.0	21.0	22.5	23.5	25.0	25.5	27.0
18.5	20.0	21.5	23.0	24.0	25.0	26.5	28.0	29.5	30.5	32.0
20.5	22.0	23.5	25.0	26.5	28.0	29.5	31.0	32.5	33.5	35.0
10.0	10.5	11.5	12.0	12.5	13.5	14.0	15.0	15.5	16.0	17.0
17.5	19.0	20.5	21.5	22.5	24.0	25.0	26.5	28.0	29.0	30.0
17.5	19.0	20.5	21.5	22.5	24.0	25.0	26.5	28.0	29.0	30.0
17.5	19.0	20.5	21.5	22.5	24.0	25.0	26.5	28.0	29.0	30.0
10.0	10.5	11.5	12.0	12.5	13.5	14.0	15.0	15.5	16.0	17.0
16.5	18.0	19.0	20.5	21.5	22.5	24.0	25.0	26.5	27.0	28.5
16.5	18.0	19.0	20.5	21.5	22.5	24.0	25.0	26.5	27.0	28.5
16.5	18.0	19.0	20.5	21.5	22.5	24.0	25.0	26.5	27.0	28.5
10.0	10.5	11.5	12.0	12.5	13.5	14.0	15.0	15.5	16.0	17.0
14.5	16.0	17.0	18.0	19.0	20.0	21.0	22.0	23.5	24.0	25.0
11.5	12.5	13.5	14.5	15.0	16.0	17.0	17.5	18.5	19.0	20.0
10.0	10.5	11.5	12.0	12.5	13.5	14.0	15.0	15.5	16.0	17.0
10.0	10.5	11.5	12.0	12.5	13.5	14.0	15.0	15.5	16.0	17.0

WEEK BEGINNING: **PLANNED WEEKLY HOURS:**

Week's goals (check off as achieved)

▓ _____ weights, 20 mins, 4d _____

▓ _____ run 4x4m + 1x10m _____

▓ _____ spin 1 class _____

MONDAY   2 / 21 / 06

Ⓕ Sleep Ⓕ Fatigue Ⓕ Stress Ⓕ Soreness

Resting heart rate 69   Weight

Workout 1

S   B   Ⓡ   O _____

Duration 39m   Weather great warm

Route subdivision

_____

Distance 4 m   Time 5:24 - 6:05

Time
by zone **1**   **2**   **3**   **(4)**   **5**

Workout rating

Notes Heart rate 138 - 162

_____

Workout 2

S   B   R   Ⓞ _____

Duration 15m   Weather

Route 2 x 12 push ups, 2 x 12

ball/back raise, 2x12 lunges

Distance   Time

Time
by zone **1**   **2**   **3**   **4**   **5**

Workout rating

Notes

_____

TUESDAY → 2 / 22 / 06

  Sleep   Fatigue   Stress   Soreness

Resting heart rate   Weight

Workout 1

S   B   R   O _____

Duration   Weather

Route

_____

Distance   Time

Time
by zone **1**   **2**   **3**   **4**   **5**

Workout rating

Notes

_____

Workout 2

S   B   R   O _____

Duration   Weather

Route

_____

Distance   Time

Time
by zone **1**   **2**   **3**   **4**   **5**

Workout rating

Notes

_____

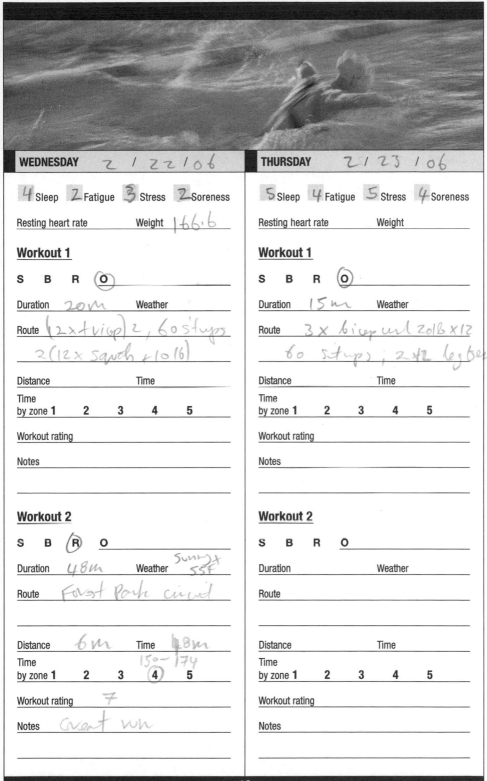

WEDNESDAY 2 / 22 / 06	THURSDAY 2 / 23 / 06

4 Sleep **2** Fatigue **3** Stress **2** Soreness

Resting heart rate   Weight **166.6**

Workout 1

S   B   R   (O)

Duration **20m**   Weather

Route **(2 x triop) 2, 60 situps**
    2 (12 x squat + 10 lb)

Distance   Time

Time by zone **1**   **2**   **3**   **4**   **5**

Workout rating

Notes

Workout 2

S   (B)   R   O

Duration **48m**   Weather **Sunny + 55F**

Route **Forest Park circuit**

Distance **6m**   Time **48m**

Time by zone **1**   **2**   **3**   (**4**)   **5**   **150 - 174**

Workout rating **7**

Notes **Great run**

---

5 Sleep **4** Fatigue **5** Stress **4** Soreness

Resting heart rate   Weight

Workout 1

S   B   R   (O)

Duration **15m**   Weather

Route **3 x bicep curl 20lb x 12**
    60 situps; 2 x 12 legbends

Distance   Time

Time by zone **1**   **2**   **3**   **4**   **5**

Workout rating

Notes

Workout 2

S   B   R   O

Duration   Weather

Route

Distance   Time

Time by zone **1**   **2**   **3**   **4**   **5**

Workout rating

Notes

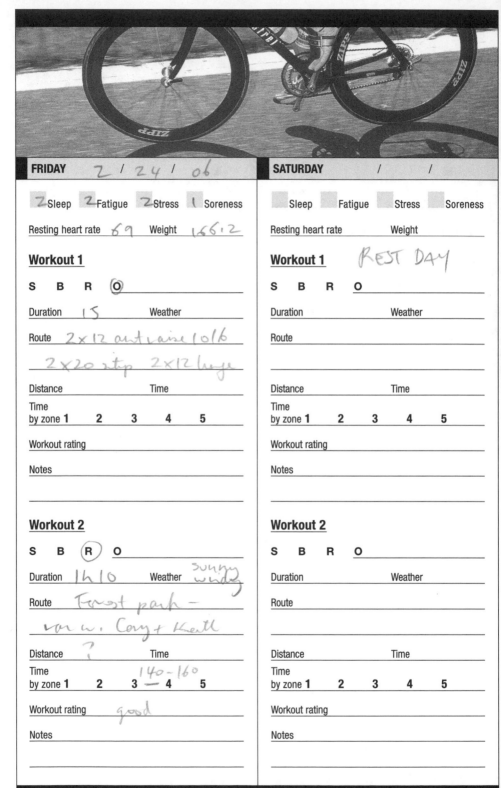

FRIDAY 2 / 24 / 06	SATURDAY / /

☑ Sleep ☑ Fatigue ☑ Stress 1 Soreness | **Sleep Fatigue Stress Soreness**

Resting heart rate 89   Weight 166.2 | Resting heart rate   Weight

Workout 1   ## Workout 1   REST DAY

S   B   R   ⊙ _____ | S   B   R   O _____

Duration 15   Weather _____ | Duration _____ Weather _____

Route 2x12 anti raise 10/6 | Route _____
2x20 rtp 2x12 huye

Distance _____ Time _____ | Distance _____ Time _____

Time by zone **1   2   3   4   5** | Time by zone **1   2   3   4   5**

Workout rating _____ | Workout rating _____

Notes _____ | Notes _____

Workout 2   ## Workout 2

S   B   ⟨R⟩   O _____ | S   B   R   O _____

Duration 1h10   Weather sunny windy | Duration _____ Weather _____

Route Forest park – | Route _____
run w. Cory + Keith

Distance ?   Time _____ | Distance _____ Time _____

Time by zone **1   2   3 —— 4   5**   140–160 | Time by zone **1   2   3   4   5**

Workout rating good | Workout rating _____

Notes _____ | Notes _____

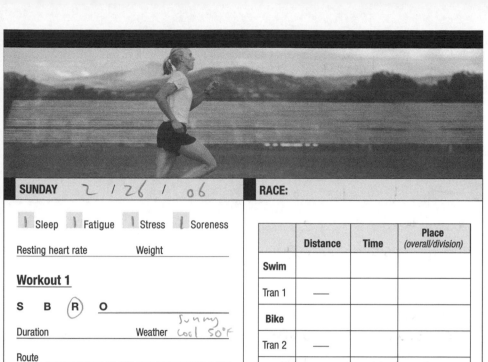

SUNDAY 2 / 26 / 06

| | Sleep | | Fatigue | | Stress | | Soreness |

Resting heart rate _____ Weight _____

Workout 1

S   B   (R)   O _____

Duration _____ Weather Cool 50°F Sunny

Route _____

_____

Distance _____ Time _____

Time
by zone **1   2   3   4   5**

Workout rating _____

Notes _____

_____

Workout 2

S   B   R   O _____

Duration _____ Weather _____

Route _____

_____

Distance _____ Time _____

Time
by zone **1   2   3   4   5**

Workout rating _____

Notes _____

_____

RACE: _____

	Distance	Time	Place *(overall/division)*
Swim			
Tran 1	—		
Bike			
Tran 2	—		
Run			
Finish	—		

Notes _____

_____

WEEKLY SUMMARY

	Time/dist.	Year to date
Swim		
Bike		
Run		
Strength		

Weekly total _____ Year-to-date total _____

Soreness _____

Notes _____

_____

WEEK BEGINNING: 1/1/07   **PLANNED WEEKLY HOURS:**

Week's goals (check off as achieved)

☐ Routine run, swim bike
☐ start setting baseline performan
☐

MONDAY 1 / 1 / 07	TUESDAY 1 / 2 / 07
4 Sleep 4 Fatigue 1 Stress 2 Soreness	4 Sleep 3 Fatigue 2 Stress 1 Soreness
Resting heart rate 65 Weight 167	Resting heart rate — Weight —

Workout 1

S   B   (R)   O _____

Duration 30m   Weather fine

Route Subdivision 1 mile

warmup then —

Distance 2.3 m   Time 17'17"

| Time by zone | 1 | 2 | 3 | 4 | 5 |

Ave 162 max 173

Workout rating great

Notes _____

_____

Workout 2   Swim

S   B   R   O _____

Duration   Weather

Route _____

_____

Distance   Time

| Time by zone | 1 | 2 | 3 | 4 | 5 |

Workout rating _____

Notes _____

_____

Workout 1

(S)   B   R   O _____

Duration 30m   Weather

Route leg technique in pool

_____

Distance ~10 lyh   Time 30m

| Time by zone | 1 | 2 | 3 | 4 | 5 |

Workout rating okay

Notes getting better at using

upper leg

Tempo

Workout 2

S   B   R   O _____

Duration   Weather

Route _____

_____

Distance   Time

| Time by zone | 1 | 2 | 3 | 4 | 5 |

Workout rating _____

Notes _____

_____

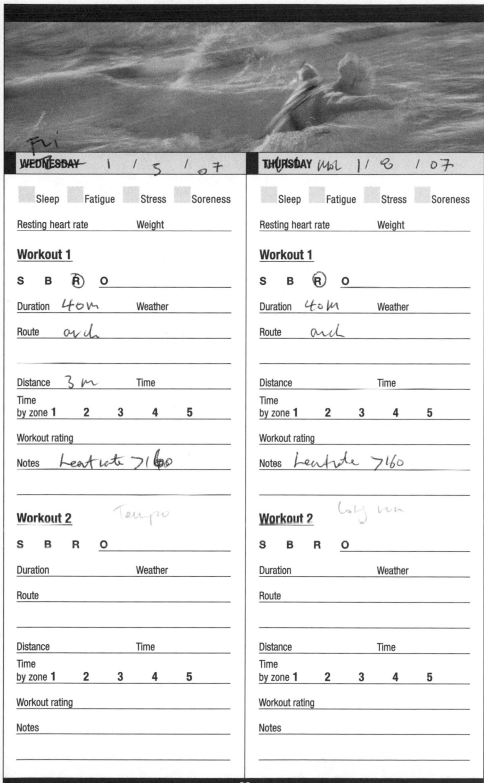

WEDNESDAY ~~~~ 1 / 3 / 07

Fri

Sleep   Fatigue   Stress   Soreness

Resting heart rate _____ Weight _____

Workout 1

S   B   (R)   O _____

Duration 40m   Weather _____

Route arch _____

_____

Distance 3 m   Time _____

Time
by zone **1**   **2**   **3**   **4**   **5**

Workout rating _____

Notes Heart rate 7160 _____

Workout 2   Tempo

S   B   R   O _____

Duration _____   Weather _____

Route _____

_____

Distance _____   Time _____

Time
by zone **1**   **2**   **3**   **4**   **5**

Workout rating _____

Notes _____

_____

THURSDAY Mar 1 / 8 / 07

Sleep   Fatigue   Stress   Soreness

Resting heart rate _____ Weight _____

Workout 1

S   B   (R)   O _____

Duration 40m   Weather _____

Route arch _____

_____

Distance _____   Time _____

Time
by zone **1**   **2**   **3**   **4**   **5**

Workout rating _____

Notes Heart rate 7160 _____

Workout 2   long run

S   B   R   O _____

Duration _____   Weather _____

Route _____

_____

Distance _____   Time _____

Time
by zone **1**   **2**   **3**   **4**   **5**

Workout rating _____

Notes _____

_____

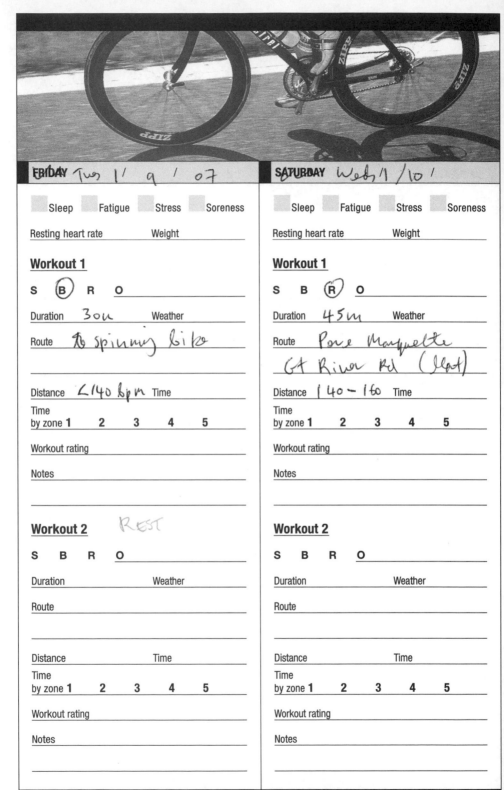

FRIDAY Tues 1 / 9 / 07

Sleep   Fatigue   Stress   Soreness

Resting heart rate _____ Weight _____

Workout 1

S (B) R O _____

Duration 30u   Weather _____

Route To spinning bike _____

_____

Distance <140 bpm Time _____

Time
by zone 1   2   3   4   5

Workout rating _____

Notes _____

_____

Workout 2   REST

S   B   R   O _____

Duration _____   Weather _____

Route _____

_____

Distance _____   Time _____

Time
by zone 1   2   3   4   5

Workout rating _____

Notes _____

_____

SATURDAY Wed 1 / 10 /

Sleep   Fatigue   Stress   Soreness

Resting heart rate _____ Weight _____

Workout 1

S B (R) O _____

Duration 45m   Weather _____

Route Pere Marquette
GT River Rd (flat)

Distance 140 - 160 Time _____

Time
by zone 1   2   3   4   5

Workout rating _____

Notes _____

_____

Workout 2

S   B   R   O _____

Duration _____   Weather _____

Route _____

_____

Distance _____   Time _____

Time
by zone 1   2   3   4   5

Workout rating _____

Notes _____

_____

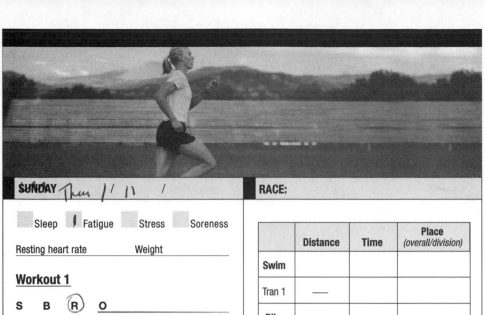

SUNDAY Thur / / / /

RACE:

Sleep | Fatigue | Stress | Soreness

Resting heart rate _____ Weight _____

Workout 1

S B (R) O _____

Duration 55m Weather _____

Route Pere Marquette
  trails 7186 bpm

Distance ? Time _____

Time
by zone **1** **2** **3** **4** **5**

Workout rating _____

Notes _____

Workout 2

S B R O _____

Duration _____ Weather _____

Route _____

_____

Distance _____ Time _____

Time
by zone **1** **2** **3** **4** **5**

Workout rating _____

Notes _____

_____

	Distance	Time	Place *(overall/division)*
Swim			
Tran 1	—		
Bike			
Tran 2	—		
Run			
Finish	—		

Notes _____

_____

WEEKLY SUMMARY

	Time/dist.	Year to date
Swim		
Bike		
Run		
Strength		

Weekly   Year-to-date
total   total

Soreness _____

Notes _____

WEEK BEGINNING: **PLANNED WEEKLY HOURS:**

Week's goals (check off as achieved)

☐ _____

☐ _____

☐ _____

MONDAY 1 / 14 / 07	**TUESDAY** 1 / 16 / 07
☐ Sleep ☐ Fatigue ☐ Stress ☐ Soreness	☐ Sleep ☐ Fatigue ☐ Stress ☐ Soreness
Resting heart rate _____ Weight 167	Resting heart rate _____ Weight 165

Workout 1

S (B) R O _____

Duration 40   Weather _____

Route   Spinning

_____

Distance _____ Time _____

Time
by zone **1**   **2**   **3**   **4**   **5**

Workout rating _____

Notes   HR >150

Workout 2

S   B   R   O _____

Duration _____ Weather _____

Route _____

_____

Distance _____ Time _____

Time
by zone **1**   **2**   **3**   **4**   **5**

Workout rating _____

Notes _____

Workout 1

S   B   (R)   O _____

Duration 45m   Weather _____

Route   30m <140BPM

        2.9m   0 incline

Distance _____ Time _____

Time
by zone **1**   **2**   **3**   **4**   **5**

Workout rating _____

Notes .

Workout 2

S   B   R   O _____

Duration _____ Weather _____

Route _____

_____

Distance _____ Time _____

Time
by zone **1**   **2**   **3**   **4**   **5**

Workout rating _____

Notes _____

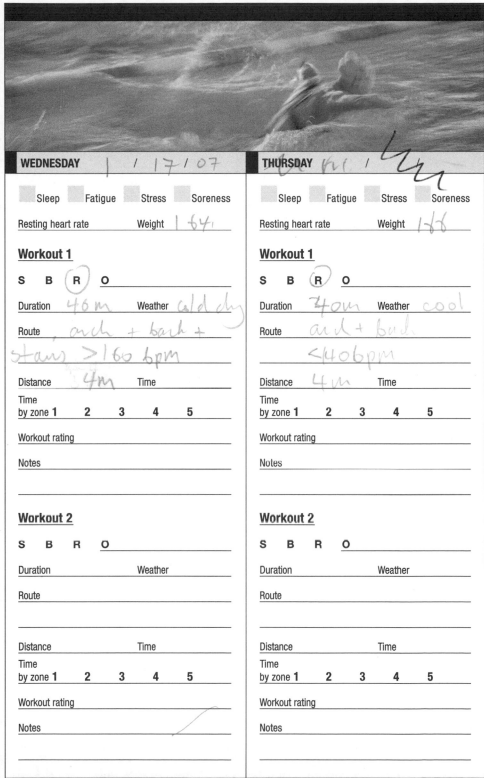

WEDNESDAY / 17 / 07

Sleep   Fatigue   Stress   Soreness

Resting heart rate   Weight 164,

Workout 1

S   B   (R)   O _____

Duration 40 m   Weather cold dry

Route , arch + back +

stairs >160 bpm

Distance 4m   Time _____

Time
by zone **1   2   3   4   5**

Workout rating _____

Notes _____

Workout 2

S   B   R   O _____

Duration   Weather _____

Route _____

Distance   Time _____

Time
by zone **1   2   3   4   5**

Workout rating _____

Notes _____

THURSDAY / /

Sleep   Fatigue   Stress   Soreness

Resting heart rate   Weight 168

Workout 1

S   B   (R)   O _____

Duration 40m   Weather cool

Route ard + back

<40 bpm

Distance 4 m   Time _____

Time
by zone **1   2   3   4   5**

Workout rating _____

Notes _____

Workout 2

S   B   R   O _____

Duration   Weather _____

Route _____

Distance   Time _____

Time
by zone **1   2   3   4   5**

Workout rating _____

Notes _____

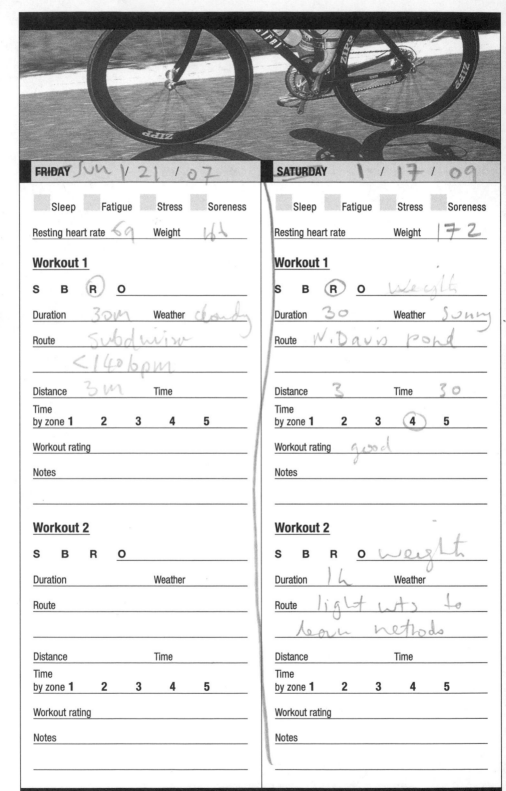

FRIDAY Jun / 21 / 07

Sleep   Fatigue   Stress   Soreness

Resting heart rate 69   Weight 161

Workout 1

S   B   (R)   O _____

Duration 30M   Weather cloudy

Route subdivision
        <140 bpm

Distance 3 m   Time _____

Time
by zone **1   2   3   4   5**

Workout rating _____

Notes _____

Workout 2

S   B   R   O _____

Duration _____   Weather _____

Route _____

Distance _____   Time _____

Time
by zone **1   2   3   4   5**

Workout rating _____

Notes _____

SATURDAY 1 / 17 / 09

Sleep   Fatigue   Stress   Soreness

Resting heart rate ___   Weight 172

Workout 1

S   B   (R)   O weight

Duration 30   Weather Sunny

Route N. Davis pond

Distance 3   Time 30

Time
by zone **1   2   3   (4)   5**

Workout rating good

Notes _____

Workout 2

S   B   R   O weight

Duration 1h   Weather _____

Route light wts to
      learn methods

Distance _____   Time _____

Time
by zone **1   2   3   4   5**

Workout rating _____

Notes _____

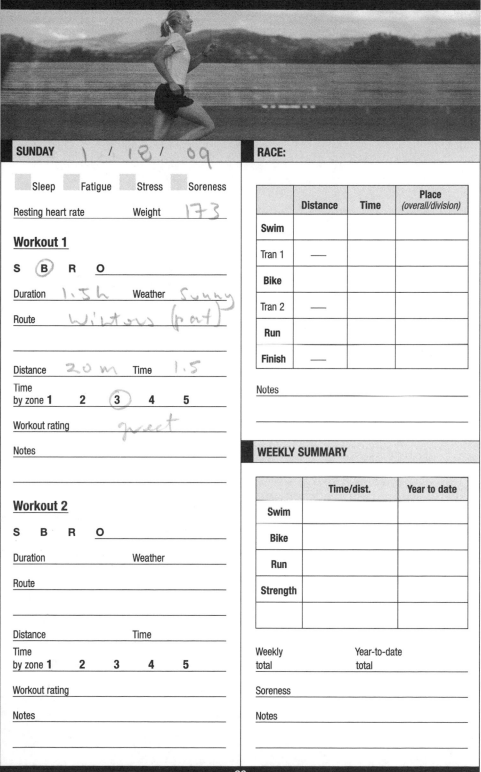

SUNDAY   1 / 18 / 09

RACE:

Sleep   Fatigue   Stress   Soreness

Resting heart rate   Weight   173

Workout 1

S   (B)   R   O _____

Duration   1.5h   Weather   Sunny

Route   Wiltons (part)

_____

Distance   20 m   Time   1.5

Time
by zone   **1**   **2**   **(3)**   **4**   **5**

Workout rating   great

Notes _____

_____

Workout 2

S   B   R   O _____

Duration   Weather _____

Route _____

_____

Distance   Time _____

Time
by zone   **1**   **2**   **3**   **4**   **5**

Workout rating _____

Notes _____

_____

	Distance	Time	Place (overall/division)
Swim			
Tran 1	—		
Bike			
Tran 2	—		
Run			
Finish	—		

Notes _____

_____

WEEKLY SUMMARY

	Time/dist.	Year to date
Swim		
Bike		
Run		
Strength		

Weekly   Year-to-date
total   total _____

Soreness _____

Notes _____

_____

WEEK BEGINNING: **PLANNED WEEKLY HOURS:**

Week's goals (check off as achieved)

☐ ___Weights - Tue + Sat___
☐ ___Run - Mon + Weds___
☐ ___Bike - Thurs + Sun___

MONDAY 1 / 19 / 09	**TUESDAY** 1 / 20 / 09
☐ Sleep ☐ Fatigue ☐ Stress ☐ Soreness	☐ Sleep ☐ Fatigue ☐ Stress ☐ Soreness
Resting heart rate ____ Weight ____	Resting heart rate ____ Weight ____
Workout 1 Walk up	**Workout 1**
S B R Ⓞ rt. Sonoma	Ⓢ B R O _____
Duration ____ Weather ____	Duration ____ Weather ____
Route _____	Route _____
_____	_____
Distance ____ Time ____	Distance ____ Time ____
Time by zone **1 2 3 4 5**	Time by zone **1 2 3 4 5**
Workout rating ____	Workout rating ____
Notes ____	Notes ____
_____	_____
Workout 2	**Workout 2**
~~S~~ B R O _____	S B R O _____
Duration ____ Weather ____	Duration ____ Weather ____
Route _____	Route _____
_____	_____
Distance ____ Time ____	Distance ____ Time ____
Time by zone **1 2 3 4 5**	Time by zone **1 2 3 4 5**
Workout rating ____	Workout rating ____
Notes ____	Notes ____
_____	_____

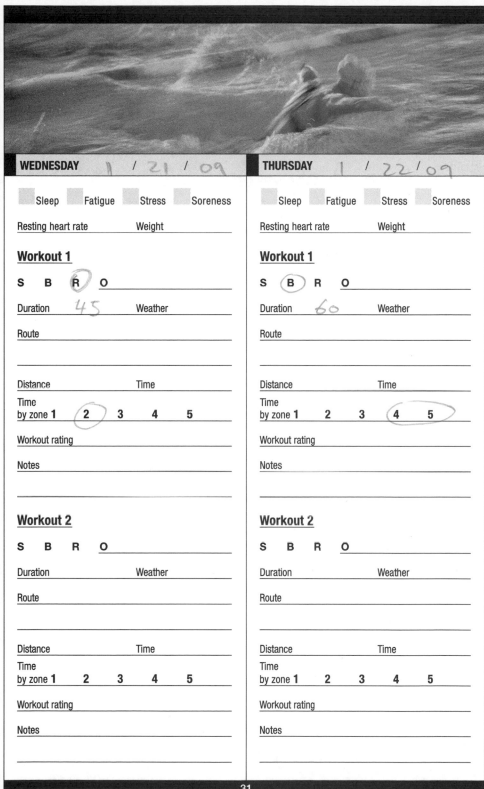

Sleep ▮ Fatigue ▮ Stress ▮ Soreness

Resting heart rate _____ Weight _____

Workout 1

S B (R) O _____

Duration _45_ Weather _____

Route _____

_____

Distance _____ Time _____

Time
by zone **1** (**2**) **3** **4** **5**

Workout rating _____

Notes _____

_____

Workout 2

S B R O _____

Duration _____ Weather _____

Route _____

_____

Distance _____ Time _____

Time
by zone **1** **2** **3** **4** **5**

Workout rating _____

Notes _____

_____

Sleep ▮ Fatigue ▮ Stress ▮ Soreness

Resting heart rate _____ Weight _____

Workout 1

S (B) R O _____

Duration _60_ Weather _____

Route _____

_____

Distance _____ Time _____

Time
by zone **1** **2** **3** (**4** **5**)

Workout rating _____

Notes _____

_____

Workout 2

S B R O _____

Duration _____ Weather _____

Route _____

_____

Distance _____ Time _____

Time
by zone **1** **2** **3** **4** **5**

Workout rating _____

Notes _____

_____

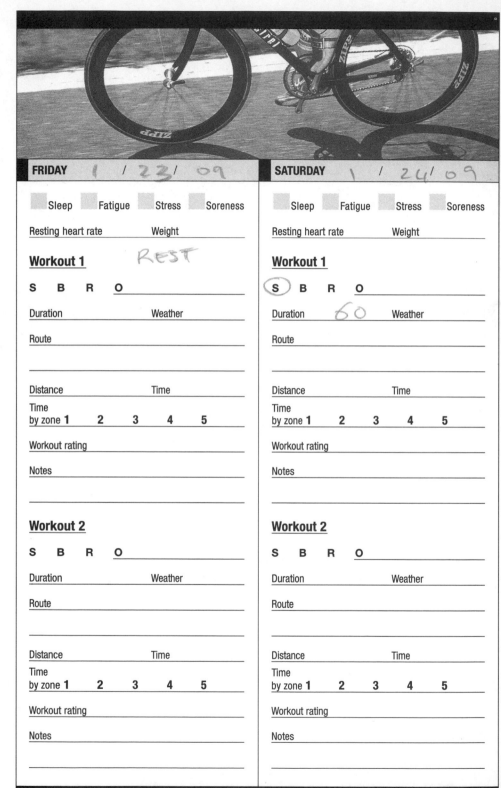

FRIDAY 1 / 23 / 09

Sleep Fatigue Stress Soreness

Resting heart rate _____ Weight _____

Workout 1   REST

S   B   R   O _____

Duration _____ Weather _____

Route _____

_____

Distance _____ Time _____

Time
by zone **1**   **2**   **3**   **4**   **5**

Workout rating _____

Notes _____

_____

Workout 2

S   B   R   O _____

Duration _____ Weather _____

Route _____

_____

Distance _____ Time _____

Time
by zone **1**   **2**   **3**   **4**   **5**

Workout rating _____

Notes _____

_____

SATURDAY 1 / 24 / 09

Sleep Fatigue Stress Soreness

Resting heart rate _____ Weight _____

Workout 1

(S)   B   R   O _____

Duration _60_ Weather _____

Route _____

_____

Distance _____ Time _____

Time
by zone **1**   **2**   **3**   **4**   **5**

Workout rating _____

Notes _____

_____

Workout 2

S   B   R   O _____

Duration _____ Weather _____

Route _____

_____

Distance _____ Time _____

Time
by zone **1**   **2**   **3**   **4**   **5**

Workout rating _____

Notes _____

_____

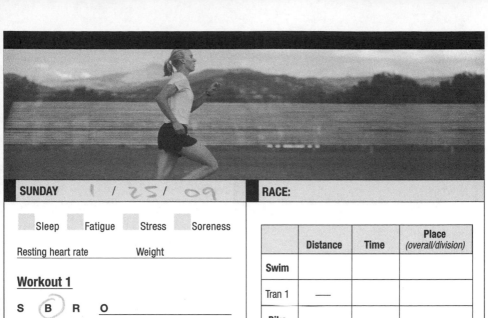

SUNDAY 1 / 25 / 09

RACE:

Sleep ▢ Fatigue ▢ Stress ▢ Soreness

Resting heart rate _____ Weight _____

Workout 1

S (B) R O _____

Duration 2-3h Weather _____

Route _____

_____

Distance _____ Time _____

Time
by zone **1** **2** (**3**) **4** **5** _____

Workout rating _____

Notes _____

_____

Workout 2

S B R O _____

Duration _____ Weather _____

Route _____

_____

Distance _____ Time _____

Time
by zone **1** **2** **3** **4** **5** _____

Workout rating _____

Notes _____

_____

	Distance	Time	Place *(overall/division)*
Swim			
Tran 1	—		
Bike			
Tran 2	—		
Run			
Finish	—		

Notes _____

_____

	Time/dist.	Year to date
Swim		
Bike		
Run		
Strength		

Weekly _____ Year-to-date _____
total   total

Soreness _____

Notes _____

_____

WEEK BEGINNING: **PLANNED WEEKLY HOURS:**

Week's goals (check off as achieved)

☐ _____

☐ _____

☐ _____

| MONDAY | / | / |

☐ Sleep ☐ Fatigue ☐ Stress ☐ Soreness

Resting heart rate _____ Weight _____

Workout 1

S   B   R   O _____

Duration _____ Weather _____

Route _____

_____

Distance _____ Time _____

Time
by zone **1**   **2**   **3**   **4**   **5**

Workout rating _____

Notes _____

_____

Workout 2

S   B   R   O _____

Duration _____ Weather _____

Route _____

_____

Distance _____ Time _____

Time
by zone **1**   **2**   **3**   **4**   **5**

Workout rating _____

Notes _____

_____

| TUESDAY | / | / |

☐ Sleep ☐ Fatigue ☐ Stress ☐ Soreness

Resting heart rate _____ Weight _____

Workout 1

S   B   R   O _____

Duration _____ Weather _____

Route _____

_____

Distance _____ Time _____

Time
by zone **1**   **2**   **3**   **4**   **5**

Workout rating _____

Notes _____

_____

Workout 2

S   B   R   O _____

Duration _____ Weather _____

Route _____

_____

Distance _____ Time _____

Time
by zone **1**   **2**   **3**   **4**   **5**

Workout rating _____

Notes _____

_____

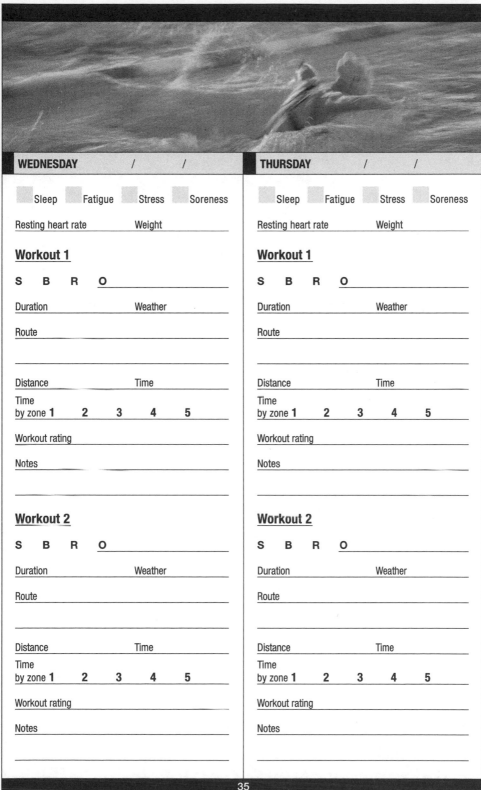

WEDNESDAY / /

Sleep Fatigue Stress Soreness

Resting heart rate   Weight

Workout 1

S   B   R   O

Duration   Weather

Route

Distance   Time

Time
by zone **1   2   3   4   5**

Workout rating

Notes

Workout 2

S   B   R   O

Duration   Weather

Route

Distance   Time

Time
by zone **1   2   3   4   5**

Workout rating

Notes

THURSDAY / /

Sleep Fatigue Stress Soreness

Resting heart rate   Weight

Workout 1

S   B   R   O

Duration   Weather

Route

Distance   Time

Time
by zone **1   2   3   4   5**

Workout rating

Notes

Workout 2

S   B   R   O

Duration   Weather

Route

Distance   Time

Time
by zone **1   2   3   4   5**

Workout rating

Notes

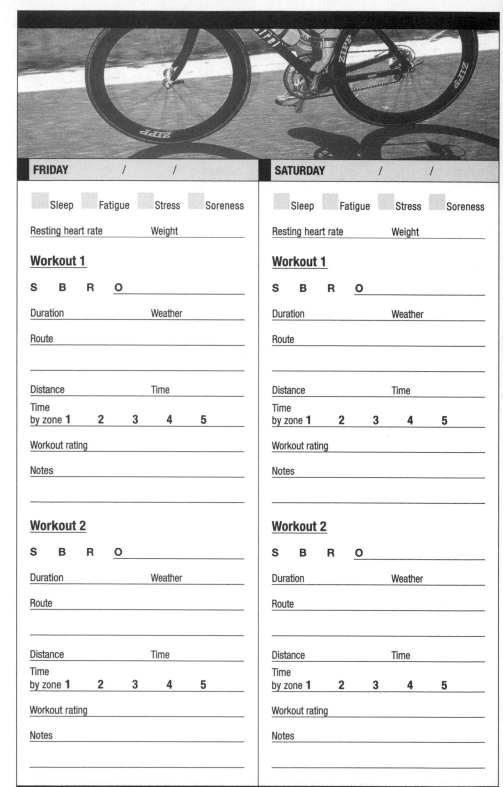

FRIDAY / /

Sleep Fatigue Stress Soreness

Resting heart rate _____ Weight _____

Workout 1

S B R O _____

Duration _____ Weather _____

Route _____

_____

Distance _____ Time _____

Time
by zone **1** **2** **3** **4** **5**

Workout rating _____

Notes _____

_____

Workout 2

S B R O _____

Duration _____ Weather _____

Route _____

_____

Distance _____ Time _____

Time
by zone **1** **2** **3** **4** **5**

Workout rating _____

Notes _____

_____

SATURDAY / /

Sleep Fatigue Stress Soreness

Resting heart rate _____ Weight _____

Workout 1

S B R O _____

Duration _____ Weather _____

Route _____

_____

Distance _____ Time _____

Time
by zone **1** **2** **3** **4** **5**

Workout rating _____

Notes _____

_____

Workout 2

S B R O _____

Duration _____ Weather _____

Route _____

_____

Distance _____ Time _____

Time
by zone **1** **2** **3** **4** **5**

Workout rating _____

Notes _____

_____

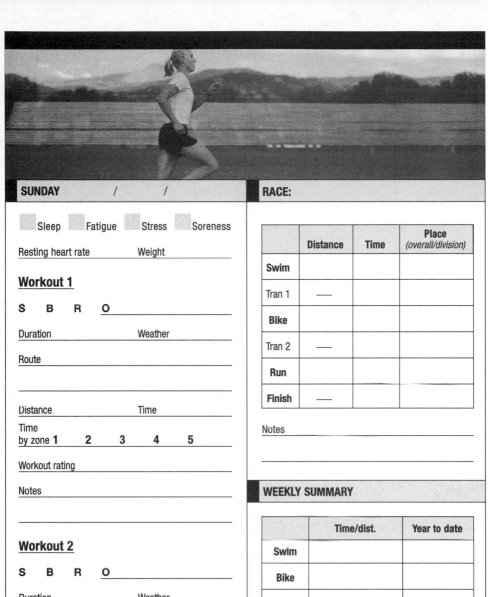

SUNDAY	/	/

RACE:

Sleep   Fatigue   Stress   Soreness

Resting heart rate   Weight

Workout 1

S   B   R   O

Duration   Weather

Route

Distance   Time

Time
by zone **1**   **2**   **3**   **4**   **5**

Workout rating

Notes

Workout 2

S   B   R   O

Duration   Weather

Route

Distance   Time

Time
by zone **1**   **2**   **3**   **4**   **5**

Workout rating

Notes

	Distance	Time	Place *(overall/division)*
Swim			
Tran 1	—		
Bike			
Tran 2	—		
Run			
Finish	—		

Notes

WEEKLY SUMMARY

	Time/dist.	Year to date
Swim		
Bike		
Run		
Strength		

Weekly
total   Year-to-date
total

Soreness

Notes

WEEK BEGINNING: **PLANNED WEEKLY HOURS:**

Week's goals (check off as achieved)

☐ _____

☐ _____

☐ _____

MONDAY / /	TUESDAY / /

☐ Sleep ☐ Fatigue ☐ Stress ☐ Soreness

Resting heart rate _____ Weight _____

Workout 1

S B R O _____

Duration _____ Weather _____

Route _____

_____

Distance _____ Time _____

Time
by zone **1   2   3   4   5**

Workout rating _____

Notes _____

_____

Workout 2

S B R O _____

Duration _____ Weather _____

Route _____

_____

Distance _____ Time _____

Time
by zone **1   2   3   4   5**

Workout rating _____

Notes _____

_____

☐ Sleep ☐ Fatigue ☐ Stress ☐ Soreness

Resting heart rate _____ Weight _____

Workout 1

S B R O _____

Duration _____ Weather _____

Route _____

_____

Distance _____ Time _____

Time
by zone **1   2   3   4   5**

Workout rating _____

Notes _____

_____

Workout 2

S B R O _____

Duration _____ Weather _____

Route _____

_____

Distance _____ Time _____

Time
by zone **1   2   3   4   5**

Workout rating _____

Notes _____

_____

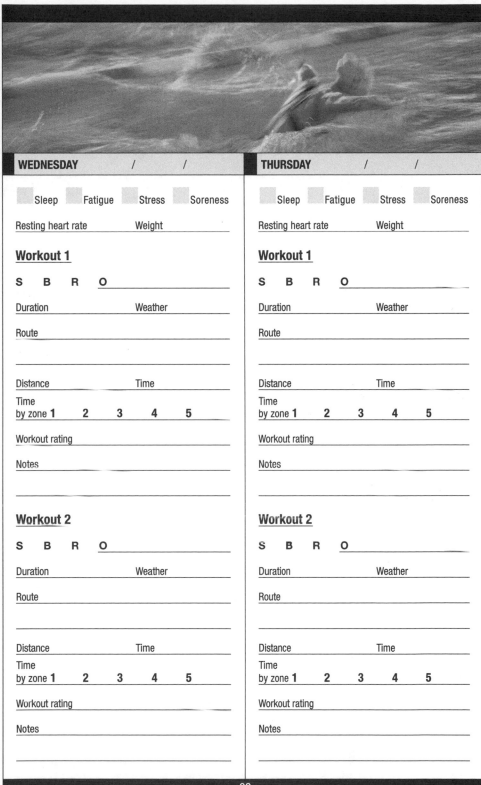

WEDNESDAY	/	/

Sleep Fatigue Stress Soreness

Resting heart rate _____ Weight _____

Workout 1

S B R O _____

Duration _____ Weather _____

Route _____

_____

Distance _____ Time _____

Time
by zone **1** **2** **3** **4** **5** _____

Workout rating _____

Notes _____

_____

Workout 2

S B R O _____

Duration _____ Weather _____

Route _____

_____

Distance _____ Time _____

Time
by zone **1** **2** **3** **4** **5** _____

Workout rating _____

Notes _____

_____

THURSDAY	/	/

Sleep Fatigue Stress Soreness

Resting heart rate _____ Weight _____

Workout 1

S B R O _____

Duration _____ Weather _____

Route _____

_____

Distance _____ Time _____

Time
by zone **1** **2** **3** **4** **5** _____

Workout rating _____

Notes _____

_____

Workout 2

S B R O _____

Duration _____ Weather _____

Route _____

_____

Distance _____ Time _____

Time
by zone **1** **2** **3** **4** **5** _____

Workout rating _____

Notes _____

_____

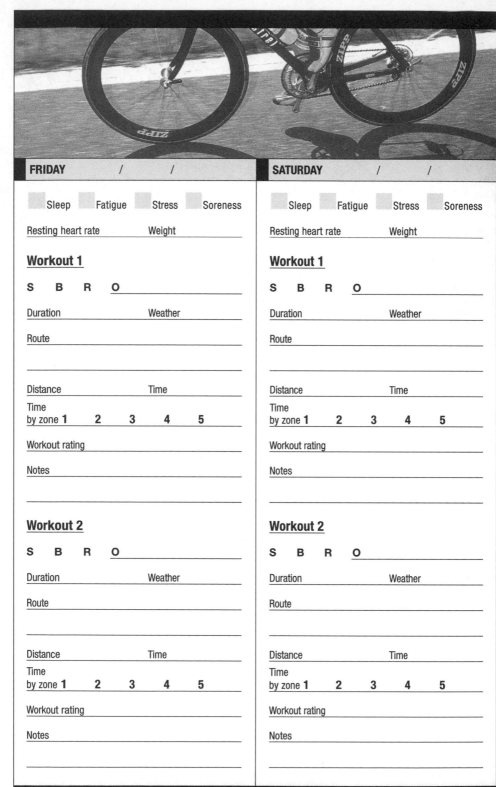

FRIDAY / /

Sleep Fatigue Stress Soreness

Resting heart rate _____ Weight _____

Workout 1

S   B   R   O _____

Duration _____ Weather _____

Route _____

_____

Distance _____ Time _____

Time
by zone **1   2   3   4   5**

Workout rating _____

Notes _____

_____

Workout 2

S   B   R   O _____

Duration _____ Weather _____

Route _____

_____

Distance _____ Time _____

Time
by zone **1   2   3   4   5**

Workout rating _____

Notes _____

_____

SATURDAY / /

Sleep Fatigue Stress Soreness

Resting heart rate _____ Weight _____

Workout 1

S   B   R   O _____

Duration _____ Weather _____

Route _____

_____

Distance _____ Time _____

Time
by zone **1   2   3   4   5**

Workout rating _____

Notes _____

_____

Workout 2

S   B   R   O _____

Duration _____ Weather _____

Route _____

_____

Distance _____ Time _____

Time
by zone **1   2   3   4   5**

Workout rating _____

Notes _____

_____

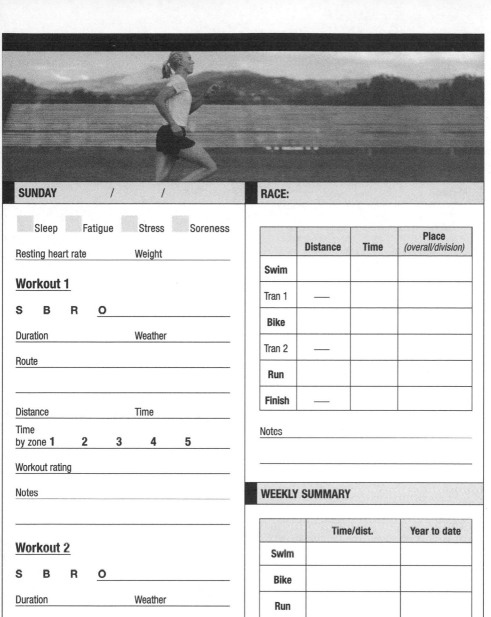

Sleep   Fatigue   Stress   Soreness

Resting heart rate   Weight

Workout 1

S   B   R   O

Duration   Weather

Route

Distance   Time

Time
by zone 1   2   3   4   5

Workout rating

Notes

Workout 2

S   B   R   O

Duration   Weather

Route

Distance   Time

Time
by zone 1   2   3   4   5

Workout rating

Notes

RACE:

	Distance	Time	Place *(overall/division)*
Swim			
Tran 1	—		
Bike			
Tran 2	—		
Run			
Finish	—		

Notes

WEEKLY SUMMARY

	Time/dist.	Year to date
Swim		
Bike		
Run		
Strength		

Weekly   Year-to-date
total   total

Soreness

Notes

WEEK BEGINNING:　　　　　　　　**PLANNED WEEKLY HOURS:**

Week's goals (check off as achieved)

▨ _____

▨ _____

▨ _____

| **MONDAY** | / | / | **TUESDAY** | / | / |

▨ Sleep　▨ Fatigue　▨ Stress　▨ Soreness

Resting heart rate _____ Weight _____

Workout 1

S　　B　　R　　O _____

Duration _____ Weather _____

Route _____

_____

Distance _____ Time _____

Time
by zone **1**　　**2**　　**3**　　**4**　　**5**

Workout rating _____

Notes _____

_____

Workout 2

S　　B　　R　　O _____

Duration _____ Weather _____

Route _____

_____

Distance _____ Time _____

Time
by zone **1**　　**2**　　**3**　　**4**　　**5**

Workout rating _____

Notes _____

_____

▨ Sleep　▨ Fatigue　▨ Stress　▨ Soreness

Resting heart rate _____ Weight _____

Workout 1

S　　B　　R　　O _____

Duration _____ Weather _____

Route _____

_____

Distance _____ Time _____

Time
by zone **1**　　**2**　　**3**　　**4**　　**5**

Workout rating _____

Notes _____

_____

Workout 2

S　　B　　R　　O _____

Duration _____ Weather _____

Route _____

_____

Distance _____ Time _____

Time
by zone **1**　　**2**　　**3**　　**4**　　**5**

Workout rating _____

Notes _____

_____

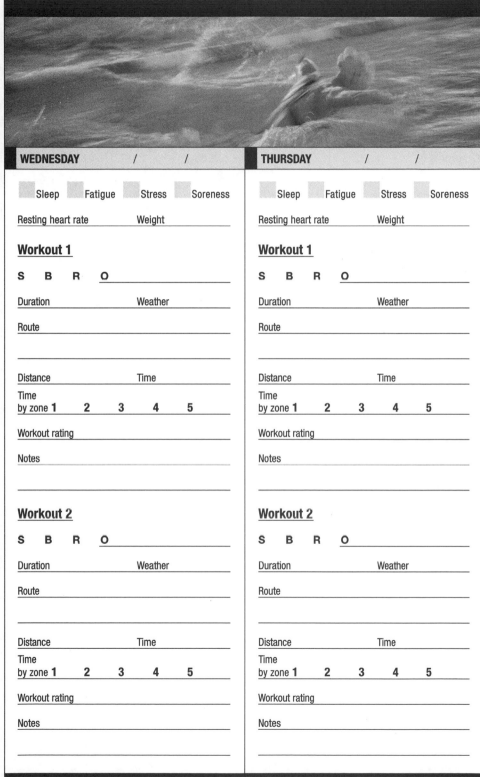

WEDNESDAY	/	/

Sleep   Fatigue   Stress   Soreness

Resting heart rate _____ Weight _____

Workout 1

S   B   R   O   _____

Duration _____ Weather _____

Route _____

_____

Distance _____ Time _____

Time
by zone **1**   **2**   **3**   **4**   **5**

Workout rating _____

Notes _____

_____

Workout 2

S   B   R   O   _____

Duration _____ Weather _____

Route _____

_____

Distance _____ Time _____

Time
by zone **1**   **2**   **3**   **4**   **5**

Workout rating _____

Notes _____

_____

THURSDAY	/	/

Sleep   Fatigue   Stress   Soreness

Resting heart rate _____ Weight _____

Workout 1

S   B   R   O   _____

Duration _____ Weather _____

Route _____

_____

Distance _____ Time _____

Time
by zone **1**   **2**   **3**   **4**   **5**

Workout rating _____

Notes _____

_____

Workout 2

S   B   R   O   _____

Duration _____ Weather _____

Route _____

_____

Distance _____ Time _____

Time
by zone **1**   **2**   **3**   **4**   **5**

Workout rating _____

Notes _____

_____

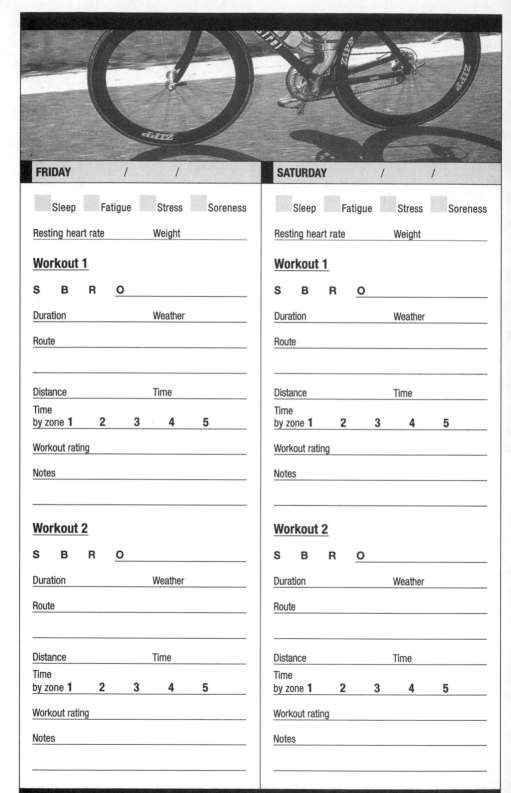

FRIDAY   /   /

Sleep   Fatigue   Stress   Soreness

Resting heart rate _____   Weight _____

Workout 1

S   B   R   O _____

Duration _____   Weather _____

Route _____

_____

Distance _____   Time _____

Time
by zone **1   2   3   4   5**

Workout rating _____

Notes _____

_____

Workout 2

S   B   R   O _____

Duration _____   Weather _____

Route _____

_____

Distance _____   Time _____

Time
by zone **1   2   3   4   5**

Workout rating _____

Notes _____

_____

SATURDAY   /   /

Sleep   Fatigue   Stress   Soreness

Resting heart rate _____   Weight _____

Workout 1

S   B   R   O _____

Duration _____   Weather _____

Route _____

_____

Distance _____   Time _____

Time
by zone **1   2   3   4   5**

Workout rating _____

Notes _____

_____

Workout 2

S   B   R   O _____

Duration _____   Weather _____

Route _____

_____

Distance _____   Time _____

Time
by zone **1   2   3   4   5**

Workout rating _____

Notes _____

_____

SUNDAY   /   /

Sleep   Fatigue   Stress   Soreness

Resting heart rate _____ Weight _____

Workout 1

S   B   R   O   _____

Duration _____ Weather _____

Route _____

_____

Distance _____ Time _____

Time
by zone **1   2   3   4   5** _____

Workout rating _____

Notes _____

_____

Workout 2

S   B   R   O   _____

Duration _____ Weather _____

Route _____

_____

Distance _____ Time _____

Time
by zone **1   2   3   4   5** _____

Workout rating _____

Notes _____

_____

RACE:

	Distance	Time	Place *(overall/division)*
Swim			
Tran 1	—		
Bike			
Tran 2	—		
Run			
Finish	—		

Notes _____

_____

WEEKLY SUMMARY

	Time/dist.	Year to date
Swim		
Bike		
Run		
Strength		

Weekly   Year-to-date
total   total _____

Soreness _____

Notes _____

_____

WEEK BEGINNING: **PLANNED WEEKLY HOURS:**

Week's goals (check off as achieved)

☐ _____

☐ _____

☐ _____

MONDAY / /	TUESDAY / /

☐ Sleep ☐ Fatigue ☐ Stress ☐ Soreness

Resting heart rate _____ Weight _____

Workout 1

S   B   R   O _____

Duration _____ Weather _____

Route _____

_____

Distance _____ Time _____

Time
by zone **1   2   3   4   5**

Workout rating _____

Notes _____

_____

Workout 2

S   B   R   O _____

Duration _____ Weather _____

Route _____

_____

Distance _____ Time _____

Time
by zone **1   2   3   4   5**

Workout rating _____

Notes _____

_____

☐ Sleep ☐ Fatigue ☐ Stress ☐ Soreness

Resting heart rate _____ Weight _____

Workout 1

S   B   R   O _____

Duration _____ Weather _____

Route _____

_____

Distance _____ Time _____

Time
by zone **1   2   3   4   5**

Workout rating _____

Notes _____

_____

Workout 2

S   B   R   O _____

Duration _____ Weather _____

Route _____

_____

Distance _____ Time _____

Time
by zone **1   2   3   4   5**

Workout rating _____

Notes _____

_____

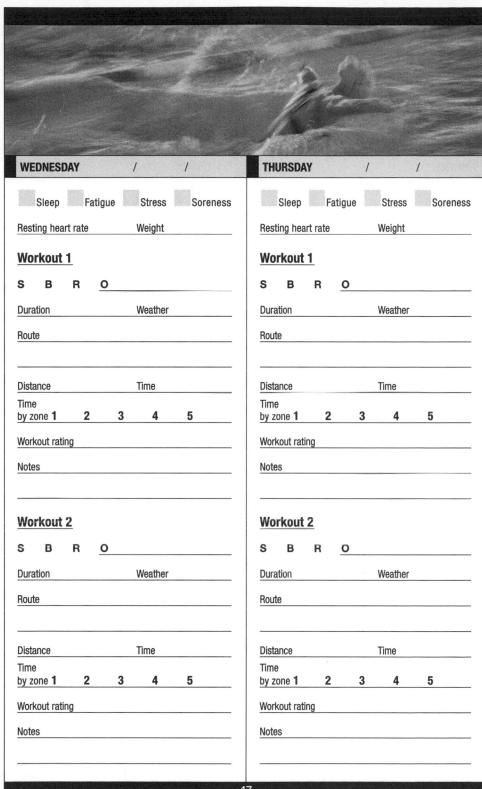

Sleep   Fatigue   Stress   Soreness

Resting heart rate _____ Weight _____

Workout 1

S   B   R   O _____

Duration _____ Weather _____

Route _____

_____

Distance _____ Time _____

Time
by zone **1   2   3   4   5** _____

Workout rating _____

Notes _____

_____

Workout 2

S   B   R   O _____

Duration _____ Weather _____

Route _____

_____

Distance _____ Time _____

Time
by zone **1   2   3   4   5** _____

Workout rating _____

Notes _____

_____

Sleep   Fatigue   Stress   Soreness

Resting heart rate _____ Weight _____

Workout 1

S   B   R   O _____

Duration _____ Weather _____

Route _____

_____

Distance _____ Time _____

Time
by zone **1   2   3   4   5** _____

Workout rating _____

Notes _____

_____

Workout 2

S   B   R   O _____

Duration _____ Weather _____

Route _____

_____

Distance _____ Time _____

Time
by zone **1   2   3   4   5** _____

Workout rating _____

Notes _____

_____

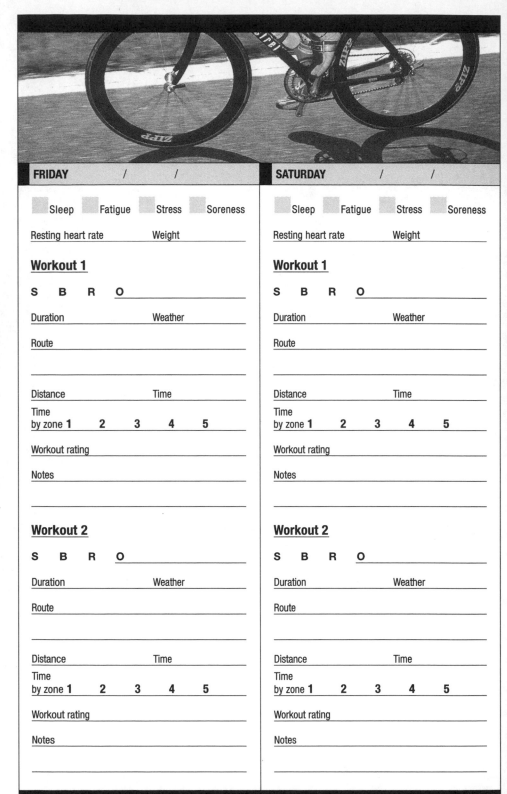

FRIDAY / /

Sleep Fatigue Stress Soreness

Resting heart rate _____ Weight _____

Workout 1

S B R O _____

Duration _____ Weather _____

Route _____

_____

Distance _____ Time _____

Time
by zone **1   2   3   4   5**

Workout rating _____

Notes _____

_____

Workout 2

S B R O _____

Duration _____ Weather _____

Route _____

_____

Distance _____ Time _____

Time
by zone **1   2   3   4   5**

Workout rating _____

Notes _____

_____

SATURDAY / /

Sleep Fatigue Stress Soreness

Resting heart rate _____ Weight _____

Workout 1

S B R O _____

Duration _____ Weather _____

Route _____

_____

Distance _____ Time _____

Time
by zone **1   2   3   4   5**

Workout rating _____

Notes _____

_____

Workout 2

S B R O _____

Duration _____ Weather _____

Route _____

_____

Distance _____ Time _____

Time
by zone **1   2   3   4   5**

Workout rating _____

Notes _____

_____

SUNDAY	/	/

Sleep   Fatigue   Stress   Soreness

Resting heart rate _____ Weight _____

Workout 1

S   B   R   O _____

Duration _____ Weather _____

Route _____

_____

Distance _____ Time _____

Time
by zone **1**   **2**   **3**   **4**   **5**

Workout rating _____

Notes _____

_____

Workout 2

S   B   R   O _____

Duration _____ Weather _____

Route _____

_____

Distance _____ Time _____

Time
by zone **1**   **2**   **3**   **4**   **5**

Workout rating _____

Notes _____

_____

RACE: _____

	Distance	Time	Place *(overall/division)*
Swim			
Tran 1	—		
Bike			
Tran 2	—		
Run			
Finish	—		

Notes _____

_____

WEEKLY SUMMARY

	Time/dist.	Year to date
Swim		
Bike		
Run		
Strength		

Weekly total _____ Year-to-date total _____

Soreness _____

Notes _____

_____

WEEK BEGINNING: **PLANNED WEEKLY HOURS:**

Week's goals (check off as achieved)

▨ _____

▨ _____

▨ _____

MONDAY / /	**TUESDAY** / /
▨ Sleep ▨ Fatigue ▨ Stress ▨ Soreness	▨ Sleep ▨ Fatigue ▨ Stress ▨ Soreness
Resting heart rate _____ Weight _____	Resting heart rate _____ Weight _____

Workout 1   **Workout 1**

S   B   R   O _____   S   B   R   O _____

Duration _____ Weather _____   Duration _____ Weather _____

Route _____   Route _____

_____   _____

Distance _____ Time _____   Distance _____ Time _____

Time by zone **1**   **2**   **3**   **4**   **5**   Time by zone **1**   **2**   **3**   **4**   **5**

Workout rating _____   Workout rating _____

Notes _____   Notes _____

_____   _____

Workout 2   **Workout 2**

S   B   R   O _____   S   B   R   O _____

Duration _____ Weather _____   Duration _____ Weather _____

Route _____   Route _____

_____   _____

Distance _____ Time _____   Distance _____ Time _____

Time by zone **1**   **2**   **3**   **4**   **5**   Time by zone **1**   **2**   **3**   **4**   **5**

Workout rating _____   Workout rating _____

Notes _____   Notes _____

_____   _____

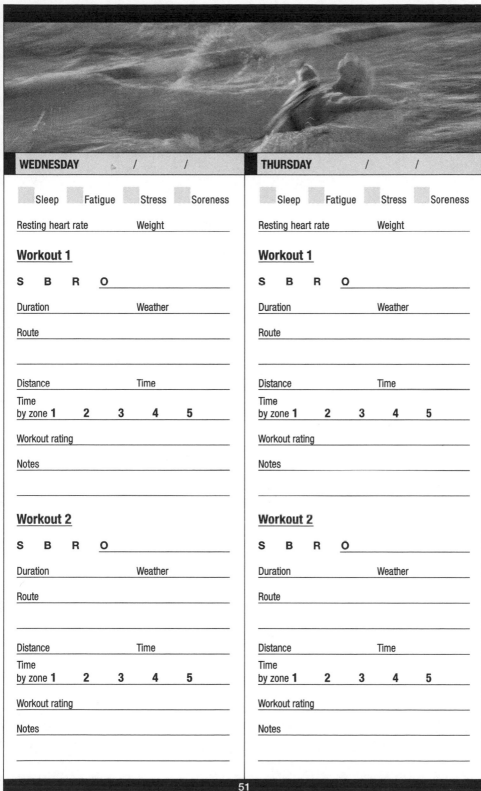

WEDNESDAY   /   /

Sleep   Fatigue   Stress   Soreness

Resting heart rate   Weight

Workout 1

S   B   R   O

Duration   Weather

Route

Distance   Time

Time
by zone 1   2   3   4   5

Workout rating

Notes

Workout 2

S   B   R   O

Duration   Weather

Route

Distance   Time

Time
by zone 1   2   3   4   5

Workout rating

Notes

THURSDAY   /   /

Sleep   Fatigue   Stress   Soreness

Resting heart rate   Weight

Workout 1

S   B   R   O

Duration   Weather

Route

Distance   Time

Time
by zone 1   2   3   4   5

Workout rating

Notes

Workout 2

S   B   R   O

Duration   Weather

Route

Distance   Time

Time
by zone 1   2   3   4   5

Workout rating

Notes

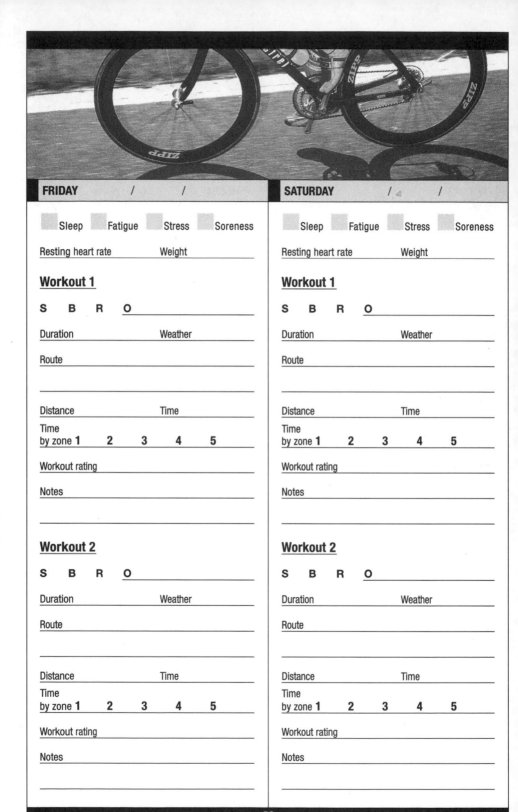

FRIDAY / /

Sleep Fatigue Stress Soreness

Resting heart rate _____ Weight _____

Workout 1

S   B   R   O _____

Duration _____ Weather _____

Route _____
_____

Distance _____ Time _____

Time
by zone **1   2   3   4   5**

Workout rating _____

Notes _____
_____

Workout 2

S   B   R   O _____

Duration _____ Weather _____

Route _____
_____

Distance _____ Time _____

Time
by zone **1   2   3   4   5**

Workout rating _____

Notes _____
_____

SATURDAY / /

Sleep Fatigue Stress Soreness

Resting heart rate _____ Weight _____

Workout 1

S   B   R   O _____

Duration _____ Weather _____

Route _____
_____

Distance _____ Time _____

Time
by zone **1   2   3   4   5**

Workout rating _____

Notes _____
_____

Workout 2

S   B   R   O _____

Duration _____ Weather _____

Route _____
_____

Distance _____ Time _____

Time
by zone **1   2   3   4   5**

Workout rating _____

Notes _____
_____

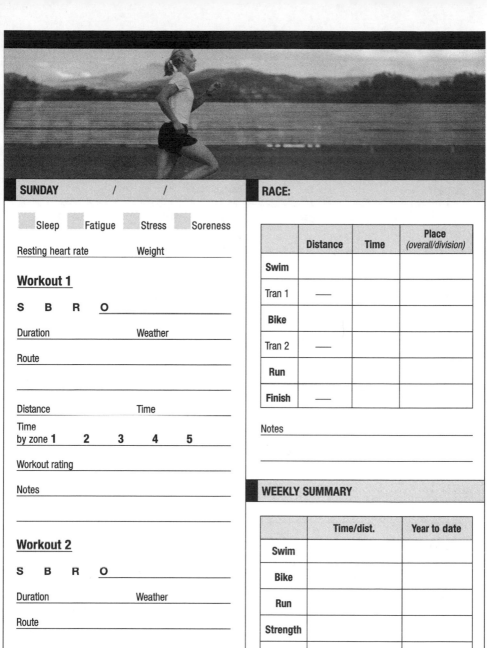

SUNDAY / /

Sleep ▢ Fatigue ▢ Stress ▢ Soreness ▢

Resting heart rate _____ Weight _____

Workout 1

S   B   R   O _____

Duration _____ Weather _____

Route _____
_____

Distance _____ Time _____

Time
by zone **1   2   3   4   5** _____

Workout rating _____

Notes _____
_____

Workout 2

S   B   R   O _____

Duration _____ Weather _____

Route _____
_____

Distance _____ Time _____

Time
by zone **1   2   3   4   5** _____

Workout rating _____

Notes _____
_____

RACE: _____

	Distance	Time	Place *(overall/division)*
Swim			
Tran 1	—		
Bike			
Tran 2	—		
Run			
Finish	—		

Notes _____
_____

WEEKLY SUMMARY

	Time/dist.	Year to date
Swim		
Bike		
Run		
Strength		

Weekly total _____   Year-to-date total _____

Soreness _____

Notes _____
_____

WEEK BEGINNING: **PLANNED WEEKLY HOURS:**

Week's goals (check off as achieved)

☐ _____

☐ _____

☐ _____

MONDAY / /	**TUESDAY** / /

☐ Sleep ☐ Fatigue ☐ Stress ☐ Soreness

Resting heart rate _____ Weight _____

Workout 1

S   B   R   O _____

Duration _____ Weather _____

Route _____

_____

Distance _____ Time _____

Time
by zone **1**   **2**   **3**   **4**   **5**

Workout rating _____

Notes _____

_____

Workout 2

S   B   R   O _____

Duration _____ Weather _____

Route _____

_____

Distance _____ Time _____

Time
by zone **1**   **2**   **3**   **4**   **5**

Workout rating _____

Notes _____

_____

☐ Sleep ☐ Fatigue ☐ Stress ☐ Soreness

Resting heart rate _____ Weight _____

Workout 1

S   B   R   O _____

Duration _____ Weather _____

Route _____

_____

Distance _____ Time _____

Time
by zone **1**   **2**   **3**   **4**   **5**

Workout rating _____

Notes _____

_____

Workout 2

S   B   R   O _____

Duration _____ Weather _____

Route _____

_____

Distance _____ Time _____

Time
by zone **1**   **2**   **3**   **4**   **5**

Workout rating _____

Notes _____

_____

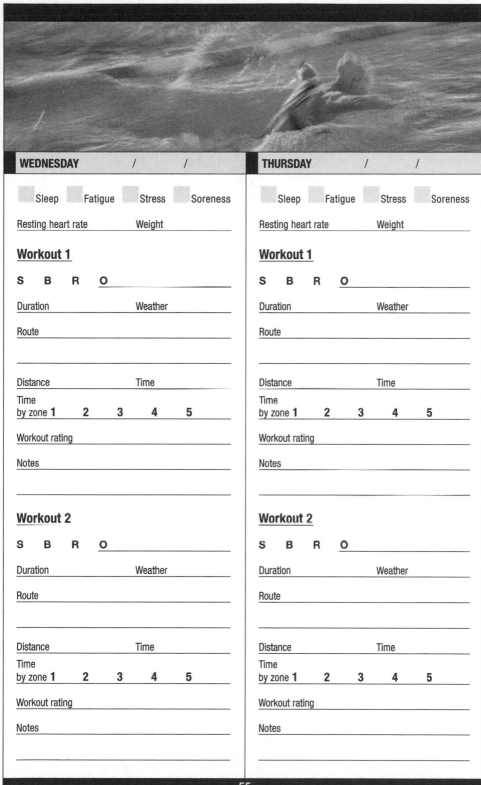

WEDNESDAY	/	/

Sleep   Fatigue   Stress   Soreness

Resting heart rate _____ Weight _____

Workout 1

S   B   R   O _____

Duration _____ Weather _____

Route _____

_____

Distance _____ Time _____

Time
by zone 1   2   3   4   5

Workout rating _____

Notes _____

_____

Workout 2

S   B   R   O _____

Duration _____ Weather _____

Route _____

_____

Distance _____ Time _____

Time
by zone 1   2   3   4   5

Workout rating _____

Notes _____

_____

THURSDAY	/	/

Sleep   Fatigue   Stress   Soreness

Resting heart rate _____ Weight _____

Workout 1

S   B   R   O _____

Duration _____ Weather _____

Route _____

_____

Distance _____ Time _____

Time
by zone 1   2   3   4   5

Workout rating _____

Notes _____

_____

Workout 2

S   B   R   O _____

Duration _____ Weather _____

Route _____

_____

Distance _____ Time _____

Time
by zone 1   2   3   4   5

Workout rating _____

Notes _____

_____

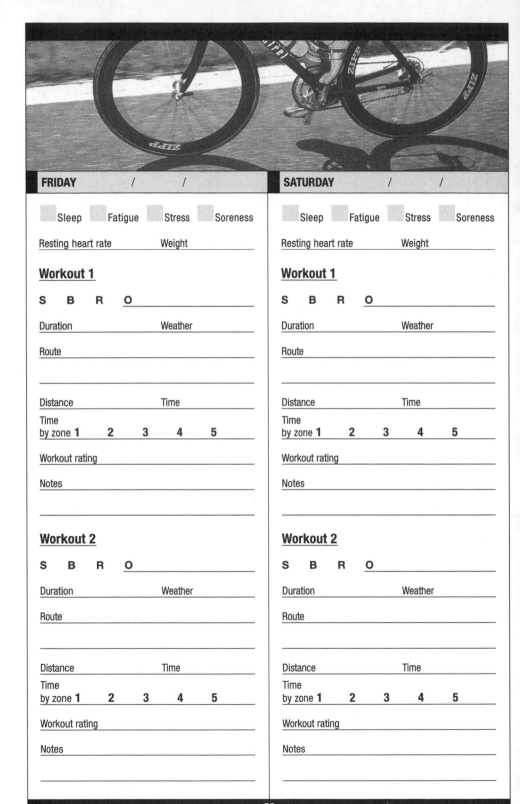

| FRIDAY | / | / | | SATURDAY | / | / |

Sleep ▢ Fatigue ▢ Stress ▢ Soreness ▢

Resting heart rate _____ Weight _____

Workout 1

S   B   R   O _____

Duration _____ Weather _____

Route _____

_____

Distance _____ Time _____

Time
by zone **1   2   3   4   5**

Workout rating _____

Notes _____

_____

Workout 2

S   B   R   O _____

Duration _____ Weather _____

Route _____

_____

Distance _____ Time _____

Time
by zone **1   2   3   4   5**

Workout rating _____

Notes _____

_____

Sleep ▢ Fatigue ▢ Stress ▢ Soreness ▢

Resting heart rate _____ Weight _____

Workout 1

S   B   R   O _____

Duration _____ Weather _____

Route _____

_____

Distance _____ Time _____

Time
by zone **1   2   3   4   5**

Workout rating _____

Notes _____

_____

Workout 2

S   B   R   O _____

Duration _____ Weather _____

Route _____

_____

Distance _____ Time _____

Time
by zone **1   2   3   4   5**

Workout rating _____

Notes _____

_____

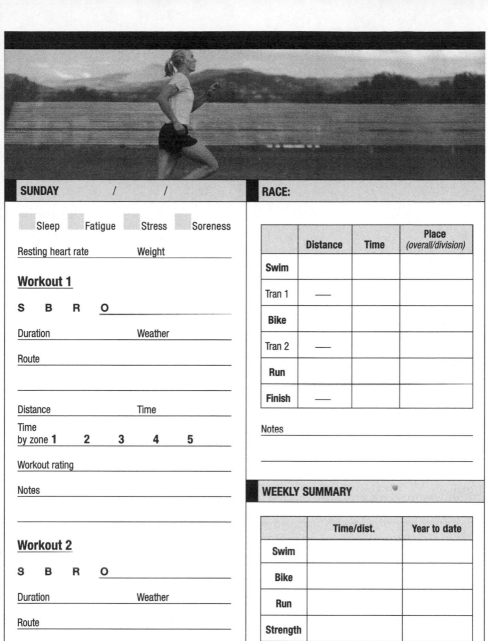

SUNDAY / /

RACE:

Sleep Fatigue Stress Soreness

Resting heart rate _____ Weight _____

Workout 1

S   B   R   O _____

Duration _____ Weather _____

Route _____

_____

Distance _____ Time _____

Time
by zone **1**   **2**   **3**   **4**   **5**

Workout rating _____

Notes _____

_____

Workout 2

S   B   R   O _____

Duration _____ Weather _____

Route _____

_____

Distance _____ Time _____

Time
by zone **1**   **2**   **3**   **4**   **5**

Workout rating _____

Notes _____

_____

	Distance	Time	Place *(overall/division)*
Swim			
Tran 1	—		
Bike			
Tran 2	—		
Run			
Finish	—		

Notes _____

_____

WEEKLY SUMMARY

	Time/dist.	Year to date
Swim		
Bike		
Run		
Strength		

Weekly
total _____

Year-to-date
total _____

Soreness _____

Notes _____

_____

WEEK BEGINNING: PLANNED WEEKLY HOURS:

Week's goals (check off as achieved)

▨ _____

▨ _____

▨ _____

MONDAY / /	TUESDAY / /
▨ Sleep ▨ Fatigue ▨ Stress ▨ Soreness	▨ Sleep ▨ Fatigue ▨ Stress ▨ Soreness
Resting heart rate Weight	Resting heart rate Weight

Workout 1

S   B   R   O _____

Duration _____ Weather _____

Route _____

_____

Distance _____ Time _____

Time
by zone **1   2   3   4   5** _____

Workout rating _____

Notes _____

_____

Workout 2

S   B   R   O _____

Duration _____ Weather _____

Route _____

_____

Distance _____ Time _____

Time
by zone **1   2   3   4   5** _____

Workout rating _____

Notes _____

_____

Workout 1

S   B   R   O _____

Duration _____ Weather _____

Route _____

_____

Distance _____ Time _____

Time
by zone **1   2   3   4   5** _____

Workout rating _____

Notes _____

_____

Workout 2

S   B   R   O _____

Duration _____ Weather _____

Route _____

_____

Distance _____ Time _____

Time
by zone **1   2   3   4   5** _____

Workout rating _____

Notes _____

_____

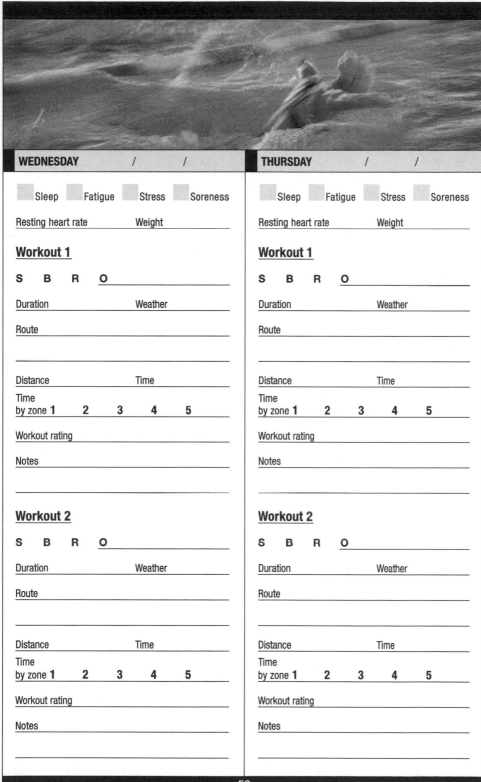

| WEDNESDAY | / | / | | THURSDAY | / | / |

Sleep   Fatigue   Stress   Soreness

Resting heart rate   Weight

Workout 1

S   B   R   O

Duration   Weather

Route

Distance   Time

Time
by zone **1   2   3   4   5**

Workout rating

Notes

Workout 2

S   B   R   O

Duration   Weather

Route

Distance   Time

Time
by zone **1   2   3   4   5**

Workout rating

Notes

Sleep   Fatigue   Stress   Soreness

Resting heart rate   Weight

Workout 1

S   B   R   O

Duration   Weather

Route

Distance   Time

Time
by zone **1   2   3   4   5**

Workout rating

Notes

Workout 2

S   B   R   O

Duration   Weather

Route

Distance   Time

Time
by zone **1   2   3   4   5**

Workout rating

Notes

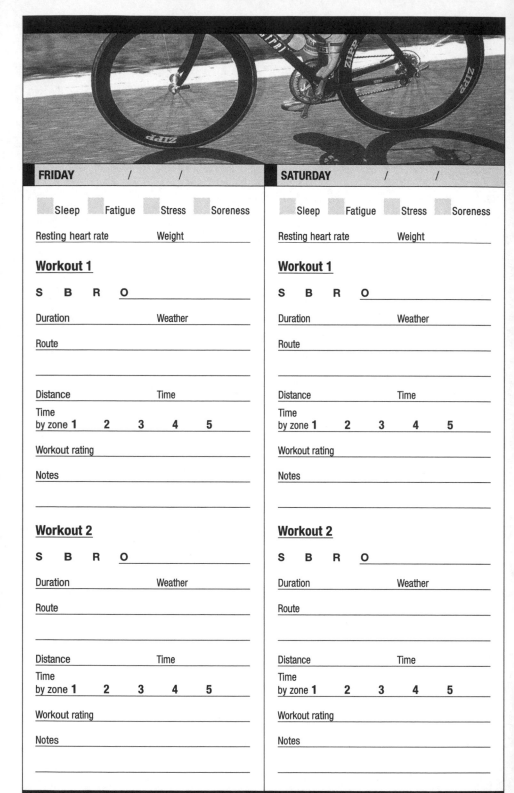

FRIDAY	/	/

Sleep Fatigue Stress Soreness

Resting heart rate _____ Weight _____

Workout 1

S B R O _____

Duration _____ Weather _____

Route _____

_____

Distance _____ Time _____

Time
by zone **1   2   3   4   5**

Workout rating _____

Notes _____

_____

Workout 2

S B R O _____

Duration _____ Weather _____

Route _____

_____

Distance _____ Time _____

Time
by zone **1   2   3   4   5**

Workout rating _____

Notes _____

_____

SATURDAY	/	/

Sleep Fatigue Stress Soreness

Resting heart rate _____ Weight _____

Workout 1

S B R O _____

Duration _____ Weather _____

Route _____

_____

Distance _____ Time _____

Time
by zone **1   2   3   4   5**

Workout rating _____

Notes _____

_____

Workout 2

S B R O _____

Duration _____ Weather _____

Route _____

_____

Distance _____ Time _____

Time
by zone **1   2   3   4   5**

Workout rating _____

Notes _____

_____

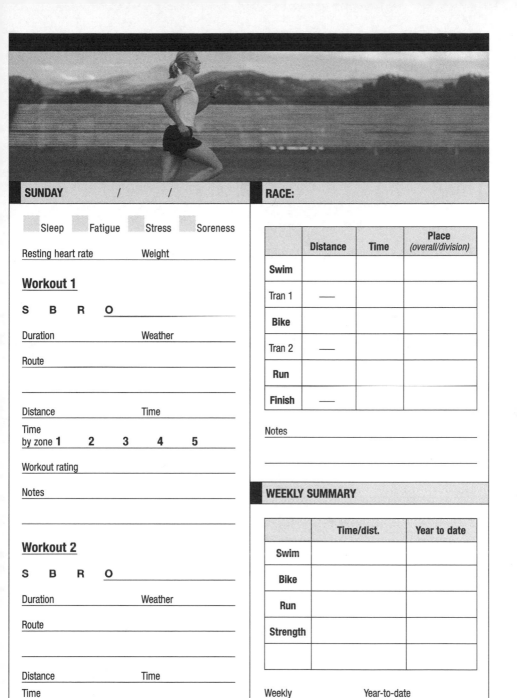

SUNDAY / /

Sleep   Fatigue   Stress   Soreness

Resting heart rate _____   Weight _____

Workout 1

S   B   R   O _____

Duration _____   Weather _____

Route _____

_____

Distance _____   Time _____

Time
by zone **1   2   3   4   5**

Workout rating _____

Notes _____

_____

Workout 2

S   B   R   O _____

Duration _____   Weather _____

Route _____

_____

Distance _____   Time _____

Time
by zone **1   2   3   4   5**

Workout rating _____

Notes _____

_____

RACE: _____

	Distance	Time	Place (overall/division)
Swim			
Tran 1	—		
Bike			
Tran 2	—		
Run			
Finish	—		

Notes _____

_____

WEEKLY SUMMARY

	Time/dist.	Year to date
Swim		
Bike		
Run		
Strength		

Weekly total _____   Year-to-date total _____

Soreness _____

Notes _____

_____

WEEK BEGINNING:　　　　　　　　**PLANNED WEEKLY HOURS:**

Week's goals (check off as achieved)

☐ _____

☐ _____

☐ _____

MONDAY / /	TUESDAY / /

☐ Sleep ☐ Fatigue ☐ Stress ☐ Soreness　　　☐ Sleep ☐ Fatigue ☐ Stress ☐ Soreness

Resting heart rate　　　　Weight　　　　　　Resting heart rate　　　　Weight

Workout 1

S　　B　　R　　O _____

Duration _____ Weather _____

Route _____

_____

Distance _____ Time _____

Time
by zone **1**　　**2**　　**3**　　**4**　　**5**

Workout rating _____

Notes _____

_____

Workout 2

S　　B　　R　　O _____

Duration _____ Weather _____

Route _____

_____

Distance _____ Time _____

Time
by zone **1**　　**2**　　**3**　　**4**　　**5**

Workout rating _____

Notes _____

_____

Workout 1

S　　B　　R　　O _____

Duration _____ Weather _____

Route _____

_____

Distance _____ Time _____

Time
by zone **1**　　**2**　　**3**　　**4**　　**5**

Workout rating _____

Notes _____

_____

Workout 2

S　　B　　R　　O _____

Duration _____ Weather _____

Route _____

_____

Distance _____ Time _____

Time
by zone **1**　　**2**　　**3**　　**4**　　**5**

Workout rating _____

Notes _____

_____

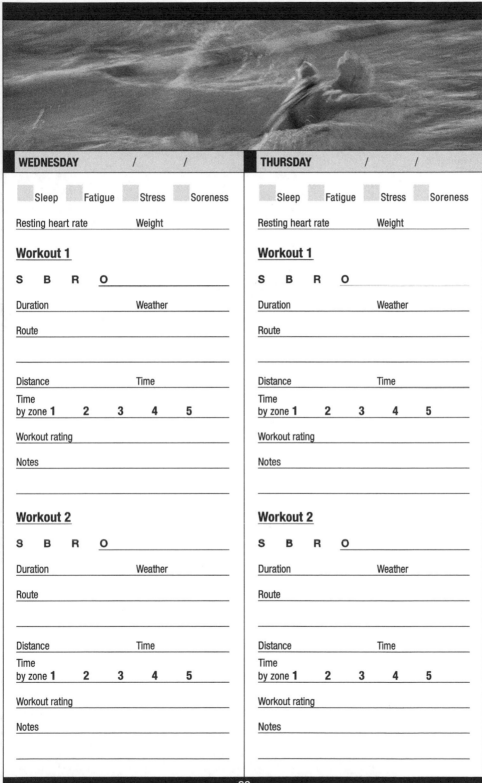

WEDNESDAY / /

Sleep Fatigue Stress Soreness

Resting heart rate _____ Weight _____

Workout 1

S B R O _____

Duration _____ Weather _____

Route _____

_____

Distance _____ Time _____

Time
by zone **1 2 3 4 5**

Workout rating _____

Notes _____

_____

Workout 2

S B R O _____

Duration _____ Weather _____

Route _____

_____

Distance _____ Time _____

Time
by zone **1 2 3 4 5**

Workout rating _____

Notes _____

_____

THURSDAY / /

Sleep Fatigue Stress Soreness

Resting heart rate _____ Weight _____

Workout 1

S B R O _____

Duration _____ Weather _____

Route _____

_____

Distance _____ Time _____

Time
by zone **1 2 3 4 5**

Workout rating _____

Notes _____

_____

Workout 2

S B R O _____

Duration _____ Weather _____

Route _____

_____

Distance _____ Time _____

Time
by zone **1 2 3 4 5**

Workout rating _____

Notes _____

_____

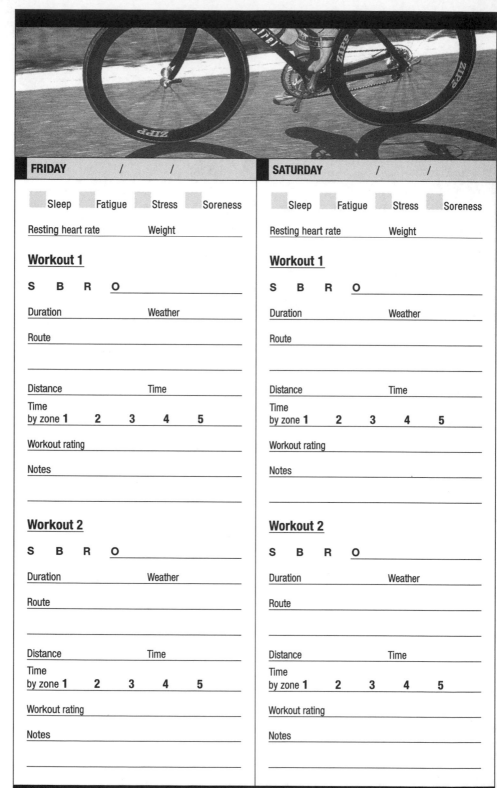

FRIDAY / /

Sleep Fatigue Stress Soreness

Resting heart rate _____ Weight _____

Workout 1

S   B   R   O _____

Duration _____ Weather _____

Route _____

_____

Distance _____ Time _____

Time
by zone **1**   **2**   **3**   **4**   **5**

Workout rating _____

Notes _____

_____

Workout 2

S   B   R   O _____

Duration _____ Weather _____

Route _____

_____

Distance _____ Time _____

Time
by zone **1**   **2**   **3**   **4**   **5**

Workout rating _____

Notes _____

_____

SATURDAY / /

Sleep Fatigue Stress Soreness

Resting heart rate _____ Weight _____

Workout 1

S   B   R   O _____

Duration _____ Weather _____

Route _____

_____

Distance _____ Time _____

Time
by zone **1**   **2**   **3**   **4**   **5**

Workout rating _____

Notes _____

_____

Workout 2

S   B   R   O _____

Duration _____ Weather _____

Route _____

_____

Distance _____ Time _____

Time
by zone **1**   **2**   **3**   **4**   **5**

Workout rating _____

Notes _____

_____

SUNDAY   /   /

RACE:

Sleep   Fatigue   Stress   Soreness

Resting heart rate   Weight

Workout 1

S   B   R   O

Duration   Weather

Route

Distance   Time

Time
by zone **1**   **2**   **3**   **4**   **5**

Workout rating

Notes

Workout 2

S   B   R   O

Duration   Weather

Route

Distance   Time

Time
by zone **1**   **2**   **3**   **4**   **5**

Workout rating

Notes

	Distance	Time	Place *(overall/division)*
Swim			
Tran 1	—		
Bike			
Tran 2	—		
Run			
Finish	—		

Notes

WEEKLY SUMMARY

	Time/dist.	Year to date
Swim		
Bike		
Run		
Strength		

Weekly
total   Year-to-date
total

Soreness

Notes

Week's goals (check off as achieved)

☐ _____

☐ _____

☐ _____

MONDAY / /	**TUESDAY** / /

☐ Sleep ☐ Fatigue ☐ Stress ☐ Soreness   ☐ Sleep ☐ Fatigue ☐ Stress ☐ Soreness

Resting heart rate _____ Weight _____   Resting heart rate _____ Weight _____

Workout 1

S   B   R   O _____

Duration _____ Weather _____

Route _____

_____

Distance _____ Time _____

Time
by zone **1**   **2**   **3**   **4**   **5**

Workout rating _____

Notes _____

_____

Workout 2

S   B   R   O _____

Duration _____ Weather _____

Route _____

_____

Distance _____ Time _____

Time
by zone **1**   **2**   **3**   **4**   **5**

Workout rating _____

Notes _____

_____

Workout 1

S   B   R   O _____

Duration _____ Weather _____

Route _____

_____

Distance _____ Time _____

Time
by zone **1**   **2**   **3**   **4**   **5**

Workout rating _____

Notes _____

_____

Workout 2

S   B   R   O _____

Duration _____ Weather _____

Route _____

_____

Distance _____ Time _____

Time
by zone **1**   **2**   **3**   **4**   **5**

Workout rating _____

Notes _____

_____

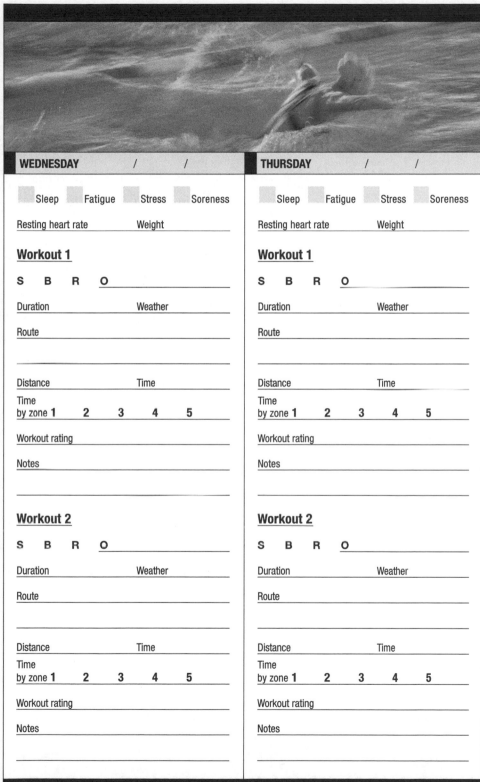

WEDNESDAY   /   /

Sleep   Fatigue   Stress   Soreness

Resting heart rate _____ Weight _____

Workout 1

S   B   R   O _____

Duration _____ Weather _____

Route _____

_____

Distance _____ Time _____

Time
by zone **1   2   3   4   5**

Workout rating _____

Notes _____

_____

Workout 2

S   B   R   O _____

Duration _____ Weather _____

Route _____

_____

Distance _____ Time _____

Time
by zone **1   2   3   4   5**

Workout rating _____

Notes _____

_____

THURSDAY   /   /

Sleep   Fatigue   Stress   Soreness

Resting heart rate _____ Weight _____

Workout 1

S   B   R   O _____

Duration _____ Weather _____

Route _____

_____

Distance _____ Time _____

Time
by zone **1   2   3   4   5**

Workout rating _____

Notes _____

_____

Workout 2

S   B   R   O _____

Duration _____ Weather _____

Route _____

_____

Distance _____ Time _____

Time
by zone **1   2   3   4   5**

Workout rating _____

Notes _____

_____

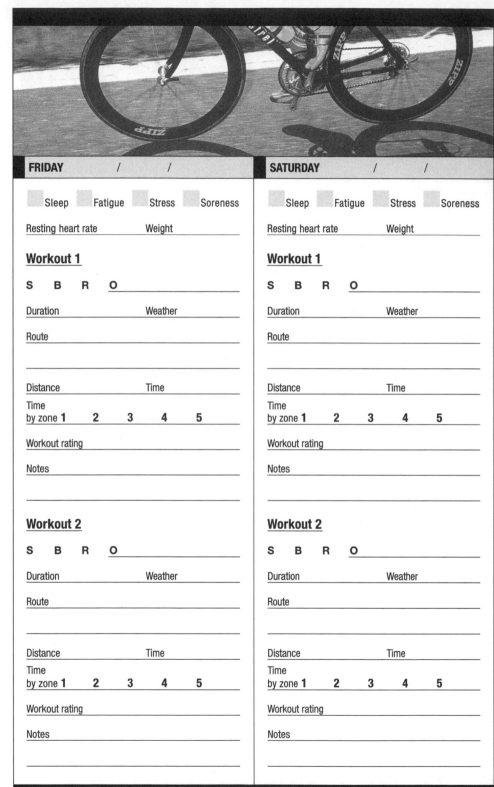

FRIDAY / /

Sleep Fatigue Stress Soreness

Resting heart rate _____ Weight _____

Workout 1

S   B   R   O _____

Duration _____ Weather _____

Route _____

_____

Distance _____ Time _____

Time
by zone **1** **2** **3** **4** **5**

Workout rating _____

Notes _____

_____

Workout 2

S   B   R   O _____

Duration _____ Weather _____

Route _____

_____

Distance _____ Time _____

Time
by zone **1** **2** **3** **4** **5**

Workout rating _____

Notes _____

_____

SATURDAY / /

Sleep Fatigue Stress Soreness

Resting heart rate _____ Weight _____

Workout 1

S   B   R   O _____

Duration _____ Weather _____

Route _____

_____

Distance _____ Time _____

Time
by zone **1** **2** **3** **4** **5**

Workout rating _____

Notes _____

_____

Workout 2

S   B   R   O _____

Duration _____ Weather _____

Route _____

_____

Distance _____ Time _____

Time
by zone **1** **2** **3** **4** **5**

Workout rating _____

Notes _____

_____

RACE:

	Distance	Time	Place *(overall/division)*
Swim			
Tran 1	—		
Bike			
Tran 2	—		
Run			
Finish	—		

Notes _____

_____

Sleep ___ Fatigue ___ Stress ___ Soreness

Resting heart rate _____ Weight _____

Workout 1

S   B   R   O _____

Duration _____ Weather _____

Route _____

_____

Distance _____ Time _____

Time
by zone 1   2   3   4   5

Workout rating _____

Notes _____

_____

Workout 2

S   B   R   O _____

Duration _____ Weather _____

Route _____

_____

Distance _____ Time _____

Time
by zone 1   2   3   4   5

Workout rating _____

Notes _____

_____

WEEKLY SUMMARY

	Time/dist.	Year to date
Swim		
Bike		
Run		
Strength		

Weekly   Year-to-date
total   total _____

Soreness _____

Notes _____

WEEK BEGINNING: **PLANNED WEEKLY HOURS:**

Week's goals (check off as achieved)

- [ ] _____
- [ ] _____
- [ ] _____

MONDAY / /	TUESDAY / /

Sleep   Fatigue   Stress   Soreness | **Sleep   Fatigue   Stress   Soreness**

Resting heart rate   Weight | Resting heart rate   Weight

Workout 1

S   B   R   O _____

Duration _____ Weather _____

Route _____

_____

Distance _____ Time _____

Time
by zone **1   2   3   4   5**

Workout rating _____

Notes _____

_____

Workout 2

S   B   R   O _____

Duration _____ Weather _____

Route _____

_____

Distance _____ Time _____

Time
by zone **1   2   3   4   5**

Workout rating _____

Notes _____

_____

Workout 1

S   B   R   O _____

Duration _____ Weather _____

Route _____

_____

Distance _____ Time _____

Time
by zone **1   2   3   4   5**

Workout rating _____

Notes _____

_____

Workout 2

S   B   R   O _____

Duration _____ Weather _____

Route _____

_____

Distance _____ Time _____

Time
by zone **1   2   3   4   5**

Workout rating _____

Notes _____

_____

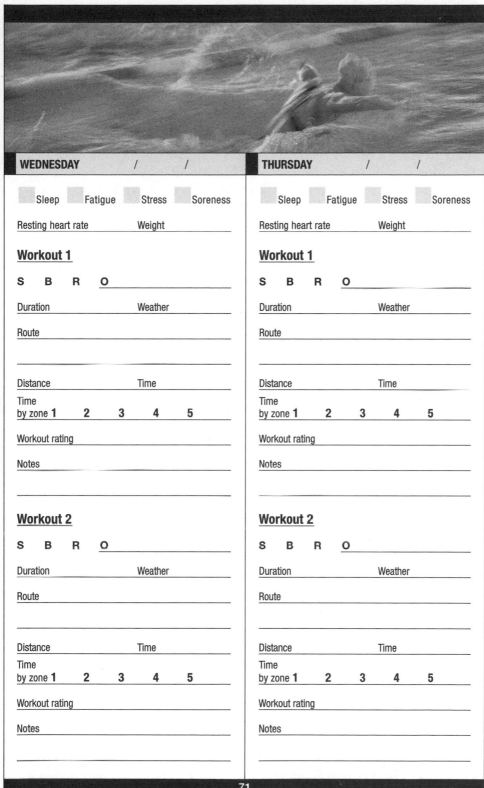

WEDNESDAY / /

Sleep   Fatigue   Stress   Soreness

Resting heart rate   Weight

Workout 1

S   B   R   O

Duration   Weather

Route

Distance   Time

Time
by zone 1   2   3   4   5

Workout rating

Notes

Workout 2

S   B   R   O

Duration   Weather

Route

Distance   Time

Time
by zone 1   2   3   4   5

Workout rating

Notes

THURSDAY / /

Sleep   Fatigue   Stress   Soreness

Resting heart rate   Weight

Workout 1

S   B   R   O

Duration   Weather

Route

Distance   Time

Time
by zone 1   2   3   4   5

Workout rating

Notes

Workout 2

S   B   R   O

Duration   Weather

Route

Distance   Time

Time
by zone 1   2   3   4   5

Workout rating

Notes

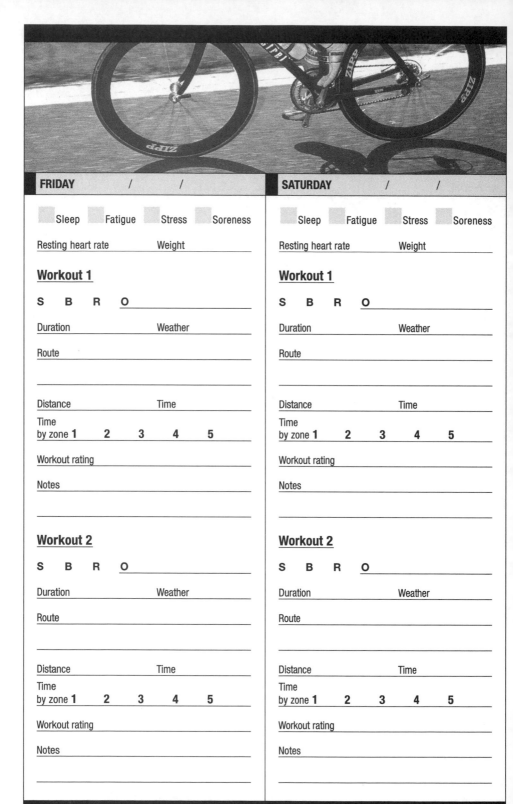

| FRIDAY | / | / | SATURDAY | / | / |

Sleep   Fatigue   Stress   Soreness

Resting heart rate   Weight

Workout 1

S   B   R   O

Duration   Weather

Route

Distance   Time

Time
by zone **1**   **2**   **3**   **4**   **5**

Workout rating

Notes

Workout 2

S   B   R   O

Duration   Weather

Route

Distance   Time

Time
by zone **1**   **2**   **3**   **4**   **5**

Workout rating

Notes

Sleep   Fatigue   Stress   Soreness

Resting heart rate   Weight

Workout 1

S   B   R   O

Duration   Weather

Route

Distance   Time

Time
by zone **1**   **2**   **3**   **4**   **5**

Workout rating

Notes

Workout 2

S   B   R   O

Duration   Weather

Route

Distance   Time

Time
by zone **1**   **2**   **3**   **4**   **5**

Workout rating

Notes

SUNDAY	/	/

Sleep Fatigue Stress Soreness

Resting heart rate _____ Weight _____

Workout 1

S   B   R   O _____

Duration _____ Weather _____

Route _____

_____

Distance _____ Time _____

Time
by zone **1   2   3   4   5** _____

Workout rating _____

Notes _____

_____

Workout 2

S   B   R   O _____

Duration _____ Weather _____

Route _____

_____

Distance _____ Time _____

Time
by zone **1   2   3   4   5** _____

Workout rating _____

Notes _____

_____

RACE:

	Distance	Time	Place (overall/division)
Swim			
Tran 1	—		
Bike			
Tran 2	—		
Run			
Finish	—		

Notes _____

_____

WEEKLY SUMMARY

	Time/dist.	Year to date
Swim		
Bike		
Run		
Strength		

Weekly   Year-to-date
total   total

Soreness _____

Notes _____

_____

WEEK BEGINNING: **PLANNED WEEKLY HOURS:**

Week's goals (check off as achieved)

☐ _____

☐ _____

☐ _____

MONDAY / /	**TUESDAY** / /

☐ Sleep ☐ Fatigue ☐ Stress ☐ Soreness   ☐ Sleep ☐ Fatigue ☐ Stress ☐ Soreness

Resting heart rate _____ Weight _____   Resting heart rate _____ Weight _____

Workout 1

S   B   R   O _____

Duration _____ Weather _____

Route _____

_____

Distance _____ Time _____

Time
by zone **1   2   3   4   5**

Workout rating _____

Notes _____

_____

Workout 2

S   B   R   O _____

Duration _____ Weather _____

Route _____

_____

Distance _____ Time _____

Time
by zone **1   2   3   4   5**

Workout rating _____

Notes _____

_____

Workout 1

S   B   R   O _____

Duration _____ Weather _____

Route _____

_____

Distance _____ Time _____

Time
by zone **1   2   3   4   5**

Workout rating _____

Notes _____

_____

Workout 2

S   B   R   O _____

Duration _____ Weather _____

Route _____

_____

Distance _____ Time _____

Time
by zone **1   2   3   4   5**

Workout rating _____

Notes _____

_____

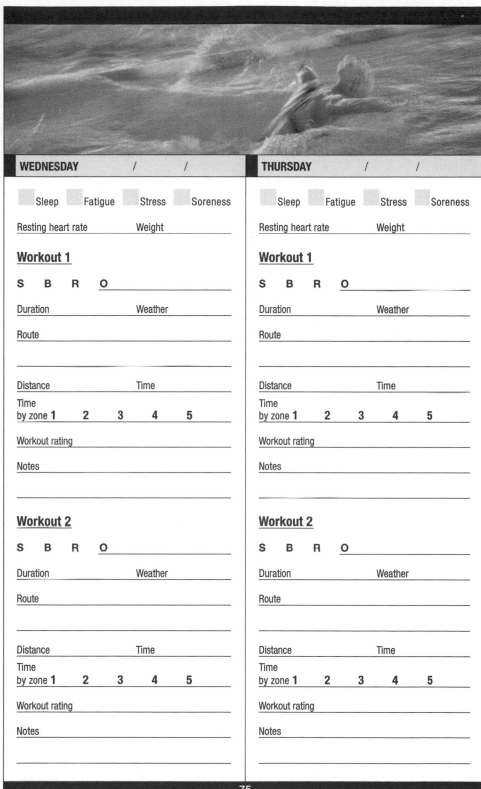

WEDNESDAY   /   /

Sleep   Fatigue   Stress   Soreness

Resting heart rate _____ Weight _____

Workout 1

S   B   R   O _____

Duration _____ Weather _____

Route _____

_____

Distance _____ Time _____

Time
by zone 1   2   3   4   5

Workout rating _____

Notes _____

_____

Workout 2

S   B   R   O _____

Duration _____ Weather _____

Route _____

_____

Distance _____ Time _____

Time
by zone 1   2   3   4   5

Workout rating _____

Notes _____

_____

THURSDAY   /   /

Sleep   Fatigue   Stress   Soreness

Resting heart rate _____ Weight _____

Workout 1

S   B   R   O _____

Duration _____ Weather _____

Route _____

_____

Distance _____ Time _____

Time
by zone 1   2   3   4   5

Workout rating _____

Notes _____

_____

Workout 2

S   B   R   O _____

Duration _____ Weather _____

Route _____

_____

Distance _____ Time _____

Time
by zone 1   2   3   4   5

Workout rating _____

Notes _____

_____

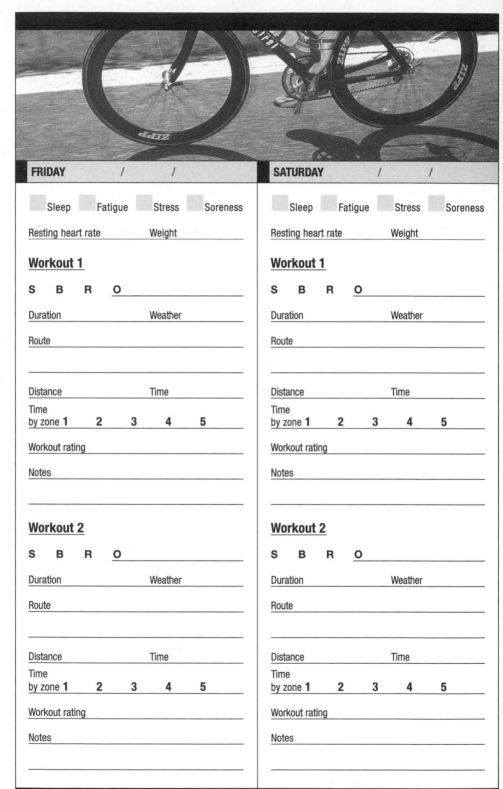

FRIDAY / /

Sleep Fatigue Stress Soreness

Resting heart rate _____ Weight _____

Workout 1

S   B   R   O _____

Duration _____ Weather _____

Route _____

_____

Distance _____ Time _____

Time
by zone 1   2   3   4   5

Workout rating _____

Notes _____

_____

Workout 2

S   B   R   O _____

Duration _____ Weather _____

Route _____

_____

Distance _____ Time _____

Time
by zone 1   2   3   4   5

Workout rating _____

Notes _____

_____

SATURDAY / /

Sleep Fatigue Stress Soreness

Resting heart rate _____ Weight _____

Workout 1

S   B   R   O _____

Duration _____ Weather _____

Route _____

_____

Distance _____ Time _____

Time
by zone 1   2   3   4   5

Workout rating _____

Notes _____

_____

Workout 2

S   B   R   O _____

Duration _____ Weather _____

Route _____

_____

Distance _____ Time _____

Time
by zone 1   2   3   4   5

Workout rating _____

Notes _____

_____

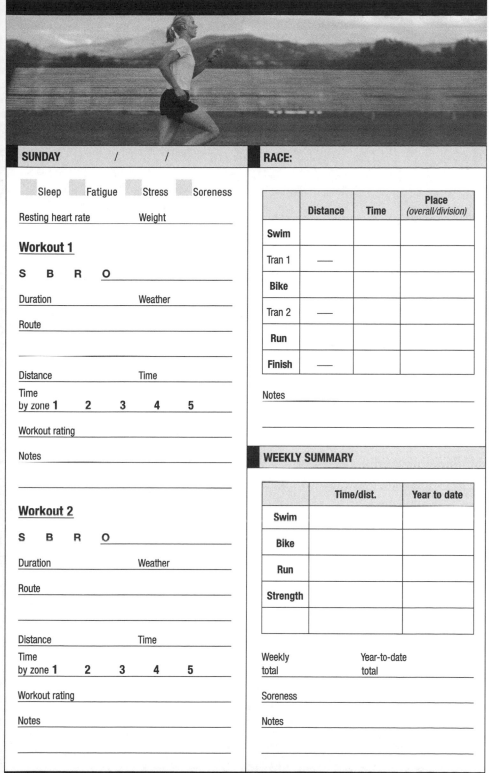

SUNDAY / /

Sleep Fatigue Stress Soreness

Resting heart rate _____ Weight _____

Workout 1

S   B   R   O _____

Duration _____ Weather _____

Route _____

_____

Distance _____ Time _____

Time
by zone **1   2   3   4   5** _____

Workout rating _____

Notes _____

_____

Workout 2

S   B   R   O _____

Duration _____ Weather _____

Route _____

_____

Distance _____ Time _____

Time
by zone **1   2   3   4   5** _____

Workout rating _____

Notes _____

_____

RACE: _____

	Distance	Time	Place *(overall/division)*
Swim			
Tran 1	—		
Bike			
Tran 2	—		
Run			
Finish	—		

Notes _____

_____

WEEKLY SUMMARY

	Time/dist.	Year to date
Swim		
Bike		
Run		
Strength		

Weekly
total _____ Year-to-date
total _____

Soreness _____

Notes _____

WEEK BEGINNING: **PLANNED WEEKLY HOURS:**

Week's goals (check off as achieved)

☐ _____

☐ _____

☐ _____

MONDAY / /	TUESDAY / /

☐ Sleep ☐ Fatigue ☐ Stress ☐ Soreness

Resting heart rate _____ Weight _____

Workout 1

S   B   R   O _____

Duration _____ Weather _____

Route _____

_____

Distance _____ Time _____

Time
by zone **1   2   3   4   5**

Workout rating _____

Notes _____

_____

Workout 2

S   B   R   O _____

Duration _____ Weather _____

Route _____

_____

Distance _____ Time _____

Time
by zone **1   2   3   4   5**

Workout rating _____

Notes _____

_____

☐ Sleep ☐ Fatigue ☐ Stress ☐ Soreness

Resting heart rate _____ Weight _____

Workout 1

S   B   R   O _____

Duration _____ Weather _____

Route _____

_____

Distance _____ Time _____

Time
by zone **1   2   3   4   5**

Workout rating _____

Notes _____

_____

Workout 2

S   B   R   O _____

Duration _____ Weather _____

Route _____

_____

Distance _____ Time _____

Time
by zone **1   2   3   4   5**

Workout rating _____

Notes _____

_____

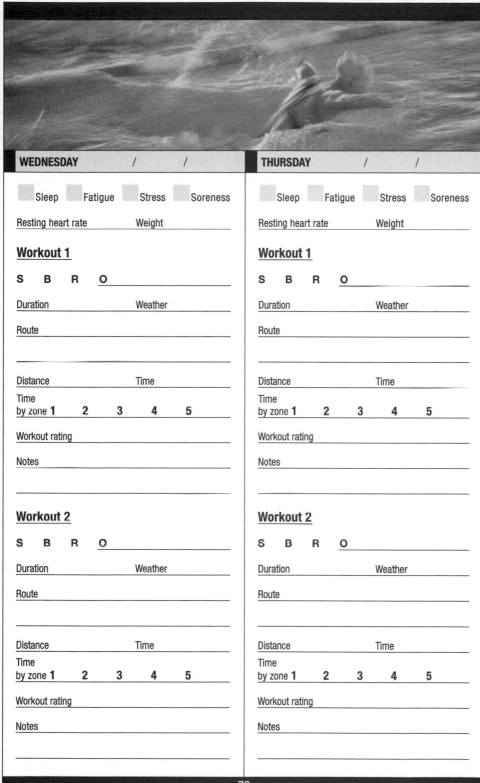

WEDNESDAY / /

Sleep   Fatigue   Stress   Soreness

Resting heart rate _____ Weight _____

Workout 1

S   B   R   O _____

Duration _____ Weather _____

Route _____

_____

Distance _____ Time _____

Time by zone **1   2   3   4   5**

Workout rating _____

Notes _____

_____

Workout 2

S   B   R   O _____

Duration _____ Weather _____

Route _____

_____

Distance _____ Time _____

Time by zone **1   2   3   4   5**

Workout rating _____

Notes _____

_____

THURSDAY / /

Sleep   Fatigue   Stress   Soreness

Resting heart rate _____ Weight _____

Workout 1

S   B   R   O _____

Duration _____ Weather _____

Route _____

_____

Distance _____ Time _____

Time by zone **1   2   3   4   5**

Workout rating _____

Notes _____

_____

Workout 2

S   B   R   O _____

Duration _____ Weather _____

Route _____

_____

Distance _____ Time _____

Time by zone **1   2   3   4   5**

Workout rating _____

Notes _____

_____

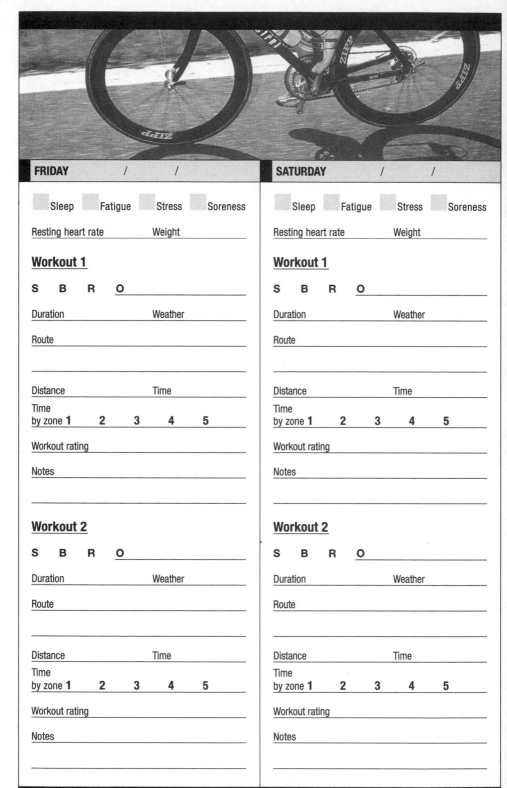

| FRIDAY | / | / |

Sleep Fatigue Stress Soreness

Resting heart rate _____ Weight _____

Workout 1

S B R O _____

Duration _____ Weather _____

Route _____

_____

Distance _____ Time _____

Time
by zone **1** **2** **3** **4** **5**

Workout rating _____

Notes _____

_____

Workout 2

S B R O _____

Duration _____ Weather _____

Route _____

_____

Distance _____ Time _____

Time
by zone **1** **2** **3** **4** **5**

Workout rating _____

Notes _____

_____

| SATURDAY | / | / |

Sleep Fatigue Stress Soreness

Resting heart rate _____ Weight _____

Workout 1

S B R O _____

Duration _____ Weather _____

Route _____

_____

Distance _____ Time _____

Time
by zone **1** **2** **3** **4** **5**

Workout rating _____

Notes _____

_____

Workout 2

S B R O _____

Duration _____ Weather _____

Route _____

_____

Distance _____ Time _____

Time
by zone **1** **2** **3** **4** **5**

Workout rating _____

Notes _____

_____

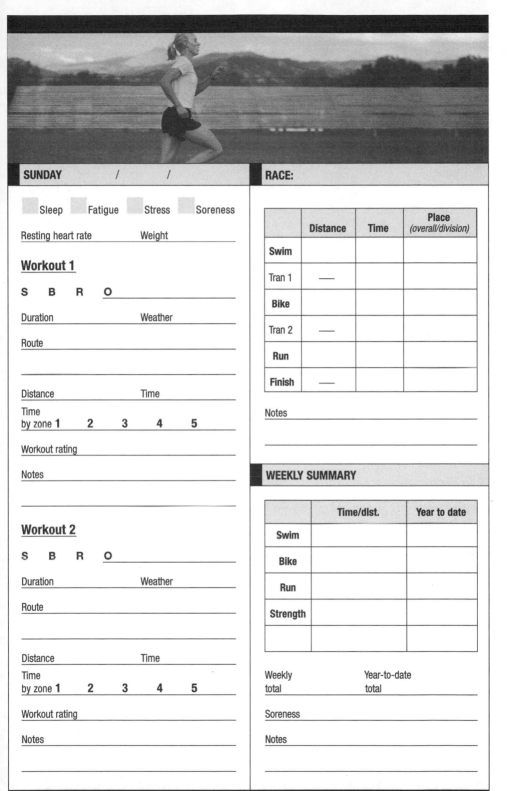

SUNDAY / /

Sleep Fatigue Stress Soreness

Resting heart rate _____ Weight _____

Workout 1

S   B   R   O   _____

Duration _____ Weather _____

Route _____

_____

Distance _____ Time _____

Time
by zone **1   2   3   4   5** _____

Workout rating _____

Notes _____

_____

Workout 2

S   B   R   O   _____

Duration _____ Weather _____

Route _____

_____

Distance _____ Time _____

Time
by zone **1   2   3   4   5** _____

Workout rating _____

Notes _____

_____

RACE: _____

	Distance	Time	Place (overall/division)
Swim			
Tran 1	—		
Bike			
Tran 2	—		
Run			
Finish	—		

Notes _____

_____

WEEKLY SUMMARY

	Time/dist.	Year to date
Swim		
Bike		
Run		
Strength		

Weekly total _____ Year-to-date total _____

Soreness _____

Notes _____

_____

81

WEEK BEGINNING: **PLANNED WEEKLY HOURS:**

Week's goals (check off as achieved)

- _____
- _____
- _____

MONDAY / /	TUESDAY / /

Sleep　Fatigue　Stress　Soreness	Sleep　Fatigue　Stress　Soreness
Resting heart rate　　　Weight	Resting heart rate　　　Weight

Workout 1

S　B　R　O _____

Duration _____ Weather _____

Route _____

_____

Distance _____ Time _____

Time by zone **1**　**2**　**3**　**4**　**5**

Workout rating _____

Notes _____

_____

Workout 1

S　B　R　O _____

Duration _____ Weather _____

Route _____

_____

Distance _____ Time _____

Time by zone **1**　**2**　**3**　**4**　**5**

Workout rating _____

Notes _____

_____

Workout 2

S　B　R　O _____

Duration _____ Weather _____

Route _____

_____

Distance _____ Time _____

Time by zone **1**　**2**　**3**　**4**　**5**

Workout rating _____

Notes _____

_____

Workout 2

S　B　R　O _____

Duration _____ Weather _____

Route _____

_____

Distance _____ Time _____

Time by zone **1**　**2**　**3**　**4**　**5**

Workout rating _____

Notes _____

_____

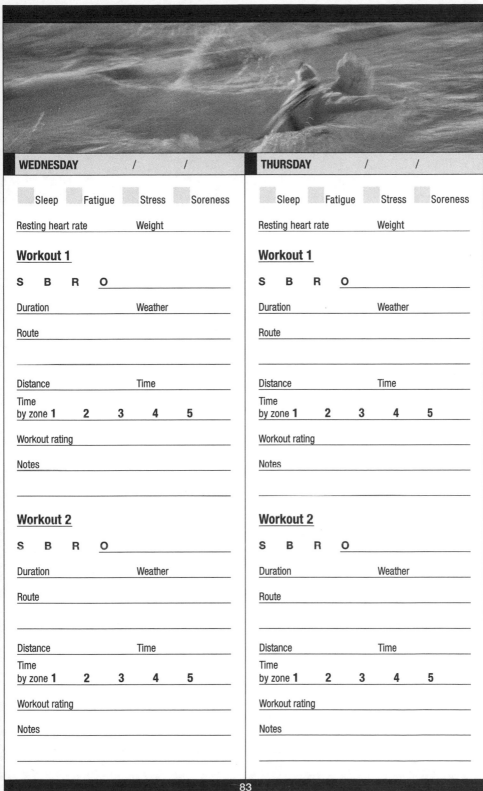

WEDNESDAY	/	/		**THURSDAY**	/	/

Sleep   Fatigue   Stress   Soreness

Resting heart rate   Weight

Workout 1

S   B   R   O

Duration   Weather

Route

_____

Distance   Time

Time
by zone **1   2   3   4   5**

Workout rating

Notes

_____

Workout 2

S   B   R   O

Duration   Weather

Route

_____

Distance   Time

Time
by zone **1   2   3   4   5**

Workout rating

Notes

_____

Sleep   Fatigue   Stress   Soreness

Resting heart rate   Weight

Workout 1

S   B   R   O

Duration   Weather

Route

_____

Distance   Time

Time
by zone **1   2   3   4   5**

Workout rating

Notes

_____

Workout 2

S   B   R   O

Duration   Weather

Route

_____

Distance   Time

Time
by zone **1   2   3   4   5**

Workout rating

Notes

_____

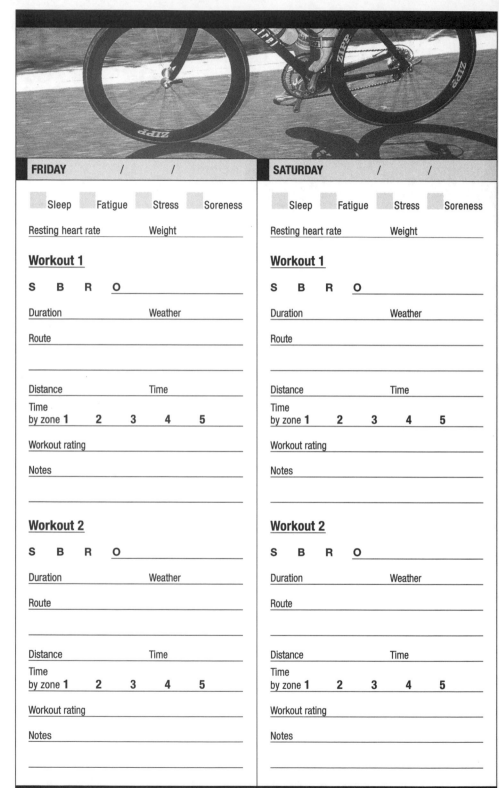

FRIDAY / /

Sleep Fatigue Stress Soreness

Resting heart rate _____ Weight _____

Workout 1

S   B   R   O _____

Duration _____ Weather _____

Route _____

_____

Distance _____ Time _____

Time
by zone **1   2   3   4   5**

Workout rating _____

Notes _____

_____

Workout 2

S   B   R   O _____

Duration _____ Weather _____

Route _____

_____

Distance _____ Time _____

Time
by zone **1   2   3   4   5**

Workout rating _____

Notes _____

_____

SATURDAY / /

Sleep Fatigue Stress Soreness

Resting heart rate _____ Weight _____

Workout 1

S   B   R   O _____

Duration _____ Weather _____

Route _____

_____

Distance _____ Time _____

Time
by zone **1   2   3   4   5**

Workout rating _____

Notes _____

_____

Workout 2

S   B   R   O _____

Duration _____ Weather _____

Route _____

_____

Distance _____ Time _____

Time
by zone **1   2   3   4   5**

Workout rating _____

Notes _____

_____

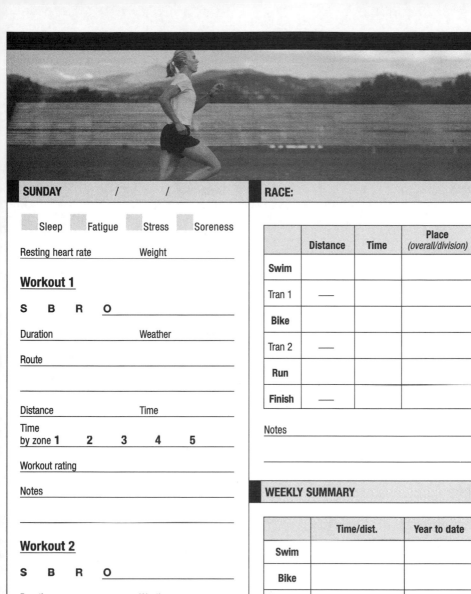

SUNDAY / /

Sleep   Fatigue   Stress   Soreness

Resting heart rate   Weight

Workout 1

S   B   R   O

Duration   Weather

Route

Distance   Time

Time
by zone 1   2   3   4   5

Workout rating

Notes

Workout 2

S   B   R   O

Duration   Weather

Route

Distance   Time

Time
by zone 1   2   3   4   5

Workout rating

Notes

RACE:

	Distance	Time	Place *(overall/division)*
Swim			
Tran 1	—		
Bike			
Tran 2	—		
Run			
Finish	—		

Notes

WEEKLY SUMMARY

	Time/dist.	Year to date
Swim		
Bike		
Run		
Strength		

Weekly   Year-to-date
total   total

Soreness

Notes

WEEK BEGINNING:　　　　　　　　**PLANNED WEEKLY HOURS:**

Week's goals (check off as achieved)

☐ _____

☐ _____

☐ _____

MONDAY / /	**TUESDAY** / /

☐ Sleep ☐ Fatigue ☐ Stress ☐ Soreness　　　☐ Sleep ☐ Fatigue ☐ Stress ☐ Soreness

Resting heart rate _____ Weight _____　　　Resting heart rate _____ Weight _____

Workout 1

S　B　R　O _____

Duration _____ Weather _____

Route _____

_____

Distance _____ Time _____

Time
by zone **1**　**2**　**3**　**4**　**5**

Workout rating _____

Notes _____

_____

Workout 2

S　B　R　O _____

Duration _____ Weather _____

Route _____

_____

Distance _____ Time _____

Time
by zone **1**　**2**　**3**　**4**　**5**

Workout rating _____

Notes _____

_____

Workout 1

S　B　R　O _____

Duration _____ Weather _____

Route _____

_____

Distance _____ Time _____

Time
by zone **1**　**2**　**3**　**4**　**5**

Workout rating _____

Notes _____

_____

Workout 2

S　B　R　O _____

Duration _____ Weather _____

Route _____

_____

Distance _____ Time _____

Time
by zone **1**　**2**　**3**　**4**　**5**

Workout rating _____

Notes _____

_____

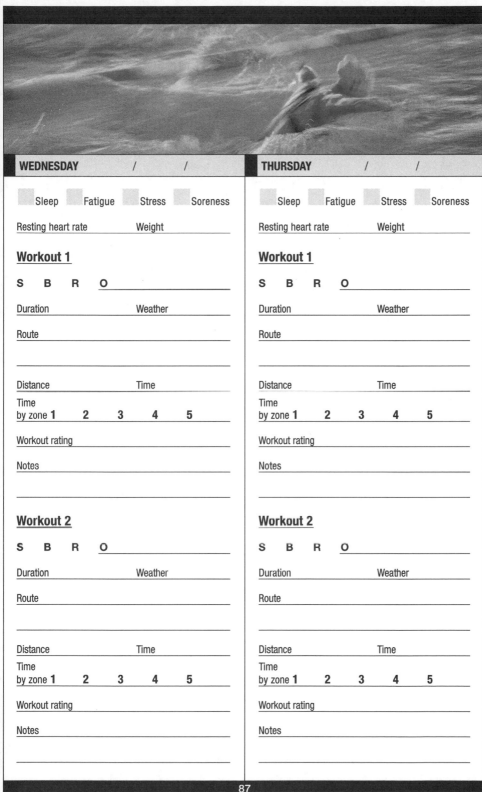

WEDNESDAY / /

■ Sleep ■ Fatigue ■ Stress ■ Soreness

Resting heart rate _____ Weight _____

Workout 1

S   B   R   O _____

Duration _____ Weather _____

Route _____

_____

Distance _____ Time _____

Time
by zone **1   2   3   4   5**

Workout rating _____

Notes _____

_____

Workout 2

S   B   R   O _____

Duration _____ Weather _____

Route _____

_____

Distance _____ Time _____

Time
by zone **1   2   3   4   5**

Workout rating _____

Notes _____

_____

THURSDAY / /

■ Sleep ■ Fatigue ■ Stress ■ Soreness

Resting heart rate _____ Weight _____

Workout 1

S   B   R   O _____

Duration _____ Weather _____

Route _____

_____

Distance _____ Time _____

Time
by zone **1   2   3   4   5**

Workout rating _____

Notes _____

_____

Workout 2

S   B   R   O _____

Duration _____ Weather _____

Route _____

_____

Distance _____ Time _____

Time
by zone **1   2   3   4   5**

Workout rating _____

Notes _____

_____

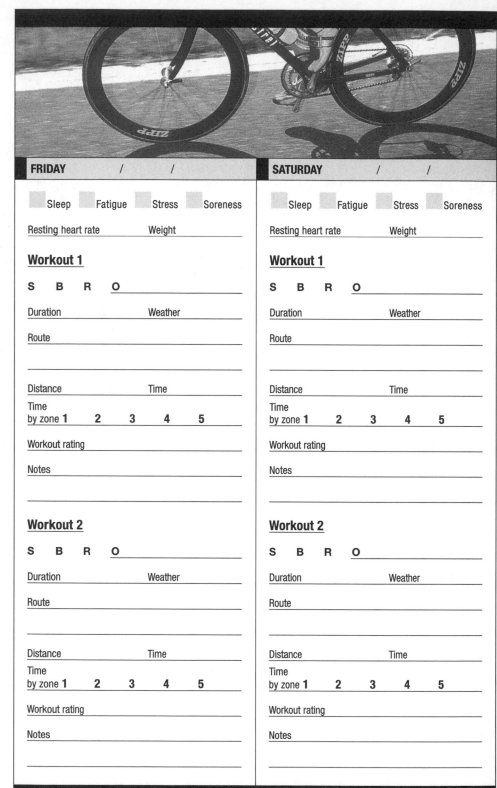

FRIDAY   /   /

Sleep   Fatigue   Stress   Soreness

Resting heart rate _____ Weight _____

Workout 1

S   B   R   O _____

Duration _____ Weather _____

Route _____

_____

Distance _____ Time _____

Time
by zone **1**   **2**   **3**   **4**   **5**

Workout rating _____

Notes _____

_____

Workout 2

S   B   R   O _____

Duration _____ Weather _____

Route _____

_____

Distance _____ Time _____

Time
by zone **1**   **2**   **3**   **4**   **5**

Workout rating _____

Notes _____

_____

SATURDAY   /   /

Sleep   Fatigue   Stress   Soreness

Resting heart rate _____ Weight _____

Workout 1

S   B   R   O _____

Duration _____ Weather _____

Route _____

_____

Distance _____ Time _____

Time
by zone **1**   **2**   **3**   **4**   **5**

Workout rating _____

Notes _____

_____

Workout 2

S   B   R   O _____

Duration _____ Weather _____

Route _____

_____

Distance _____ Time _____

Time
by zone **1**   **2**   **3**   **4**   **5**

Workout rating _____

Notes _____

_____

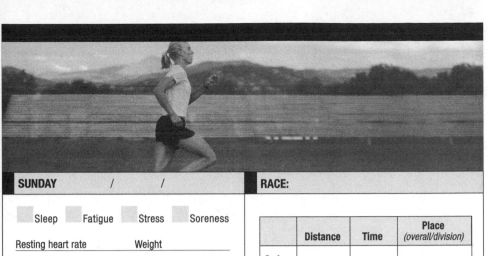

SUNDAY / /

■ Sleep ■ Fatigue ■ Stress ■ Soreness

Resting heart rate _____ Weight _____

Workout 1

S B R O _____

Duration _____ Weather _____

Route _____

_____

Distance _____ Time _____

Time
by zone **1   2   3   4   5**

Workout rating _____

Notes _____

_____

Workout 2

S B R O _____

Duration _____ Weather _____

Route _____

_____

Distance _____ Time _____

Time
by zone **1   2   3   4   5**

Workout rating _____

Notes _____

_____

RACE:

	Distance	Time	Place *(overall/division)*
Swim			
Tran 1	—		
Bike			
Tran 2	—		
Run			
Finish	—		

Notes _____

_____

WEEKLY SUMMARY

	Time/dist.	Year to date
Swim		
Bike		
Run		
Strength		

Weekly total _____ Year-to-date total _____

Soreness _____

Notes _____

_____

WEEK BEGINNING: **PLANNED WEEKLY HOURS:**

Week's goals (check off as achieved)

☐ _____

☐ _____

☐ _____

MONDAY / /	**TUESDAY** / /
☐ Sleep ☐ Fatigue ☐ Stress ☐ Soreness	☐ Sleep ☐ Fatigue ☐ Stress ☐ Soreness
Resting heart rate ____ Weight ____	Resting heart rate ____ Weight ____

Workout 1
S   B   R   O _____

Duration _____ Weather _____

Route _____

_____

Distance _____ Time _____

Time
by zone **1   2   3   4   5**

Workout rating _____

Notes _____

_____

Workout 2
S   B   R   O _____

Duration _____ Weather _____

Route _____

_____

Distance _____ Time _____

Time
by zone **1   2   3   4   5**

Workout rating _____

Notes _____

_____

Workout 1
S   B   R   O _____

Duration _____ Weather _____

Route _____

_____

Distance _____ Time _____

Time
by zone **1   2   3   4   5**

Workout rating _____

Notes _____

_____

Workout 2
S   B   R   O _____

Duration _____ Weather _____

Route _____

_____

Distance _____ Time _____

Time
by zone **1   2   3   4   5**

Workout rating _____

Notes _____

_____

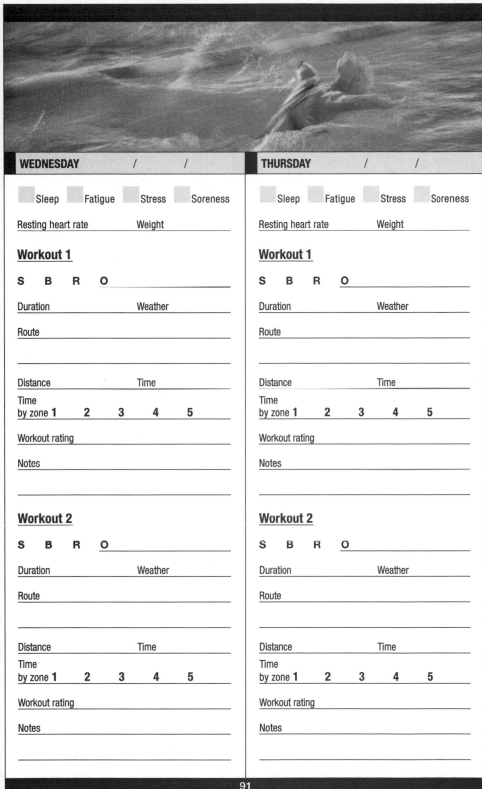

WEDNESDAY	/	/

Sleep Fatigue Stress Soreness

Resting heart rate _____ Weight _____

Workout 1

S B R O _____

Duration _____ Weather _____

Route _____

_____

Distance _____ Time _____

Time
by zone **1**   **2**   **3**   **4**   **5**

Workout rating _____

Notes _____

_____

Workout 2

S B R O _____

Duration _____ Weather _____

Route _____

_____

Distance _____ Time _____

Time
by zone **1**   **2**   **3**   **4**   **5**

Workout rating _____

Notes _____

_____

THURSDAY	/	/

Sleep Fatigue Stress Soreness

Resting heart rate _____ Weight _____

Workout 1

S B R O _____

Duration _____ Weather _____

Route _____

_____

Distance _____ Time _____

Time
by zone **1**   **2**   **3**   **4**   **5**

Workout rating _____

Notes _____

_____

Workout 2

S B R O _____

Duration _____ Weather _____

Route _____

_____

Distance _____ Time _____

Time
by zone **1**   **2**   **3**   **4**   **5**

Workout rating _____

Notes _____

_____

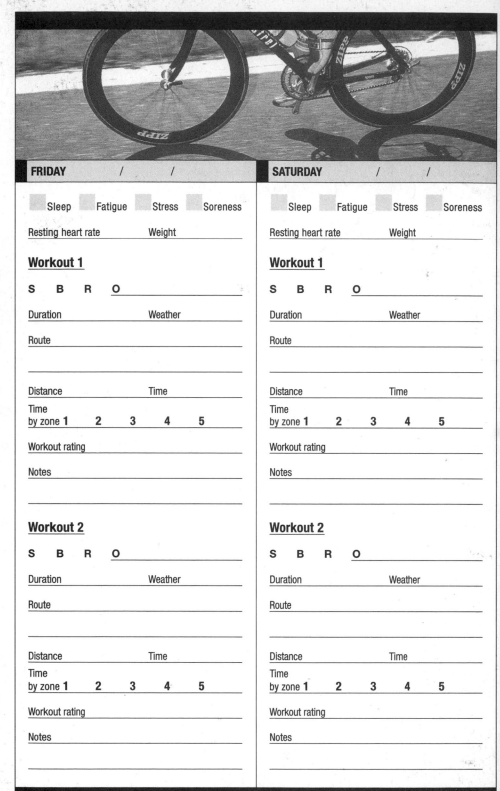

FRIDAY   /   /

Sleep   Fatigue   Stress   Soreness

Resting heart rate   Weight

Workout 1

S   B   R   O

Duration   Weather

Route

Distance   Time

Time
by zone **1**   **2**   **3**   **4**   **5**

Workout rating

Notes

Workout 2

S   B   R   O

Duration   Weather

Route

Distance   Time

Time
by zone **1**   **2**   **3**   **4**   **5**

Workout rating

Notes

SATURDAY   /   /

Sleep   Fatigue   Stress   Soreness

Resting heart rate   Weight

Workout 1

S   B   R   O

Duration   Weather

Route

Distance   Time

Time
by zone **1**   **2**   **3**   **4**   **5**

Workout rating

Notes

Workout 2

S   B   R   O

Duration   Weather

Route

Distance   Time

Time
by zone **1**   **2**   **3**   **4**   **5**

Workout rating

Notes

Achin. col
Venon   Kelly 1826
         pescond; green gans

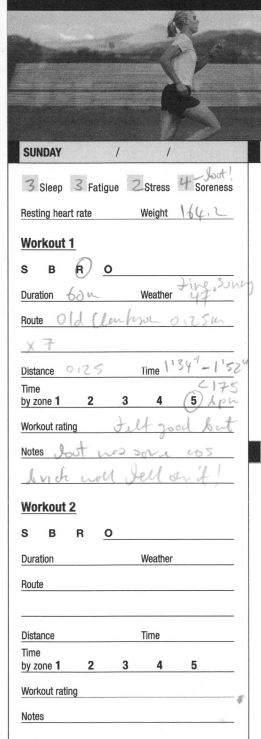

SUNDAY   /   /

3 Sleep *3* Fatigue *2* Stress *4* ~foot!~ Soreness

Resting heart rate   Weight 164.2

Workout 1

S   B   (R)   O

Duration 60m   Weather fine, sunny 47

Route Old Clarkson 0.125m

x 7

Distance 0.125   Time 1'34" - 1'52"

Time   <175
by zone **1**   **2**   **3**   **4**   (5) bpm

Workout rating felt good but

Notes foot was sore cos

Sick wall fell on it!

Workout 2

S   B   R   O

Duration   Weather

Route

Distance   Time

Time
by zone **1**   **2**   **3**   **4**   **5**

Workout rating

Notes

RACE:

	Distance	Time	Place *(overall/division)*
Swim			
Tran 1	—		
Bike			
Tran 2	—		
Run			
Finish	—		

Notes

WEEKLY SUMMARY

	Time/dist.	Year to date
Swim		
Bike		
Run		
Strength		

Weekly total   Year-to-date total

Soreness

Notes

WEEK BEGINNING: **PLANNED WEEKLY HOURS:**

Week's goals (check off as achieved)

- [ ] _____
- [ ] _____
- [ ] _____

MONDAY / /	TUESDAY 2 / 28 / 06

Z Sleep Z Fatigue Z Stress Z Soreness   Z Sleep Z Fatigue Z Stress Z Soreness

Resting heart rate ___ Weight ___   Resting heart rate ___ Weight ___

Workout 1   **Workout 1**

S B R (O) weight   S B R (O) weight

Duration ___ Weather ___   Duration ___ Weather ___

Route 2×12 upper back ball   Route 3× tricep pulls ×12
2×12 pushups, 2×12   2×20 situps , 2×12 squats
lunges 20lb   20lb

Distance ___ Time ___   Distance ___ Time ___

Time
by zone **1 2 3 4 5**   Time
by zone **1 2 3 4 5**

Workout rating ___   Workout rating ___

Notes ___   Notes ___

Workout 2   REST DAY   **Workout 2** Tempo run

S B R O   S B (R) O

Duration ___ Weather ___   Duration 1h 10n Weather sunny 80°F

Route ___   Route Forest park

Distance ___ Time ___   Distance 5.65 Time 49m
                                                                      155-165
Time
by zone **1 2 3 4 5**   Time
by zone **1 2 3 4 — 5**

Workout rating ___   Workout rating Great

Notes ___   Notes ___

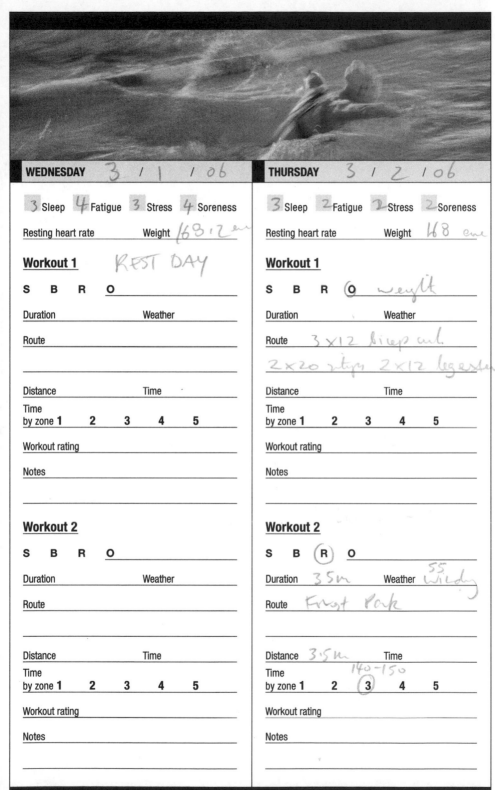

WEDNESDAY 3 / 1 / 06	THURSDAY 3 / 2 / 06

3 Sleep **4** Fatigue **3** Stress **4** Soreness

Resting heart rate   Weight *68.2 ew*

Workout 1   *REST DAY*

S   B   R   O _____

Duration _____ Weather _____

Route _____

_____

Distance _____ Time _____

Time
by zone **1   2   3   4   5**

Workout rating _____

Notes _____

_____

Workout 2

S   B   R   O _____

Duration _____ Weather _____

Route _____

_____

Distance _____ Time _____

Time
by zone **1   2   3   4   5**

Workout rating _____

Notes _____

_____

---

3 Sleep **2** Fatigue **2** Stress **2** Soreness

Resting heart rate   Weight *68 ew*

Workout 1

S   B   R   (O) *weylt*

Duration _____ Weather _____

Route *3×12 bicep curl*

2×20 ztyn 2×12 legestem

Distance _____ Time _____

Time
by zone **1   2   3   4   5**

Workout rating _____

Notes _____

_____

Workout 2

S   B   (R)   O _____

Duration *35m* Weather *55 wildy*

Route *Frwgt Park*

_____

Distance *3.5m* Time _____

Time *140-150*
by zone **1   2   (3)   4   5**

Workout rating _____

Notes _____

_____

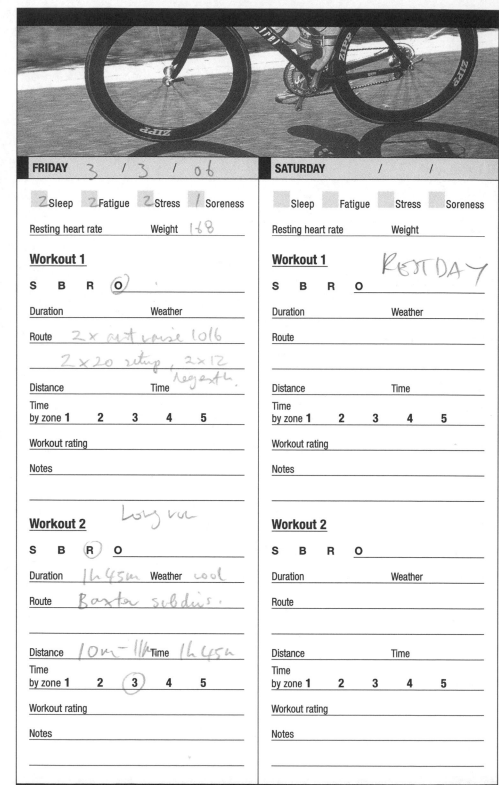

FRIDAY 3 / 3 / 06

Z Sleep Z Fatigue Z Stress 1 Soreness

Resting heart rate _____ Weight 168

Workout 1

S   B   R   (O)

Duration _____ Weather _____

Route 2× art raise 1016

2×20 situp, 2×12 regexth.

Distance _____ Time _____

Time
by zone **1**   **2**   **3**   **4**   **5**

Workout rating _____

Notes _____

Workout 2   Long run

S   B   (R)   O

Duration 1h 45m Weather cool

Route Baxter subdiv.

Distance 10m – 11m Time 1h 45m

Time
by zone **1**   **2**   **(3)**   **4**   **5**

Workout rating _____

Notes _____

SATURDAY   /   /

Sleep Fatigue Stress Soreness

Resting heart rate _____ Weight _____

Workout 1   RESTDAY

S   B   R   O

Duration _____ Weather _____

Route _____

Distance _____ Time _____

Time
by zone **1**   **2**   **3**   **4**   **5**

Workout rating _____

Notes _____

Workout 2

S   B   R   O

Duration _____ Weather _____

Route _____

Distance _____ Time _____

Time
by zone **1**   **2**   **3**   **4**   **5**

Workout rating _____

Notes _____

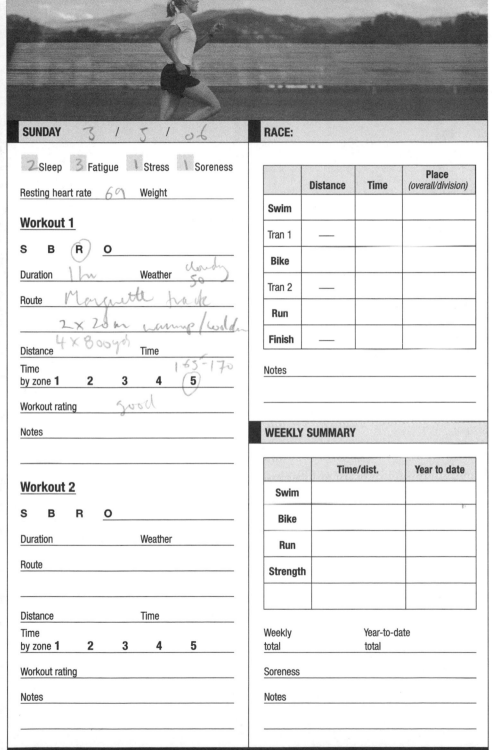

SUNDAY 3 / 5 / 06

2 Sleep   3 Fatigue   1 Stress   1 Soreness

Resting heart rate 69   Weight _____

Workout 1

S   B   (R)   O   _____

Duration 1 hr   Weather cloudy 50

Route Marquette trail

2 x 20 m warmup/cooldown

4 x 800yd

Distance _____   Time _____

Time
by zone **1**   **2**   **3**   **4**   **(5)**   165-170

Workout rating good

Notes _____

Workout 2

S   B   R   O   _____

Duration _____   Weather _____

Route _____

Distance _____   Time _____

Time
by zone **1**   **2**   **3**   **4**   **5**

Workout rating _____

Notes _____

RACE: _____

	Distance	Time	Place *(overall/division)*
Swim			
Tran 1	—		
Bike			
Tran 2	—		
Run			
Finish	—		

Notes _____

WEEKLY SUMMARY

	Time/dist.	Year to date
Swim		
Bike		
Run		
Strength		

Weekly total _____   Year-to-date total _____

Soreness _____

Notes _____

WEEK BEGINNING: _____   **PLANNED WEEKLY HOURS:** _____

Week's goals (check off as achieved)

☐ _____

☐ _____

☐ _____

MONDAY / /	TUESDAY / /

☐ Sleep ☐ Fatigue ☐ Stress ☐ Soreness

Resting heart rate _____ Weight _____

Workout 1   *Rest day*

S   B   R   O _Weights_ _____

Duration _____ Weather _____

Route _Weights_ _____

_____

Distance _____ Time _____

Time by zone **1**   **2**   **3**   **4**   **5**

Workout rating _____

Notes _____

_____

Workout 2

S   B   R   O _____

Duration _____ Weather _____

Route _____

_____

Distance _____ Time _____

Time by zone **1**   **2**   **3**   **4**   **5**

Workout rating _____

Notes _____

_____

☐ Sleep ☐ Fatigue ☐ Stress ☐ Soreness

Resting heart rate _____ Weight _____

Workout 1

S   B   R   O _weight_ _____

Duration _____ Weather _____

Route _weight_ _____

_____

Distance _____ Time _____

Time by zone **1**   **2**   **3**   **4**   **5**

Workout rating _____

Notes _____

_____

Workout 2

S   B   Ⓡ   O _____

Duration _L_ ____ Weather _windy_ ____

Route _downtown_ _____

_____

Distance _4-5m_ Time _45_

Time by zone **1**   **2**   **3**   **4**   **5**

Workout rating _____

Notes _____

_____

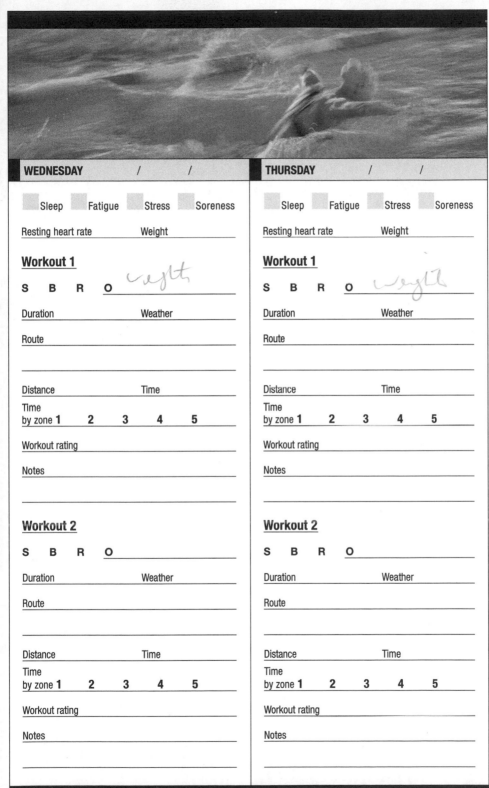

WEDNESDAY   /   /

Sleep   Fatigue   Stress   Soreness

Resting heart rate _____ Weight _____

Workout 1

S   B   R   O   _caght_ _____

Duration _____ Weather _____

Route _____

_____

Distance _____ Time _____

Time
by zone **1**   **2**   **3**   **4**   **5**

Workout rating _____

Notes _____

_____

Workout 2

S   B   R   O   _____

Duration _____ Weather _____

Route _____

_____

Distance _____ Time _____

Time
by zone **1**   **2**   **3**   **4**   **5**

Workout rating _____

Notes _____

_____

THURSDAY   /   /

Sleep   Fatigue   Stress   Soreness

Resting heart rate _____ Weight _____

Workout 1

S   B   R   O   _weyth_ _____

Duration _____ Weather _____

Route _____

_____

Distance _____ Time _____

Time
by zone **1**   **2**   **3**   **4**   **5**

Workout rating _____

Notes _____

_____

Workout 2

S   B   R   O   _____

Duration _____ Weather _____

Route _____

_____

Distance _____ Time _____

Time
by zone **1**   **2**   **3**   **4**   **5**

Workout rating _____

Notes _____

_____

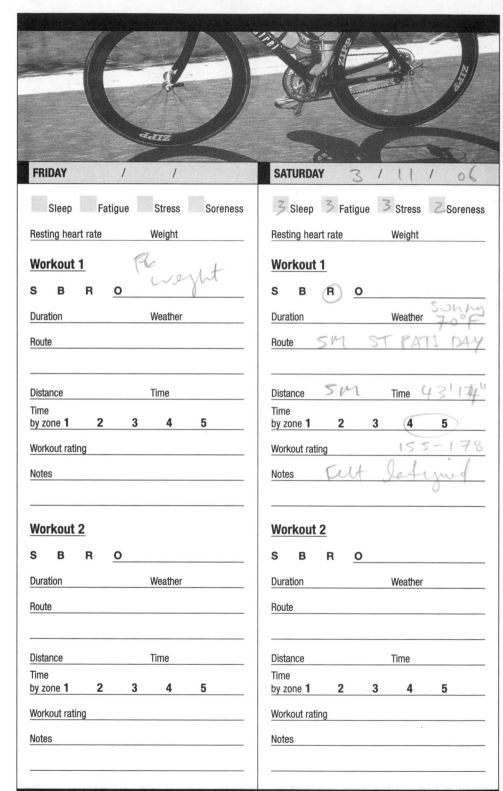

FRIDAY / /	SATURDAY 3 / 11 / 06

FRIDAY

Sleep　Fatigue　Stress　Soreness

Resting heart rate　　　Weight

Workout 1

S　B　R　O　*R weight*

Duration　　　Weather

Route

Distance　　　Time

Time
by zone 1　2　3　4　5

Workout rating

Notes

Workout 2

S　B　R　O

Duration　　　Weather

Route

Distance　　　Time

Time
by zone 1　2　3　4　5

Workout rating

Notes

SATURDAY 3 / 11 / 06

3 Sleep　3 Fatigue　3 Stress　2 Soreness

Resting heart rate　　　Weight

Workout 1

S　B　(R)　O

Duration　　　Weather　Sunny 70°F

Route　5M　ST PATS DAY

Distance　5M　Time　43'17"

Time
by zone 1　2　3　(4　5)

Workout rating　155-178

Notes　Felt fatigued

Workout 2

S　B　R　O

Duration　　　Weather

Route

Distance　　　Time

Time
by zone 1　2　3　4　5

Workout rating

Notes

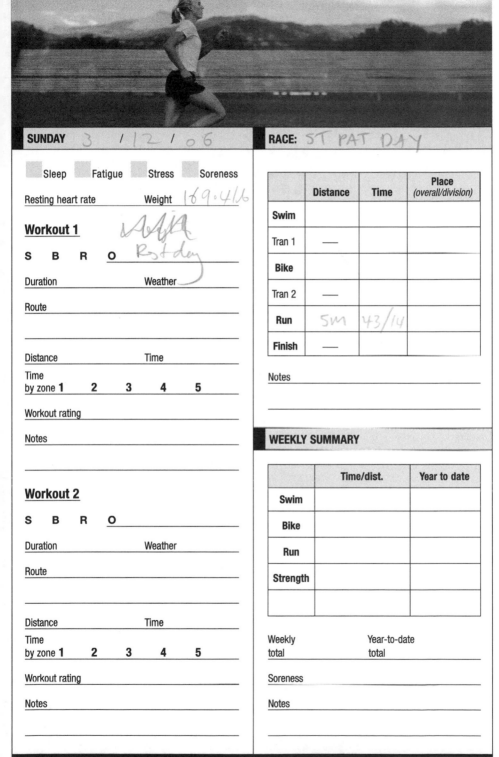

SUNDAY 3 / 12 / 06

RACE: ST PAT DAY

Sleep Fatigue Stress Soreness

Resting heart rate _____ Weight 189.4/16

Workout 1

S   B   R   O   Rst day

Duration _____ Weather _____

Route _____

_____

Distance _____ Time _____

Time
by zone **1   2   3   4   5**

Workout rating _____

Notes _____

_____

Workout 2

S   B   R   O   _____

Duration _____ Weather _____

Route _____

_____

Distance _____ Time _____

Time
by zone **1   2   3   4   5**

Workout rating _____

Notes _____

_____

	Distance	Time	Place *(overall/division)*
Swim			
Tran 1	—		
Bike			
Tran 2	—		
Run	5m	43/14	
Finish	—		

Notes _____

_____

WEEKLY SUMMARY

	Time/dist.	Year to date
Swim		
Bike		
Run		
Strength		

Weekly
total _____

Year-to-date
total _____

Soreness _____

Notes _____

_____

Week's goals (check off as achieved)

☐ _____

☐ _____

☐ _____

MONDAY 3 / 13 /	**TUESDAY** / /

☐ Sleep ☐ Fatigue ☐ Stress ☐ Soreness   ☐ Sleep ☐ Fatigue ☐ Stress ☐ Soreness

Resting heart rate _____ Weight _____   Resting heart rate _____ Weight _____

Workout 1   Wilmington   **Workout 1**   RESTDAY

S   B   R   ⓞ wts   S   B   R   O

Duration _____ Weather _____   Duration _____ Weather _____

Route _____   Route _____

_____   _____

Distance _____ Time _____   Distance _____ Time _____

Time by zone   **1**   **2**   **3**   **4**   **5**   Time by zone   **1**   **2**   **3**   **4**   **5**

Workout rating _____   Workout rating _____

Notes _____   Notes _____

Workout 2   30m bike   **Workout 2**

S   B   R   O   20m X train   S   B   R   O

Duration _____ Weather _____   Duration _____ Weather _____

Route _____   Route _____

_____   _____

Distance _____ Time _____   Distance _____ Time _____

Time by zone   **1**   **2**   **3**   **4**   **5**   Time by zone   **1**   **2**   **3**   **4**   **5**

Workout rating _____   Workout rating _____

Notes _____   Notes _____

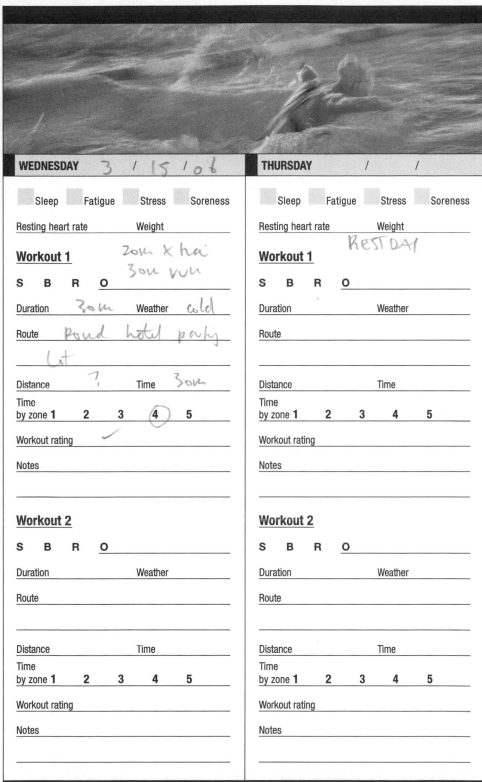

WEDNESDAY	3 / 15 / 06	THURSDAY	/ /

WEDNESDAY 3 / 15 / 06

◼ Sleep ◼ Fatigue ◼ Stress ◼ Soreness

Resting heart rate _____ Weight _____

Workout 1 _2ou x hai_
3ou vuu

S   B   R   O _____

Duration _3ou_   Weather _cold_

Route _Pond hotel party_
Lot

Distance _7,_   Time _3ou_

Time
by zone **1   2   3   (4)   5**

Workout rating _✓_

Notes _____

Workout 2

S   B   R   O _____

Duration _____ Weather _____

Route _____

Distance _____ Time _____

Time
by zone **1   2   3   4   5**

Workout rating _____

Notes _____

THURSDAY / /

◼ Sleep ◼ Fatigue ◼ Stress ◼ Soreness

Resting heart rate _____ Weight _____

Workout 1 _RESTDAY_

S   B   R   O _____

Duration _____ Weather _____

Route _____

Distance _____ Time _____

Time
by zone **1   2   3   4   5**

Workout rating _____

Notes _____

Workout 2

S   B   R   O _____

Duration _____ Weather _____

Route _____

Distance _____ Time _____

Time
by zone **1   2   3   4   5**

Workout rating _____

Notes _____

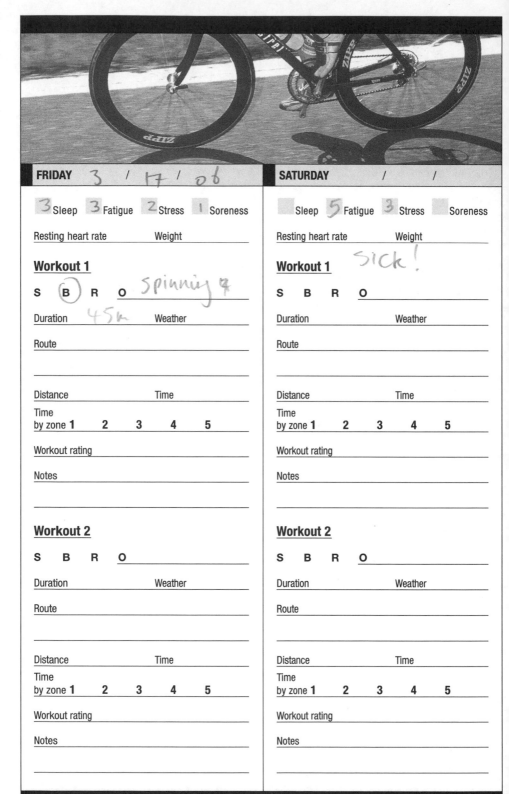

FRIDAY 3 / 17 / 06

3 Sleep   3 Fatigue   2 Stress   1 Soreness

Resting heart rate _____ Weight _____

Workout 1

S (B) R O *Spinning* ?

Duration 45m   Weather _____

Route _____

_____

Distance _____ Time _____

Time
by zone **1   2   3   4   5**

Workout rating _____

Notes _____

_____

Workout 2

S   B   R   O _____

Duration _____ Weather _____

Route _____

_____

Distance _____ Time _____

Time
by zone **1   2   3   4   5**

Workout rating _____

Notes _____

_____

SATURDAY   /   /

Sleep   5 Fatigue   3 Stress   Soreness

Resting heart rate _____ Weight _____

Workout 1   *Sick!*

S   B   R   O _____

Duration _____ Weather _____

Route _____

_____

Distance _____ Time _____

Time
by zone **1   2   3   4   5**

Workout rating _____

Notes _____

_____

Workout 2

S   B   R   O _____

Duration _____ Weather _____

Route _____

_____

Distance _____ Time _____

Time
by zone **1   2   3   4   5**

Workout rating _____

Notes _____

_____

| SUNDAY | / | / | **RACE:** |

Sleep   ⑤ Fatigue   ③ Stress   Soreness

Resting heart rate _____ Weight _____

Workout 1   SICK

S   B   R   O _____

Duration _____ Weather _____

Route _____

_____

Distance _____ Time _____

Time
by zone **1**   **2**   **3**   **4**   **5**

Workout rating _____

Notes _____

_____

Workout 2

S   B   R   O _____

Duration _____ Weather _____

Route _____

_____

Distance _____ Time _____

Time
by zone **1**   **2**   **3**   **4**   **5**

Workout rating _____

Notes _____

_____

RACE:

	Distance	**Time**	**Place** *(overall/division)*
Swim			
Tran 1	—		
Bike			
Tran 2	—		
Run			
Finish	—		

Notes _____

_____

WEEKLY SUMMARY

	Time/dist.	**Year to date**
Swim		
Bike		
Run		
Strength		

Weekly   Year-to-date
total   total

Soreness _____

Notes _____

_____

WEEK BEGINNING: PLANNED WEEKLY HOURS:

Week's goals (check off as achieved)

▨ _____

▨ _____

▨ _____

MONDAY 3 / 20 /	**TUESDAY** / /

▨ Sleep ▨ Fatigue ▨ Stress ▨ Soreness

Resting heart rate _____ Weight _____

Workout 1   SICK

S   B   R   O _____

Duration _____ Weather _____

Route _____

_____

Distance _____ Time _____

Time
by zone **1   2   3   4   5**

Workout rating _____

Notes _____

_____

Workout 2

S   B   R   O _____

Duration _____ Weather _____

Route _____

_____

Distance _____ Time _____

Time
by zone **1   2   3   4   5**

Workout rating _____

Notes _____

_____

▨ Sleep ▨ Fatigue ▨ Stress ▨ Soreness

Resting heart rate _____ Weight _____

Workout 1

S   B   R   Ⓞ Weights

Duration 15m Weather _____

Route _____

_____

Distance _____ Time _____

Time
by zone **1   2   3   4   5**

Workout rating _____

Notes _____

_____

Workout 2

S   B   R   O _____

Duration _____ Weather _____

Route _____

_____

Distance _____ Time _____

Time
by zone **1   2   3   4   5**

Workout rating _____

Notes _____

_____

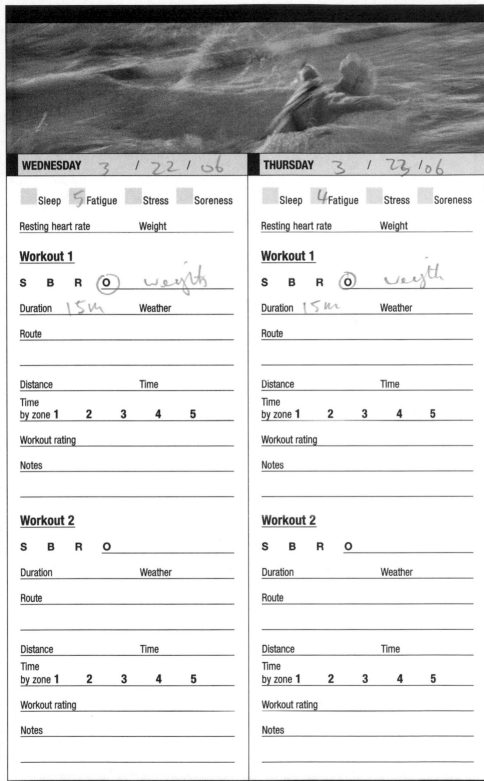

WEDNESDAY 3 / 22 / 06

▨ Sleep **5** Fatigue ▨ Stress ▨ Soreness

Resting heart rate _____ Weight _____

Workout 1

S B R (O) weyth

Duration 15m Weather _____

Route _____

_____

Distance _____ Time _____

Time
by zone **1** **2** **3** **4** **5** _____

Workout rating _____

Notes _____

_____

Workout 2

S B R O _____

Duration _____ Weather _____

Route _____

_____

Distance _____ Time _____

Time
by zone **1** **2** **3** **4** **5** _____

Workout rating _____

Notes _____

_____

THURSDAY 3 / 23 / 06

▨ Sleep **4** Fatigue ▨ Stress ▨ Soreness

Resting heart rate _____ Weight _____

Workout 1

S B R (O) weyth

Duration 15m Weather _____

Route _____

_____

Distance _____ Time _____

Time
by zone **1** **2** **3** **4** **5** _____

Workout rating _____

Notes _____

_____

Workout 2

S B R O _____

Duration _____ Weather _____

Route _____

_____

Distance _____ Time _____

Time
by zone **1** **2** **3** **4** **5** _____

Workout rating _____

Notes _____

_____

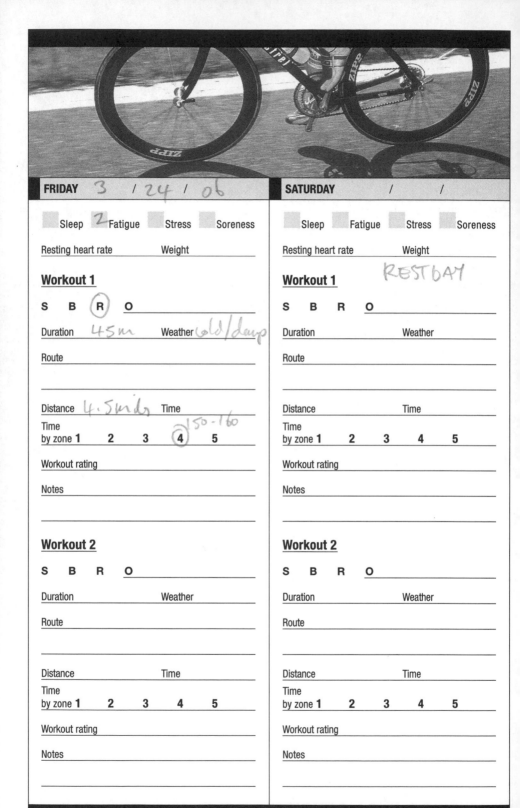

FRIDAY 3 / 24 / 06

◻ Sleep ◻ 2 Fatigue ◻ Stress ◻ Soreness

Resting heart rate _____ Weight _____

Workout 1

S   B   (R)   O _____

Duration 45m   Weather Cold/damp

Route _____

_____

Distance 4.5mds   Time _____

Time
by zone **1**   **2**   **3**   **(4)** 50-160   **5**

Workout rating _____

Notes _____

_____

Workout 2

S   B   R   O _____

Duration _____   Weather _____

Route _____

_____

Distance _____   Time _____

Time
by zone **1**   **2**   **3**   **4**   **5**

Workout rating _____

Notes _____

_____

SATURDAY / /

◻ Sleep ◻ Fatigue ◻ Stress ◻ Soreness

Resting heart rate _____ Weight _____

Workout 1   REST DAY

S   B   R   O _____

Duration _____   Weather _____

Route _____

_____

Distance _____   Time _____

Time
by zone **1**   **2**   **3**   **4**   **5**

Workout rating _____

Notes _____

_____

Workout 2

S   B   R   O _____

Duration _____   Weather _____

Route _____

_____

Distance _____   Time _____

Time
by zone **1**   **2**   **3**   **4**   **5**

Workout rating _____

Notes _____

_____

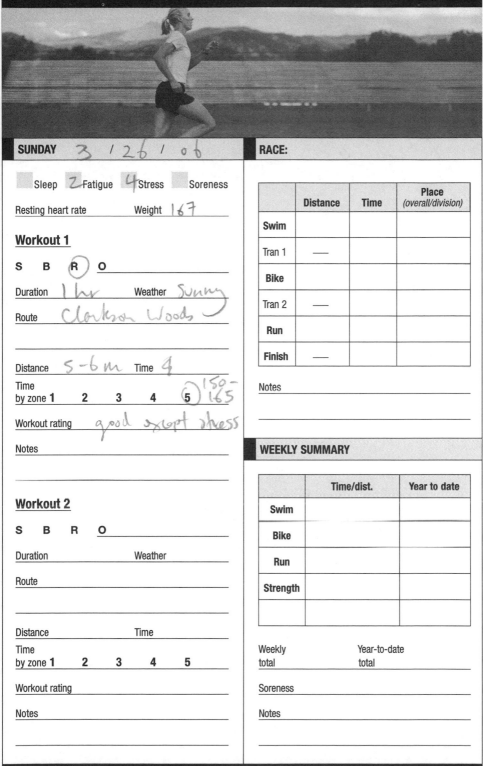

SUNDAY 3 / 26 / 06

Sleep ▢ Fatigue 2 Stress 4 Soreness ▢

Resting heart rate _____ Weight 167

Workout 1

S B (R) O _____

Duration 1 hr   Weather Sunny

Route Clarkson Woods

_____

Distance 5-6 m   Time 4

Time
by zone **1** **2** **3** **4** **⑤** 150-165

Workout rating good except stress

Notes _____

_____

Workout 2

S B R O _____

Duration _____   Weather _____

Route _____

_____

Distance _____   Time _____

Time
by zone **1** **2** **3** **4** **5**

Workout rating _____

Notes _____

_____

RACE: _____

	Distance	Time	Place (overall/division)
Swim			
Tran 1	—		
Bike			
Tran 2	—		
Run			
Finish	—		

Notes _____

_____

WEEKLY SUMMARY

	Time/dist.	Year to date
Swim		
Bike		
Run		
Strength		

Weekly total _____   Year-to-date total _____

Soreness _____

Notes _____

_____

WEEK BEGINNING:　　　　　　　**PLANNED WEEKLY HOURS:**

Week's goals (check off as achieved)

- aerobic exercise each day except Su
-
-

MONDAY 3 / 27 / 06

2 Sleep　2 Fatigue　1 Stress　3 Soreness

Resting heart rate _____ Weight _____

Workout 1

S (B) R O _exercise bike_

Duration 30m　　Weather _____

Route _____

_____

Distance _____　Time _____

Time
by zone 1　2　(3)　4　5

140 ish

Workout rating _____

Notes _____

Workout 2

S B R (O) _weight_

Duration 15m　　Weather _____

Route _____

_____

Distance _____　Time _____

Time
by zone 1　2　3　4　5

Workout rating _____

Notes _____

TUESDAY 3 / 28 / 06

Sleep　Fatigue　Stress　Soreness

Resting heart rate _____ Weight _____

Workout 1

S B R (O) _weight_

Duration 15　　Weather _____

Route _____

_____

Distance _____　Time _____

Time
by zone 1　2　3　4　5

Workout rating _____

Notes _____

Workout 2

S B R O _____

Duration _____　Weather _____

Route _____

_____

Distance _____　Time _____

Time
by zone 1　2　3　4　5

Workout rating _____

Notes _____

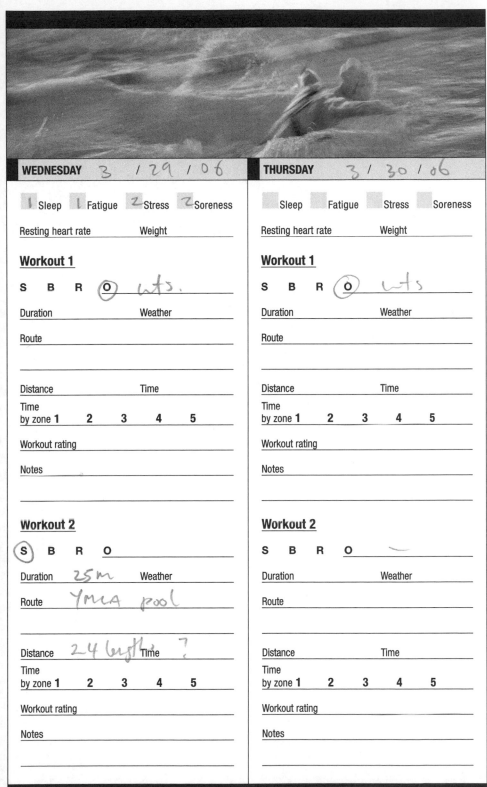

WEDNESDAY 3 / 29 / 06

☐ Sleep 1 ☐ Fatigue 1 ☐ Stress 2 ☐ Soreness 2

Resting heart rate _____ Weight _____

Workout 1

S B R (O) wts. _____

Duration _____ Weather _____

Route _____

_____

Distance _____ Time _____

Time
by zone **1**   **2**   **3**   **4**   **5**

Workout rating _____

Notes _____

_____

Workout 2

(S) B R O _____

Duration 25m Weather _____

Route YMCA pool

_____

Distance 24 lengths Time 7 _____

Time
by zone **1**   **2**   **3**   **4**   **5**

Workout rating _____

Notes _____

_____

THURSDAY 3 / 30 / 06

☐ Sleep ☐ Fatigue ☐ Stress ☐ Soreness

Resting heart rate _____ Weight _____

Workout 1

S B R (O) wts _____

Duration _____ Weather _____

Route _____

_____

Distance _____ Time _____

Time
by zone **1**   **2**   **3**   **4**   **5**

Workout rating _____

Notes _____

_____

Workout 2

S B R O _____

Duration _____ Weather _____

Route _____

_____

Distance _____ Time _____

Time
by zone **1**   **2**   **3**   **4**   **5**

Workout rating _____

Notes _____

_____

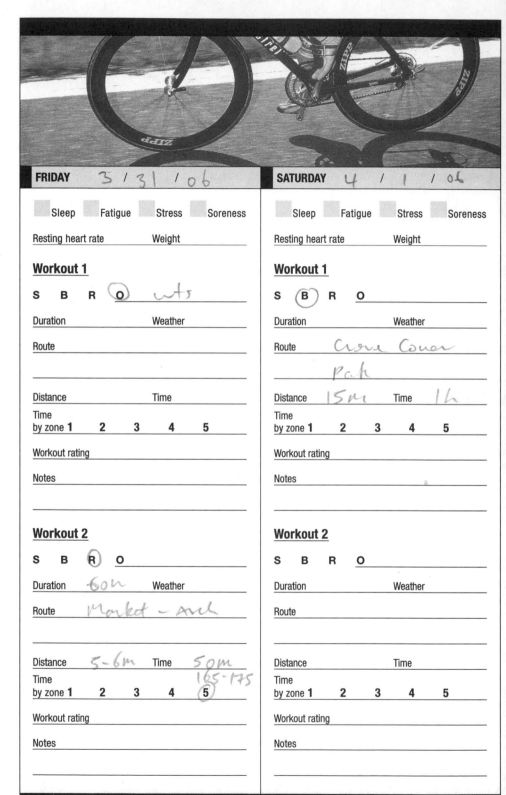

FRIDAY 3 / 31 / 06	**SATURDAY** 4 / 1 / 06

▪ Sleep ▪ Fatigue ▪ Stress ▪ Soreness	▪ Sleep ▪ Fatigue ▪ Stress ▪ Soreness

Resting heart rate _____ Weight _____ | Resting heart rate _____ Weight _____

Workout 1

S   B   R   (O)   wts

Duration _____ Weather _____

Route _____

_____

Distance _____ Time _____

Time by zone   **1**   **2**   **3**   **4**   **5**

Workout rating _____

Notes _____

_____

Workout 2

S   B   (R)   O

Duration 60 h   Weather _____

Route Market – Arch

Distance 5 – 6 m   Time 50 m   165-175

Time by zone   **1**   **2**   **3**   **4**   (**5**)

Workout rating _____

Notes _____

_____

Workout 1 (Saturday)

S   (B)   R   O

Duration _____ Weather _____

Route Crown Couer Pak

Distance 15 m   Time 1 h

Time by zone   **1**   **2**   **3**   **4**   **5**

Workout rating _____

Notes _____

_____

Workout 2 (Saturday)

S   B   R   O

Duration _____ Weather _____

Route _____

Distance _____ Time _____

Time by zone   **1**   **2**   **3**   **4**   **5**

Workout rating _____

Notes _____

_____

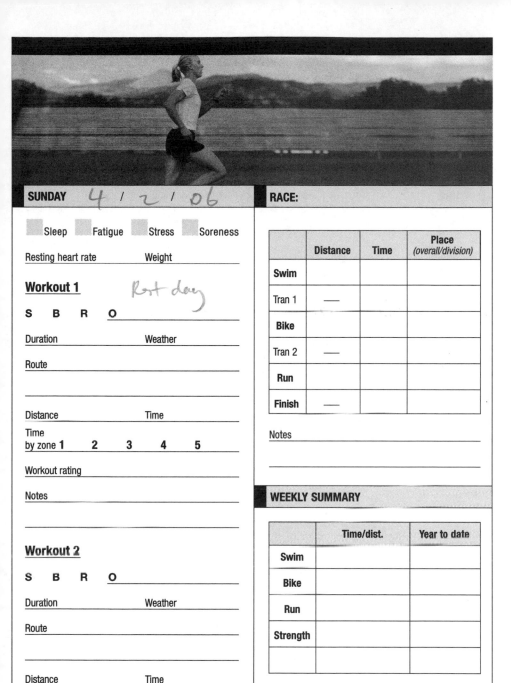

SUNDAY 4 / 2 / 06

Sleep Fatigue Stress Soreness

Resting heart rate _____ Weight _____

Workout 1   Rest day

S   B   R   O _____

Duration _____ Weather _____

Route _____

_____

Distance _____ Time _____

Time
by zone **1   2   3   4   5**

Workout rating _____

Notes _____

_____

Workout 2

S   B   R   O _____

Duration _____ Weather _____

Route _____

_____

Distance _____ Time _____

Time
by zone **1   2   3   4   5**

Workout rating _____

Notes _____

_____

RACE: _____

	Distance	Time	Place *(overall/division)*
Swim			
Tran 1	—		
Bike			
Tran 2	—		
Run			
Finish	—		

Notes _____

_____

WEEKLY SUMMARY

	Time/dist.	Year to date
Swim		
Bike		
Run		
Strength		

Weekly total _____ Year-to-date total _____

Soreness _____

Notes _____

_____

WEEK BEGINNING: **PLANNED WEEKLY HOURS:**

Week's goals (check off as achieved)

☐ _____

☐ _____

☐ _____

MONDAY 4 / 3 / 06	**TUESDAY** 4 / 4 / 06

☐ Sleep ☐ Fatigue ☐ Stress ☐ Soreness   ☐ Sleep ☐ Fatigue ☐ Stress ☐ Soreness

Resting heart rate _____ Weight 165.4   Resting heart rate _____ Weight _____

Workout 1

S   B   Ⓡ   Ⓞ ___ +t ___

Duration _____ Weather _____

Route _Arch + back to_

wah via boxball sted.

Distance 3-4 m   Time 40 M

Time by zone **1** **2** **③** **4** **5**

Workout rating ✓

Notes _____

Workout 2

S   B   R   Ⓞ   wt .

Duration _____ Weather _____

Route _____

_____

Distance _____   Time _____

Time by zone **1** **2** **3** **4** **5**

Workout rating _____

Notes _____

Workout 1

S   B   R   O ___

Duration _____ Weather _____

Route _____

_____

Distance _____   Time _____

Time by zone **1** **2** **3** **4** **5**

Workout rating _____

Notes _____

Workout 2

S   B   R   O ___

Duration _____ Weather _____

Route _____

_____

Distance _____   Time _____

Time by zone **1** **2** **3** **4** **5**

Workout rating _____

Notes _____

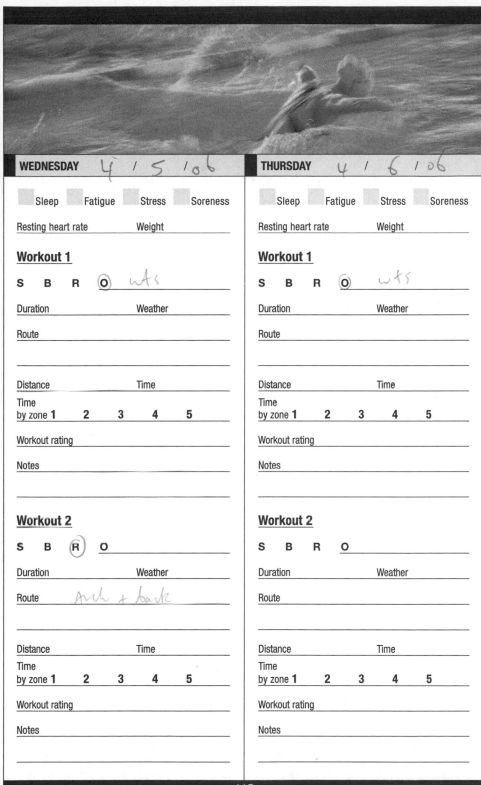

| WEDNESDAY | 4 / 5 / 06 | THURSDAY | 4 / 6 / 06 |

Sleep Fatigue Stress Soreness

Resting heart rate   Weight

Workout 1

S   B   R   Ⓞ   wts

Duration   Weather

Route

Distance   Time

Time
by zone 1   2   3   4   5

Workout rating

Notes

Workout 2

S   B   Ⓡ   O

Duration   Weather

Route   Arch + back

Distance   Time

Time
by zone 1   2   3   4   5

Workout rating

Notes

Sleep Fatigue Stress Soreness

Resting heart rate   Weight

Workout 1

S   B   R   Ⓞ   wts

Duration   Weather

Route

Distance   Time

Time
by zone 1   2   3   4   5

Workout rating

Notes

Workout 2

S   B   R   O

Duration   Weather

Route

Distance   Time

Time
by zone 1   2   3   4   5

Workout rating

Notes

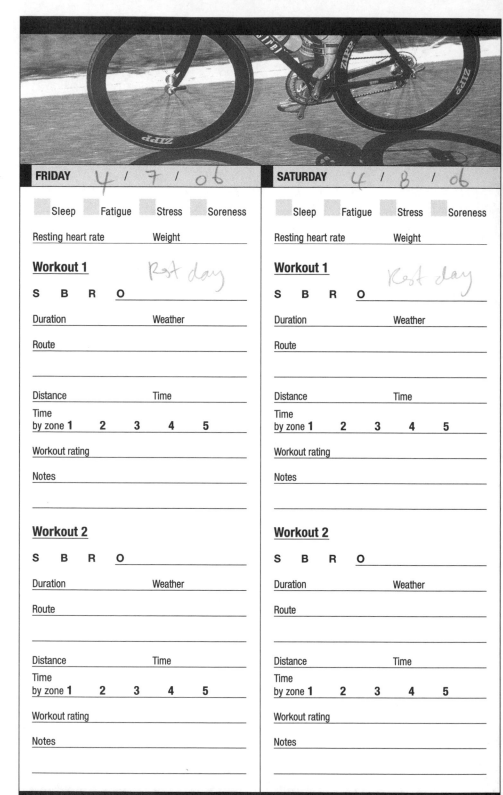

FRIDAY 4 / 7 / 06

Sleep Fatigue Stress Soreness

Resting heart rate _____ Weight _____

Workout 1

Rest day

S   B   R   O _____

Duration _____ Weather _____

Route _____

_____

Distance _____ Time _____

Time
by zone **1   2   3   4   5**

Workout rating _____

Notes _____

_____

Workout 2

S   B   R   O _____

Duration _____ Weather _____

Route _____

_____

Distance _____ Time _____

Time
by zone **1   2   3   4   5**

Workout rating _____

Notes _____

_____

SATURDAY 4 / 8 / 06

Sleep Fatigue Stress Soreness

Resting heart rate _____ Weight _____

Workout 1

Rest day

S   B   R   O _____

Duration _____ Weather _____

Route _____

_____

Distance _____ Time _____

Time
by zone **1   2   3   4   5**

Workout rating _____

Notes _____

_____

Workout 2

S   B   R   O _____

Duration _____ Weather _____

Route _____

_____

Distance _____ Time _____

Time
by zone **1   2   3   4   5**

Workout rating _____

Notes _____

_____

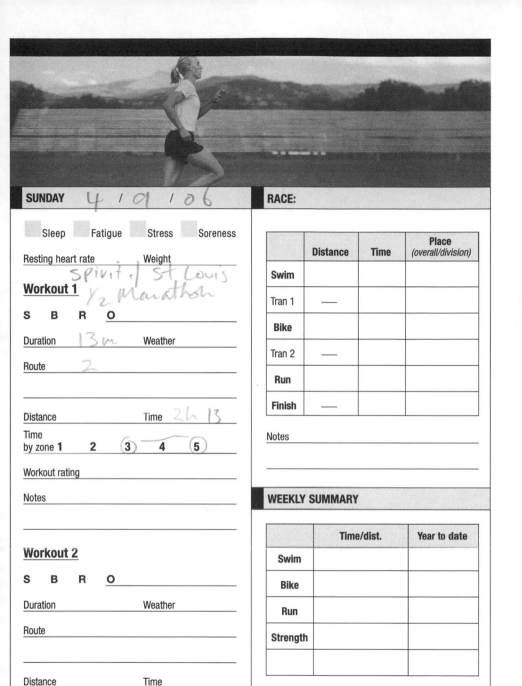

SUNDAY 4 / 9 / 06

Sleep ▢ Fatigue ▢ Stress ▢ Soreness

Resting heart rate _____ Weight _____

Spirit of St Louis

Workout 1 ½ Marathon

S   B   R   O _____

Duration 13m   Weather _____

Route 2 _____

_____

Distance _____   Time 2h 13

Time
by zone 1   2   ③   4   ⑤

Workout rating _____

Notes _____

_____

Workout 2

S   B   R   O _____

Duration _____   Weather _____

Route _____

_____

Distance _____   Time _____

Time
by zone 1   2   3   4   5

Workout rating _____

Notes _____

_____

RACE: _____

	Distance	Time	Place *(overall/division)*
Swim			
Tran 1	—		
Bike			
Tran 2	—		
Run			
Finish	—		

Notes _____

_____

WEEKLY SUMMARY

	Time/dist.	Year to date
Swim		
Bike		
Run		
Strength		

Weekly total _____   Year-to-date total _____

Soreness _____

Notes _____

_____

117

WEEK BEGINNING: **PLANNED WEEKLY HOURS:**

Week's goals (check off as achieved)

☐ _____

☐ _____

☐ _____

MONDAY 4 / 10 / 07	**TUESDAY** / /

2 Sleep 4 Fatigue 2 Stress 4 Soreness   2 Sleep 2 Fatigue 2 Stress 3 Soreness

Resting heart rate _____ Weight _____   Resting heart rate _____ Weight _____

Workout 1   Rst day

S   B   R   (O)   wts

Duration _____ Weather _____

Route _____

_____

Distance _____ Time _____

Time by zone **1   2   3   4   5**

Workout rating _____

Notes _____

_____

Workout 2

S   B   R   O _____

Duration _____ Weather _____

Route _____

_____

Distance _____ Time _____

Time by zone **1   2   3   4   5**

Workout rating _____

Notes _____

_____

Workout 1   wdi

S   B   R   (O)   wdi

Duration _____ Weather _____

Route _____

_____

Distance _____ Time _____

Time by zone **1   2   3   4   5**

Workout rating _____

Notes _____

_____

Workout 2   Stair masta

S   B   R   (O)

Duration 30u   Weather _____

Route   level 1 (O)

_____

Distance _____ Time _____

Time by zone **1   2   (3)   4   5**

Workout rating _____

Notes _____

_____

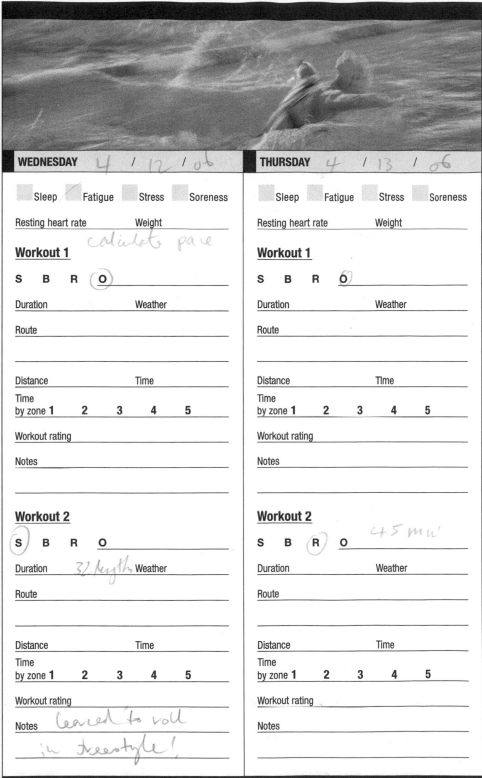

WEDNESDAY 4 / 12 / 06

☐ Sleep ☐ Fatigue ☐ Stress ☐ Soreness

Resting heart rate _____ Weight _____

calculate pace

Workout 1

S   B   R   (O) _____

Duration _____ Weather _____

Route _____

_____

Distance _____ Time _____

Time
by zone **1   2   3   4   5**

Workout rating _____

Notes _____

_____

Workout 2

(S)   B   R   O _____

Duration *32 length* Weather _____

Route _____

_____

Distance _____ Time _____

Time
by zone **1   2   3   4   5**

Workout rating _____

Notes *learned to roll*
in freestyle!

THURSDAY 4 / 13 / 06

☐ Sleep ☐ Fatigue ☐ Stress ☐ Soreness

Resting heart rate _____ Weight _____

Workout 1

S   B   R   Ø _____

Duration _____ Weather _____

Route _____

_____

Distance _____ TIme _____

Time
by zone **1   2   3   4   5**

Workout rating _____

Notes _____

_____

Workout 2

S   B   (R)   O *45 min*

Duration _____ Weather _____

Route _____

_____

Distance _____ Time _____

Time
by zone **1   2   3   4   5**

Workout rating _____

Notes _____

_____

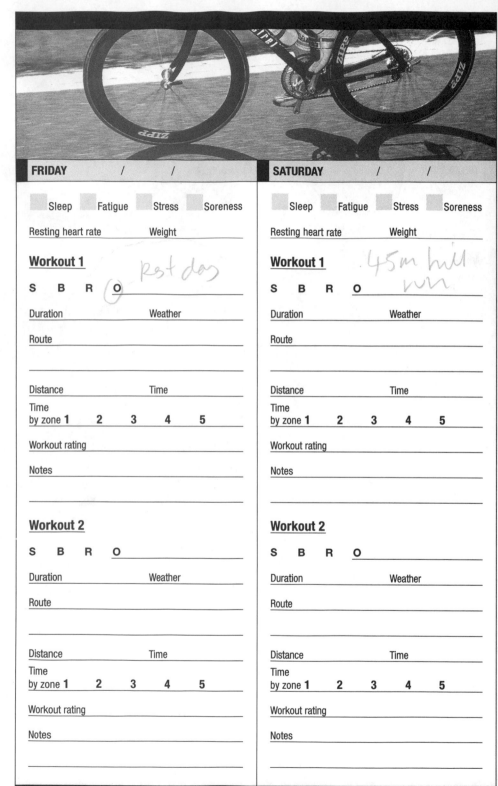

FRIDAY   /   /

■ Sleep   ■ Fatigue   ■ Stress   ■ Soreness

Resting heart rate _____   Weight _____

Workout 1

Rst day

S   B   R   Ⓞ _____

Duration _____   Weather _____

Route _____
_____

Distance _____   Time _____

Time
by zone **1   2   3   4   5**

Workout rating _____

Notes _____
_____

Workout 2

S   B   R   O _____

Duration _____   Weather _____

Route _____
_____

Distance _____   Time _____

Time
by zone **1   2   3   4   5**

Workout rating _____

Notes _____
_____

SATURDAY   /   /

■ Sleep   ■ Fatigue   ■ Stress   ■ Soreness

Resting heart rate _____   Weight _____

Workout 1

45m hill run

S   B   R   O _____

Duration _____   Weather _____

Route _____
_____

Distance _____   Time _____

Time
by zone **1   2   3   4   5**

Workout rating _____

Notes _____
_____

Workout 2

S   B   R   O _____

Duration _____   Weather _____

Route _____
_____

Distance _____   Time _____

Time
by zone **1   2   3   4   5**

Workout rating _____

Notes _____
_____

SUNDAY 4 / 16 / 04

| | RACE: |

◼ Sleep ◼ Fatigue ◼ Stress ◼ Soreness

Resting heart rate _____ Weight _____

Workout 1   45m run

S   B   R   O _____

Duration _____   Weather _____

Route _____

_____

Distance _____   Time _____

Time
by zone **1   2   3   4   5**

Workout rating _____

Notes _____

_____

Workout 2

S   B   R   O _____

Duration _____   Weather _____

Route _____

_____

Distance _____   Time _____

Time
by zone **1   2   3   4   5**

Workout rating _____

Notes _____

_____

RACE:

	Distance	Time	Place *(overall/division)*
Swim			
Tran 1	—		
Bike			
Tran 2	—		
Run			
Finish	—		

Notes _____

_____

WEEKLY SUMMARY

	Time/dist.	Year to date
Swim		
Bike		
Run		
Strength		

Weekly
total _____   Year-to-date
total _____

Soreness _____

Notes _____

_____

WEEK BEGINNING: _____   **PLANNED WEEKLY HOURS:** _____

Week's goals (check off as achieved)

☐ _____

☐ _____

☐ _____

MONDAY / /	**TUESDAY** / /

☐ Sleep ☐ Fatigue ☐ Stress ☐ Soreness   ☐ Sleep ☐ Fatigue ☐ Stress ☐ Soreness

Resting heart rate _____ Weight _____   Resting heart rate _____ Weight _____

Workout 1   *Rst day*

S   B   R   O _____

Duration _____ Weather _____

Route _____

_____

Distance _____ Time _____

Time
by zone **1   2   3   4   5**

Workout rating _____

Notes _____

_____

Workout 2

S   B   R   O _____

Duration _____ Weather _____

Route _____

_____

Distance _____ Time _____

Time
by zone **1   2   3   4   5**

Workout rating _____

Notes _____

_____

Workout 1   *800 m x 4*

S   B   R   O _____

Duration _____ Weather _____

Route _____

_____

Distance _____ Time _____

Time
by zone **1   2   3   4   5**

Workout rating _____

Notes _____

_____

Workout 2

S   B   R   O _____

Duration _____ Weather _____

Route _____

_____

Distance _____ Time _____

Time
by zone **1   2   3   4   5**

Workout rating _____

Notes _____

_____

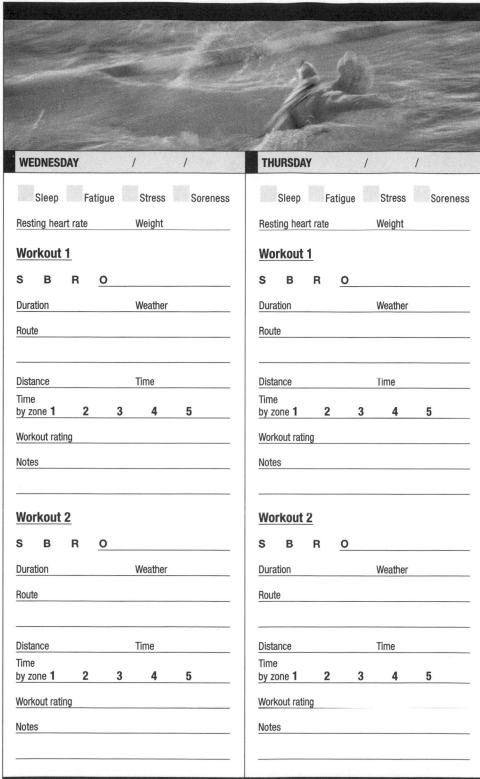

WEDNESDAY	/	/

Sleep   Fatigue   Stress   Soreness

Resting heart rate _____ Weight _____

Workout 1

S   B   R   O _____

Duration _____ Weather _____

Route _____

_____

Distance _____ Time _____

Time
by zone **1   2   3   4   5**

Workout rating _____

Notes _____

_____

Workout 2

S   B   R   O _____

Duration _____ Weather _____

Route _____

_____

Distance _____ Time _____

Time
by zone **1   2   3   4   5**

Workout rating _____

Notes _____

_____

THURSDAY	/	/

Sleep   Fatigue   Stress   Soreness

Resting heart rate _____ Weight _____

Workout 1

S   B   R   O _____

Duration _____ Weather _____

Route _____

_____

Distance _____ Time _____

Time
by zone **1   2   3   4   5**

Workout rating _____

Notes _____

_____

Workout 2

S   B   R   O _____

Duration _____ Weather _____

Route _____

_____

Distance _____ Time _____

Time
by zone **1   2   3   4   5**

Workout rating _____

Notes _____

_____

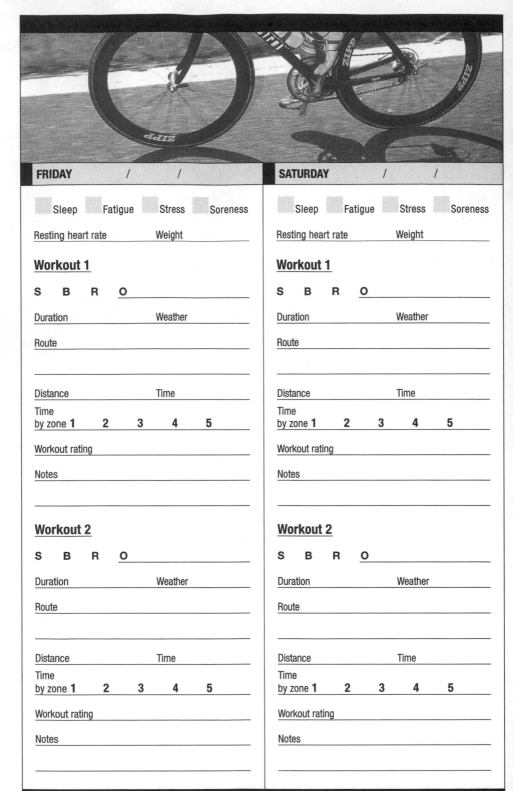

FRIDAY / /

Sleep Fatigue Stress Soreness

Resting heart rate _____ Weight _____

Workout 1

S   B   R   O _____

Duration _____ Weather _____

Route _____

_____

Distance _____ Time _____

Time
by zone **1   2   3   4   5**

Workout rating _____

Notes _____

_____

Workout 2

S   B   R   O _____

Duration _____ Weather _____

Route _____

_____

Distance _____ Time _____

Time
by zone **1   2   3   4   5**

Workout rating _____

Notes _____

_____

SATURDAY / /

Sleep Fatigue Stress Soreness

Resting heart rate _____ Weight _____

Workout 1

S   B   R   O _____

Duration _____ Weather _____

Route _____

_____

Distance _____ Time _____

Time
by zone **1   2   3   4   5**

Workout rating _____

Notes _____

_____

Workout 2

S   B   R   O _____

Duration _____ Weather _____

Route _____

_____

Distance _____ Time _____

Time
by zone **1   2   3   4   5**

Workout rating _____

Notes _____

_____

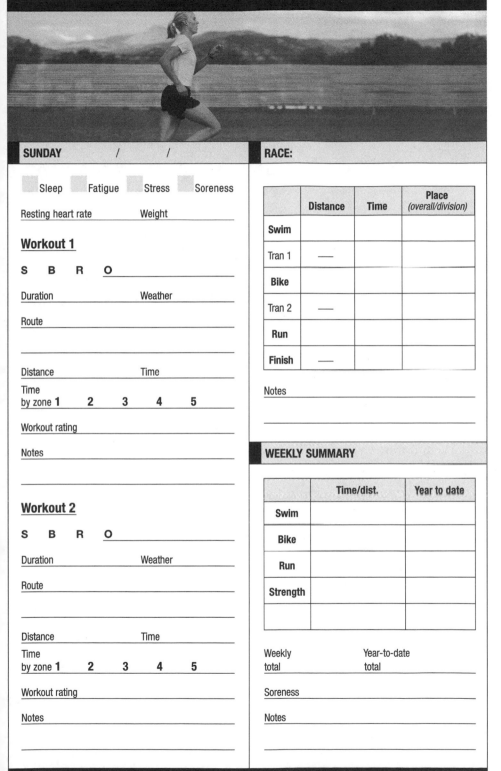

SUNDAY / /

Sleep Fatigue Stress Soreness

Resting heart rate   Weight

Workout 1

S   B   R   O

Duration   Weather

Route

Distance   Time

Time
by zone **1   2   3   4   5**

Workout rating

Notes

Workout 2

S   B   R   O

Duration   Weather

Route

Distance   Time

Time
by zone **1   2   3   4   5**

Workout rating

Notes

RACE:

	Distance	Time	Place *(overall/division)*
Swim			
Tran 1	—		
Bike			
Tran 2	—		
Run			
Finish	—		

Notes

WEEKLY SUMMARY

	Time/dist.	Year to date
Swim		
Bike		
Run		
Strength		

Weekly   Year-to-date
total   total

Soreness

Notes

WEEK BEGINNING: PLANNED WEEKLY HOURS:

Week's goals (check off as achieved)

☐ _____

☐ _____

☐ _____

MONDAY / /	TUESDAY / /

☐ Sleep ☐ Fatigue ☐ Stress ☐ Soreness   ☐ Sleep ☐ Fatigue ☐ Stress ☐ Soreness

Resting heart rate _____ Weight _____   Resting heart rate _____ Weight _____

Workout 1

S   B   R   O _____

Duration _____ Weather _____

Route _____

_____

Distance _____ Time _____

Time
by zone **1   2   3   4   5**

Workout rating _____

Notes _____

_____

Workout 2

S   B   R   O _____

Duration _____ Weather _____

Route _____

_____

Distance _____ Time _____

Time
by zone **1   2   3   4   5**

Workout rating _____

Notes _____

_____

Workout 1

S   B   R   O _____

Duration _____ Weather _____

Route _____

_____

Distance _____ Time _____

Time
by zone **1   2   3   4   5**

Workout rating _____

Notes _____

_____

Workout 2

S   B   R   O _____

Duration _____ Weather _____

Route _____

_____

Distance _____ Time _____

Time
by zone **1   2   3   4   5**

Workout rating _____

Notes _____

_____

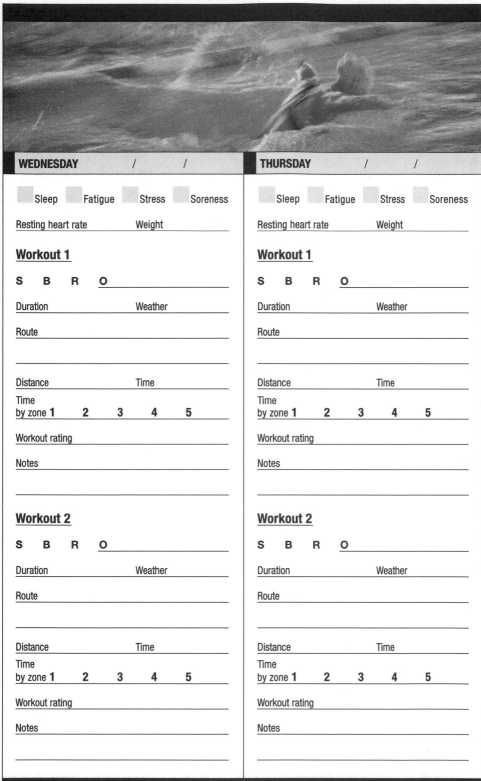

WEDNESDAY	/	/

Sleep   Fatigue   Stress   Soreness

Resting heart rate   Weight

Workout 1

S   B   R   O

Duration   Weather

Route

Distance   Time

Time
by zone **1   2   3   4   5**

Workout rating

Notes

Workout 2

S   B   R   O

Duration   Weather

Route

Distance   Time

Time
by zone **1   2   3   4   5**

Workout rating

Notes

THURSDAY	/	/

Sleep   Fatigue   Stress   Soreness

Resting heart rate   Weight

Workout 1

S   B   R   O

Duration   Weather

Route

Distance   Time

Time
by zone **1   2   3   4   5**

Workout rating

Notes

Workout 2

S   B   R   O

Duration   Weather

Route

Distance   Time

Time
by zone **1   2   3   4   5**

Workout rating

Notes

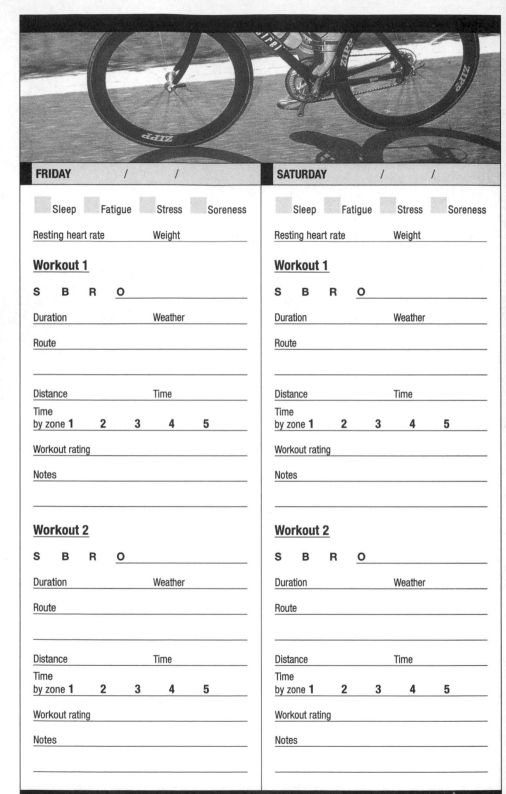

| **FRIDAY** | / | / | **SATURDAY** | / | / |

Sleep Fatigue Stress Soreness

Resting heart rate   Weight

Workout 1

S   B   R   O

Duration   Weather

Route

Distance   Time

Time
by zone **1**   **2**   **3**   **4**   **5**

Workout rating

Notes

Workout 2

S   B   R   O

Duration   Weather

Route

Distance   Time

Time
by zone **1**   **2**   **3**   **4**   **5**

Workout rating

Notes

Sleep Fatigue Stress Soreness

Resting heart rate   Weight

Workout 1

S   B   R   O

Duration   Weather

Route

Distance   Time

Time
by zone **1**   **2**   **3**   **4**   **5**

Workout rating

Notes

Workout 2

S   B   R   O

Duration   Weather

Route

Distance   Time

Time
by zone **1**   **2**   **3**   **4**   **5**

Workout rating

Notes

SUNDAY / /

RACE:

Sleep Fatigue Stress Soreness

Resting heart rate _____ Weight _____

Workout 1

S   B   R   O _____

Duration _____ Weather _____

Route _____

_____

Distance _____ Time _____

Time
by zone **1**   **2**   **3**   **4**   **5**

Workout rating _____

Notes _____

_____

Workout 2

S   B   R   O _____

Duration _____ Weather _____

Route _____

_____

Distance _____ Time _____

Time
by zone **1**   **2**   **3**   **4**   **5**

Workout rating _____

Notes _____

_____

	Distance	Time	Place *(overall/division)*
Swim			
Tran 1	—		
Bike			
Tran 2	—		
Run			
Finish	—		

Notes _____

_____

WEEKLY SUMMARY

	Time/dist.	Year to date
Swim		
Bike		
Run		
Strength		

Weekly
total _____ Year-to-date total _____

Soreness _____

Notes _____

_____

WEEK BEGINNING:　　　　**PLANNED WEEKLY HOURS:**

Week's goals (check off as achieved)

☐ _____

☐ _____

☐ _____

MONDAY / /	**TUESDAY** / /
☐ Sleep ☐ Fatigue ☐ Stress ☐ Soreness	☐ Sleep ☐ Fatigue ☐ Stress ☐ Soreness
Resting heart rate　　　Weight	Resting heart rate　　　Weight

Workout 1

S　　B　　R　　O _____

Duration　　　　Weather _____

Route _____

_____

Distance　　　　Time _____

Time
by zone **1**　　**2**　　**3**　　**4**　　**5**

Workout rating _____

Notes _____

_____

Workout 2

S　　B　　R　　O _____

Duration　　　　Weather _____

Route _____

_____

Distance　　　　Time _____

Time
by zone **1**　　**2**　　**3**　　**4**　　**5**

Workout rating _____

Notes _____

_____

Workout 1

S　　B　　R　　O _____

Duration　　　　Weather _____

Route _____

_____

Distance　　　　Time _____

Time
by zone **1**　　**2**　　**3**　　**4**　　**5**

Workout rating _____

Notes _____

_____

Workout 2

S　　B　　R　　O _____

Duration　　　　Weather _____

Route _____

_____

Distance　　　　Time _____

Time
by zone **1**　　**2**　　**3**　　**4**　　**5**

Workout rating _____

Notes _____

_____

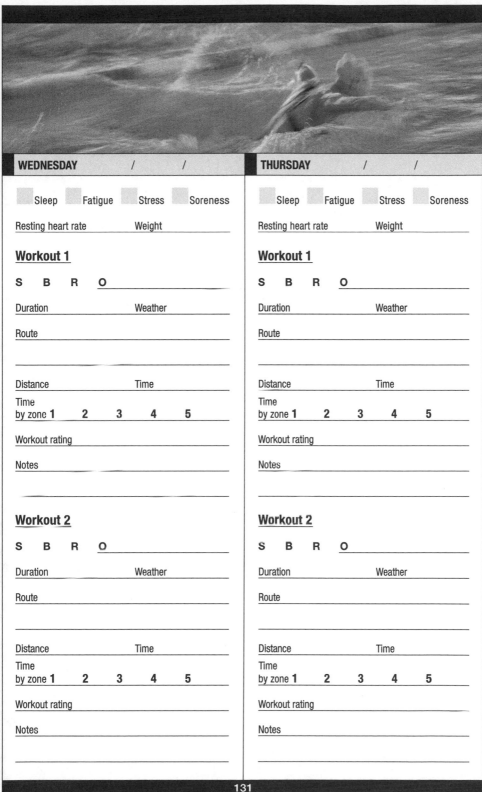

WEDNESDAY / /

Sleep   Fatigue   Stress   Soreness

Resting heart rate _____ Weight _____

Workout 1

S   B   R   O _____

Duration _____ Weather _____

Route _____

_____

Distance _____ Time _____

Time
by zone **1   2   3   4   5**

Workout rating _____

Notes _____

Workout 2

S   B   R   O _____

Duration _____ Weather _____

Route _____

_____

Distance _____ Time _____

Time
by zone **1   2   3   4   5**

Workout rating _____

Notes _____

_____

THURSDAY / /

Sleep   Fatigue   Stress   Soreness

Resting heart rate _____ Weight _____

Workout 1

S   B   R   O _____

Duration _____ Weather _____

Route _____

_____

Distance _____ Time _____

Time
by zone **1   2   3   4   5**

Workout rating _____

Notes _____

Workout 2

S   B   R   O _____

Duration _____ Weather _____

Route _____

_____

Distance _____ Time _____

Time
by zone **1   2   3   4   5**

Workout rating _____

Notes _____

_____

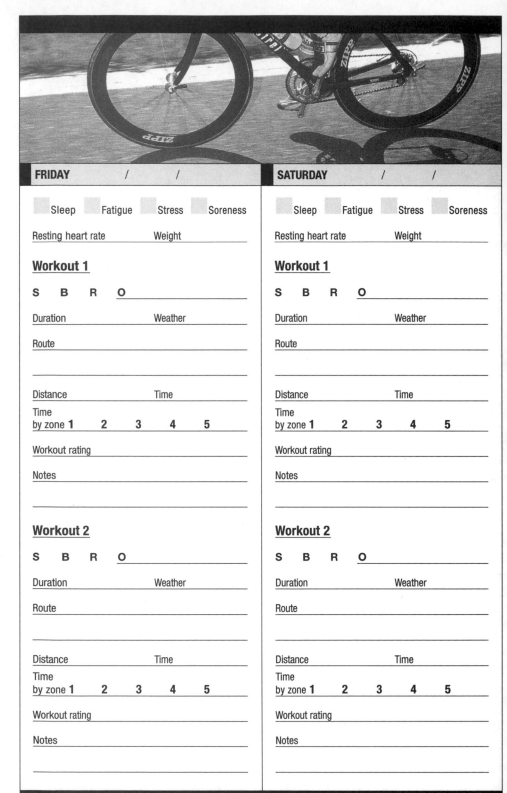

FRIDAY   /   /

Sleep   Fatigue   Stress   Soreness

Resting heart rate _____ Weight _____

Workout 1

S   B   R   O _____

Duration _____ Weather _____

Route _____
_____

Distance _____ Time _____

Time
by zone **1   2   3   4   5**

Workout rating _____

Notes _____
_____

Workout 2

S   B   R   O _____

Duration _____ Weather _____

Route _____
_____

Distance _____ Time _____

Time
by zone **1   2   3   4   5**

Workout rating _____

Notes _____
_____

SATURDAY   /   /

Sleep   Fatigue   Stress   Soreness

Resting heart rate _____ Weight _____

Workout 1

S   B   R   O _____

Duration _____ Weather _____

Route _____
_____

Distance _____ Time _____

Time
by zone **1   2   3   4   5**

Workout rating _____

Notes _____
_____

Workout 2

S   B   R   O _____

Duration _____ Weather _____

Route _____
_____

Distance _____ Time _____

Time
by zone **1   2   3   4   5**

Workout rating _____

Notes _____
_____

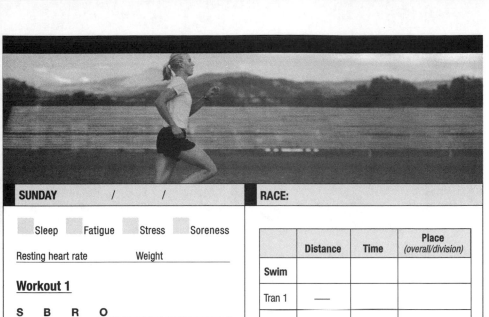

SUNDAY	/	/

Sleep   Fatigue   Stress   Soreness

Resting heart rate _____ Weight _____

Workout 1

S   B   R   O _____

Duration _____ Weather _____

Route _____

_____

Distance _____ Time _____

Time
by zone **1   2   3   4   5**

Workout rating _____

Notes _____

_____

Workout 2

S   B   R   O _____

Duration _____ Weather _____

Route _____

_____

Distance _____ Time _____

Time
by zone **1   2   3   4   5**

Workout rating _____

Notes _____

_____

RACE: _____

	Distance	Time	Place *(overall/division)*
Swim			
Tran 1	—		
Bike			
Tran 2	—		
Run			
Finish	—		

Notes _____

_____

WEEKLY SUMMARY

	Time/dist.	Year to date
Swim		
Bike		
Run		
Strength		

Weekly total _____ Year-to-date total _____

Soreness _____

Notes _____

_____

WEEK BEGINNING: _____   **PLANNED WEEKLY HOURS:** _____

Week's goals (check off as achieved)

▪ _____

▪ _____

▪ _____

MONDAY / /	**TUESDAY** / /

▪ Sleep   ▪ Fatigue   ▪ Stress   ▪ Soreness   ▪ Sleep   ▪ Fatigue   ▪ Stress   ▪ Soreness

Resting heart rate _____ Weight _____   Resting heart rate _____ Weight _____

Workout 1

S   B   R   O _____

Duration _____ Weather _____

Route _____

_____

Distance _____ Time _____

Time
by zone **1**   **2**   **3**   **4**   **5**

Workout rating _____

Notes _____

_____

Workout 2

S   B   R   O _____

Duration _____ Weather _____

Route _____

_____

Distance _____ Time _____

Time
by zone **1**   **2**   **3**   **4**   **5**

Workout rating _____

Notes _____

_____

Workout 1

S   B   R   O _____

Duration _____ Weather _____

Route _____

_____

Distance _____ Time _____

Time
by zone **1**   **2**   **3**   **4**   **5**

Workout rating _____

Notes _____

_____

Workout 2

S   B   R   O _____

Duration _____ Weather _____

Route _____

_____

Distance _____ Time _____

Time
by zone **1**   **2**   **3**   **4**   **5**

Workout rating _____

Notes _____

_____

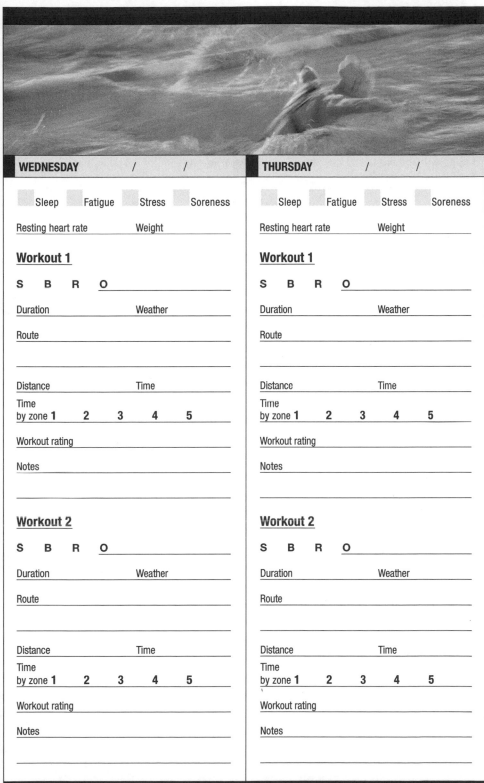

WEDNESDAY   /   /

Sleep   Fatigue   Stress   Soreness

Resting heart rate   Weight

Workout 1

S   B   R   O

Duration   Weather

Route

Distance   Time

Time
by zone 1   2   3   4   5

Workout rating

Notes

Workout 2

S   B   R   O

Duration   Weather

Route

Distance   Time

Time
by zone 1   2   3   4   5

Workout rating

Notes

THURSDAY   /   /

Sleep   Fatigue   Stress   Soreness

Resting heart rate   Weight

Workout 1

S   B   R   O

Duration   Weather

Route

Distance   Time

Time
by zone 1   2   3   4   5

Workout rating

Notes

Workout 2

S   B   R   O

Duration   Weather

Route

Distance   Time

Time
by zone 1   2   3   4   5

Workout rating

Notes

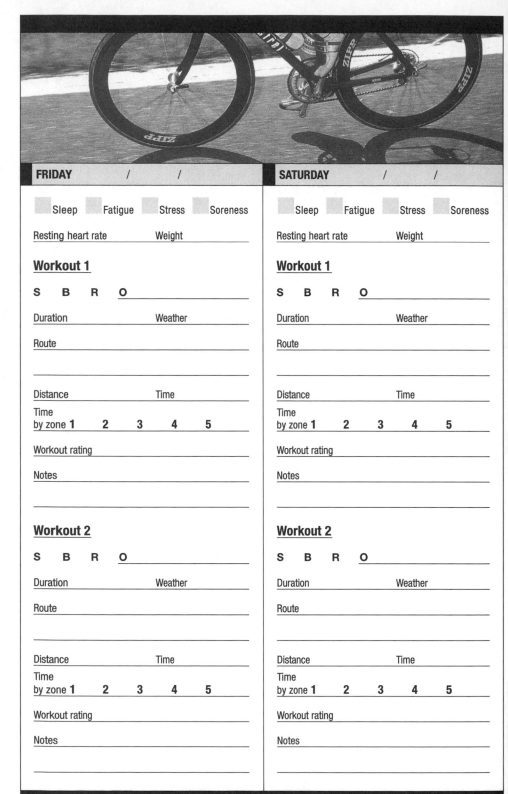

FRIDAY / /

Sleep Fatigue Stress Soreness

Resting heart rate _____ Weight _____

Workout 1

S   B   R   O _____

Duration _____ Weather _____

Route _____

_____

Distance _____ Time _____

Time
by zone **1   2   3   4   5**

Workout rating _____

Notes _____

_____

Workout 2

S   B   R   O _____

Duration _____ Weather _____

Route _____

_____

Distance _____ Time _____

Time
by zone **1   2   3   4   5**

Workout rating _____

Notes _____

_____

SATURDAY / /

Sleep Fatigue Stress Soreness

Resting heart rate _____ Weight _____

Workout 1

S   B   R   O _____

Duration _____ Weather _____

Route _____

_____

Distance _____ Time _____

Time
by zone **1   2   3   4   5**

Workout rating _____

Notes _____

_____

Workout 2

S   B   R   O _____

Duration _____ Weather _____

Route _____

_____

Distance _____ Time _____

Time
by zone **1   2   3   4   5**

Workout rating _____

Notes _____

_____

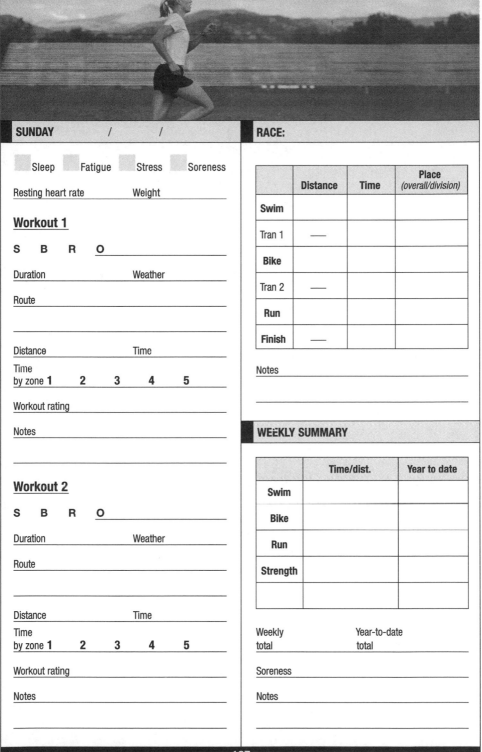

SUNDAY / /

■ Sleep ■ Fatigue ■ Stress ■ Soreness

Resting heart rate _____ Weight _____

Workout 1

S B R O _____

Duration _____ Weather _____

Route _____

_____

Distance _____ Time _____

Time
by zone **1   2   3   4   5**

Workout rating _____

Notes _____

_____

Workout 2

S B R O _____

Duration _____ Weather _____

Route _____

_____

Distance _____ Time _____

Time
by zone **1   2   3   4   5**

Workout rating _____

Notes _____

_____

RACE: _____

	Distance	Time	Place *(overall/division)*
Swim			
Tran 1	—		
Bike			
Tran 2	—		
Run			
Finish	—		

Notes _____

_____

▌WEEKLY SUMMARY

	Time/dist.	Year to date
Swim		
Bike		
Run		
Strength		

Weekly _____ Year-to-date _____
total total

Soreness _____

Notes _____

_____

Week's goals (check off as achieved)

☐ _____

☐ _____

☐ _____

MONDAY / /	**TUESDAY** / /

☐ Sleep ☐ Fatigue ☐ Stress ☐ Soreness

Resting heart rate _____ Weight _____

Workout 1

S B R O _____

Duration _____ Weather _____

Route _____

_____

Distance _____ Time _____

Time
by zone **1** **2** **3** **4** **5**

Workout rating _____

Notes _____

_____

Workout 2

S B R O _____

Duration _____ Weather _____

Route _____

_____

Distance _____ Time _____

Time
by zone **1** **2** **3** **4** **5**

Workout rating _____

Notes _____

_____

☐ Sleep ☐ Fatigue ☐ Stress ☐ Soreness

Resting heart rate _____ Weight _____

Workout 1

S B R O _____

Duration _____ Weather _____

Route _____

_____

Distance _____ Time _____

Time
by zone **1** **2** **3** **4** **5**

Workout rating _____

Notes _____

_____

Workout 2

S B R O _____

Duration _____ Weather _____

Route _____

_____

Distance _____ Time _____

Time
by zone **1** **2** **3** **4** **5**

Workout rating _____

Notes _____

_____

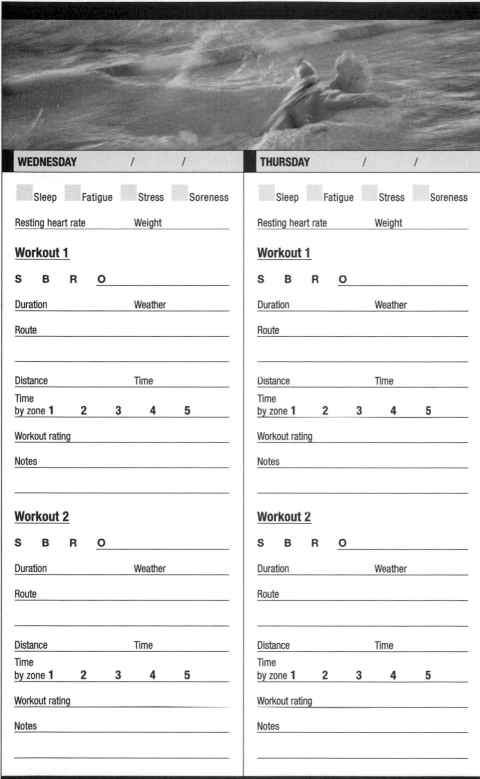

WEDNESDAY / /

Sleep   Fatigue   Stress   Soreness

Resting heart rate _____ Weight _____

Workout 1

S   B   R   O _____

Duration _____ Weather _____

Route _____

_____

Distance _____ Time _____

Time
by zone 1   2   3   4   5

Workout rating _____

Notes _____

_____

Workout 2

S   B   R   O _____

Duration _____ Weather _____

Route _____

_____

Distance _____ Time _____

Time
by zone 1   2   3   4   5

Workout rating _____

Notes _____

_____

THURSDAY / /

Sleep   Fatigue   Stress   Soreness

Resting heart rate _____ Weight _____

Workout 1

S   B   R   O _____

Duration _____ Weather _____

Route _____

_____

Distance _____ Time _____

Time
by zone 1   2   3   4   5

Workout rating _____

Notes _____

_____

Workout 2

S   B   R   O _____

Duration _____ Weather _____

Route _____

_____

Distance _____ Time _____

Time
by zone 1   2   3   4   5

Workout rating _____

Notes _____

_____

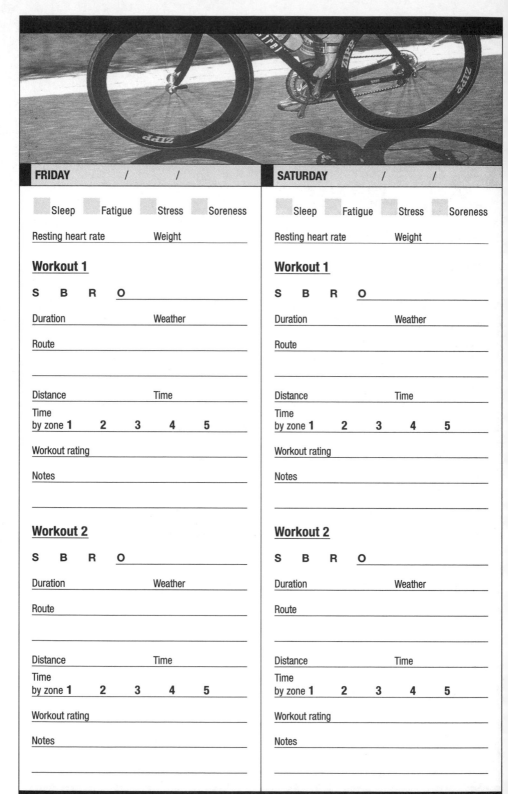

FRIDAY / /

Sleep Fatigue Stress Soreness

Resting heart rate _____ Weight _____

Workout 1

S   B   R   O _____

Duration _____ Weather _____

Route _____

_____

Distance _____ Time _____

Time
by zone **1   2   3   4   5**

Workout rating _____

Notes _____

_____

Workout 2

S   B   R   O _____

Duration _____ Weather _____

Route _____

_____

Distance _____ Time _____

Time
by zone **1   2   3   4   5**

Workout rating _____

Notes _____

_____

SATURDAY / /

Sleep Fatigue Stress Soreness

Resting heart rate _____ Weight _____

Workout 1

S   B   R   O _____

Duration _____ Weather _____

Route _____

_____

Distance _____ Time _____

Time
by zone **1   2   3   4   5**

Workout rating _____

Notes _____

_____

Workout 2

S   B   R   O _____

Duration _____ Weather _____

Route _____

_____

Distance _____ Time _____

Time
by zone **1   2   3   4   5**

Workout rating _____

Notes _____

_____

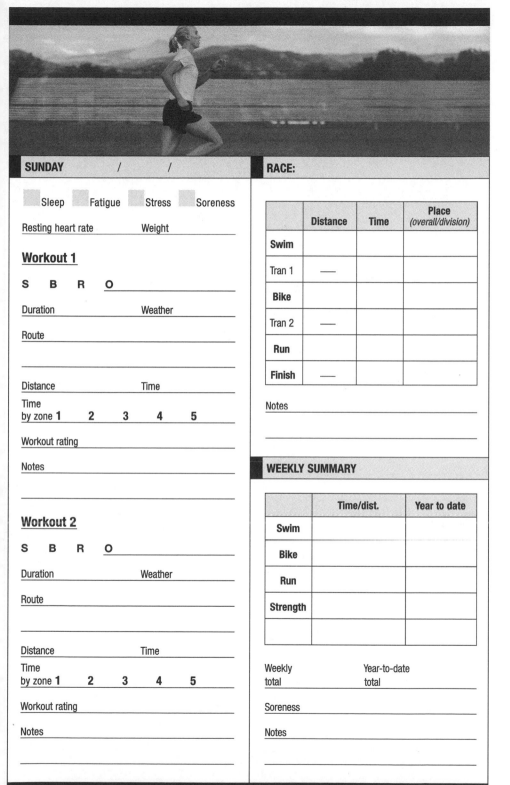

SUNDAY / /

Sleep Fatigue Stress Soreness

Resting heart rate _____ Weight _____

Workout 1

S B R O _____

Duration _____ Weather _____

Route _____

_____

Distance _____ Time _____

Time
by zone **1** **2** **3** **4** **5**

Workout rating _____

Notes _____

_____

Workout 2

S B R O _____

Duration _____ Weather _____

Route _____

_____

Distance _____ Time _____

Time
by zone **1** **2** **3** **4** **5**

Workout rating _____

Notes _____

_____

RACE:

	Distance	Time	Place (overall/division)
Swim			
Tran 1	—		
Bike			
Tran 2	—		
Run			
Finish	—		

Notes _____

_____

WEEKLY SUMMARY

	Time/dist.	Year to date
Swim		
Bike		
Run		
Strength		

Weekly total _____ Year-to-date total _____

Soreness _____

Notes _____

_____

WEEK BEGINNING: _____   **PLANNED WEEKLY HOURS:** _____

Week's goals (check off as achieved)

▨ _____

▨ _____

▨ _____

MONDAY / /	TUESDAY / /

▨ Sleep ▨ Fatigue ▨ Stress ▨ Soreness   ▨ Sleep ▨ Fatigue ▨ Stress ▨ Soreness

Resting heart rate _____ Weight _____   Resting heart rate _____ Weight _____

Workout 1   ### Workout 1

S   B   R   O _____   **S   B   R   O** _____

Duration _____ Weather _____   Duration _____ Weather _____

Route _____   Route _____

_____   _____

Distance _____ Time _____   Distance _____ Time _____

Time by zone **1   2   3   4   5**   Time by zone **1   2   3   4   5**

Workout rating _____   Workout rating _____

Notes _____   Notes _____

_____   _____

Workout 2   ### Workout 2

S   B   R   O _____   **S   B   R   O** _____

Duration _____ Weather _____   Duration _____ Weather _____

Route _____   Route _____

_____   _____

Distance _____ Time _____   Distance _____ Time _____

Time by zone **1   2   3   4   5**   Time by zone **1   2   3   4   5**

Workout rating _____   Workout rating _____

Notes _____   Notes _____

_____   _____

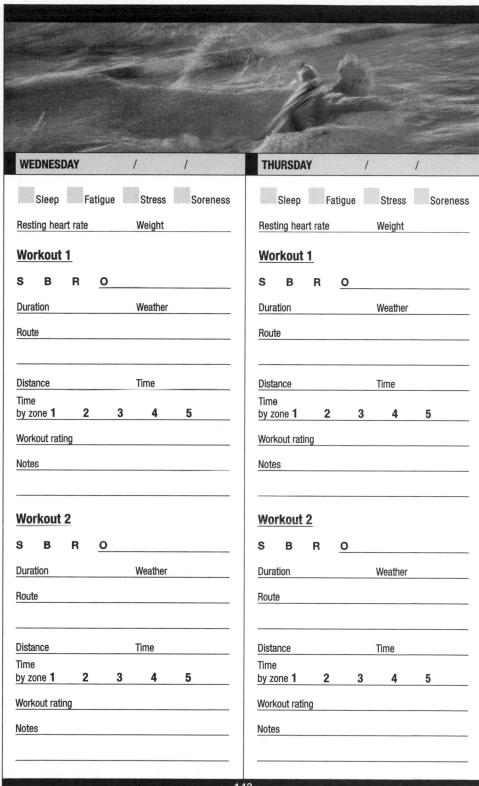

WEDNESDAY   /   /

Sleep   Fatigue   Stress   Soreness

Resting heart rate _____   Weight _____

Workout 1

S   B   R   O _____

Duration _____   Weather _____

Route _____

_____

Distance _____   Time _____

Time
by zone **1**   **2**   **3**   **4**   **5**

Workout rating _____

Notes _____

_____

Workout 2

S   B   R   O _____

Duration _____   Weather _____

Route _____

_____

Distance _____   Time _____

Time
by zone **1**   **2**   **3**   **4**   **5**

Workout rating _____

Notes _____

_____

THURSDAY   /   /

Sleep   Fatigue   Stress   Soreness

Resting heart rate _____   Weight _____

Workout 1

S   B   R   O _____

Duration _____   Weather _____

Route _____

_____

Distance _____   Time _____

Time
by zone **1**   **2**   **3**   **4**   **5**

Workout rating _____

Notes _____

_____

Workout 2

S   B   R   O _____

Duration _____   Weather _____

Route _____

_____

Distance _____   Time _____

Time
by zone **1**   **2**   **3**   **4**   **5**

Workout rating _____

Notes _____

_____

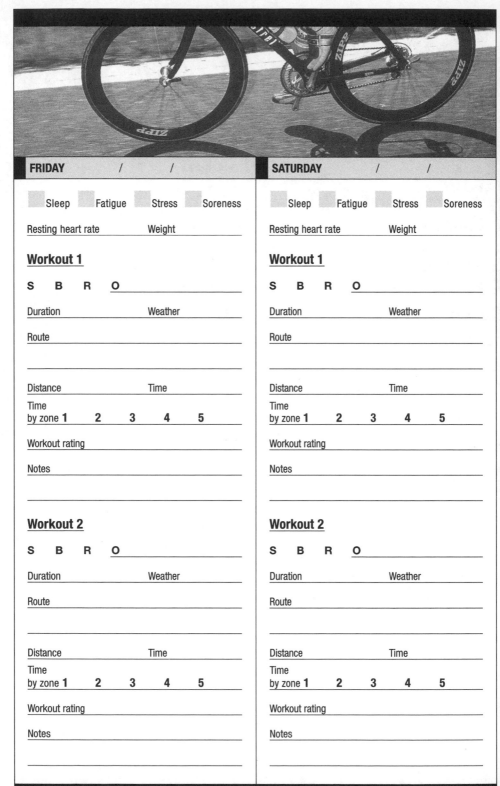

FRIDAY / /	**SATURDAY** / /

Sleep Fatigue Stress Soreness | Sleep Fatigue Stress Soreness

Resting heart rate ____ Weight ____ | Resting heart rate ____ Weight ____

Workout 1

S   B   R   O ____

Duration ____ Weather ____

Route ____

____

Distance ____ Time ____

Time
by zone **1**   **2**   **3**   **4**   **5**

Workout rating ____

Notes ____

____

Workout 2

S   B   R   O ____

Duration ____ Weather ____

Route ____

____

Distance ____ Time ____

Time
by zone **1**   **2**   **3**   **4**   **5**

Workout rating ____

Notes ____

____

Workout 1

S   B   R   O ____

Duration ____ Weather ____

Route ____

____

Distance ____ Time ____

Time
by zone **1**   **2**   **3**   **4**   **5**

Workout rating ____

Notes ____

____

Workout 2

S   B   R   O ____

Duration ____ Weather ____

Route ____

____

Distance ____ Time ____

Time
by zone **1**   **2**   **3**   **4**   **5**

Workout rating ____

Notes ____

____

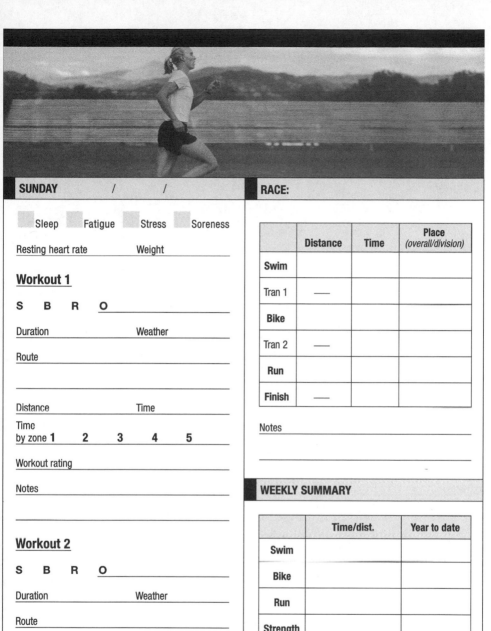

SUNDAY / /

RACE:

Sleep ▢ Fatigue ▢ Stress ▢ Soreness ▢

Resting heart rate _____ Weight _____

Workout 1

S   B   R   O _____

Duration _____ Weather _____

Route _____

_____

Distance _____ Time _____

Time
by zone **1**   **2**   **3**   **4**   **5**

Workout rating _____

Notes _____

_____

Workout 2

S   B   R   O _____

Duration _____ Weather _____

Route _____

_____

Distance _____ Time _____

Time
by zone **1**   **2**   **3**   **4**   **5**

Workout rating _____

Notes _____

_____

	Distance	Time	Place *(overall/division)*
Swim			
Tran 1	——		
Bike			
Tran 2	——		
Run			
Finish	——		

Notes _____

_____

WEEKLY SUMMARY

	Time/dist.	Year to date
Swim		
Bike		
Run		
Strength		

Weekly
total _____

Year-to-date
total _____

Soreness _____

Notes _____

_____

WEEK BEGINNING: **PLANNED WEEKLY HOURS:**

Week's goals (check off as achieved)

☐ _____

☐ _____

☐ _____

MONDAY / /	TUESDAY / /

☐ Sleep ☐ Fatigue ☐ Stress ☐ Soreness   ☐ Sleep ☐ Fatigue ☐ Stress ☐ Soreness

Resting heart rate _____ Weight _____   Resting heart rate _____ Weight _____

Workout 1

S   B   R   O _____

Duration _____ Weather _____

Route _____

_____

Distance _____ Time _____

Time
by zone **1   2   3   4   5**

Workout rating _____

Notes _____

_____

Workout 2

S   B   R   O _____

Duration _____ Weather _____

Route _____

_____

Distance _____ Time _____

Time
by zone **1   2   3   4   5**

Workout rating _____

Notes _____

_____

Workout 1

S   B   R   O _____

Duration _____ Weather _____

Route _____

_____

Distance _____ Time _____

Time
by zone **1   2   3   4   5**

Workout rating _____

Notes _____

_____

Workout 2

S   B   R   O _____

Duration _____ Weather _____

Route _____

_____

Distance _____ Time _____

Time
by zone **1   2   3   4   5**

Workout rating _____

Notes _____

_____

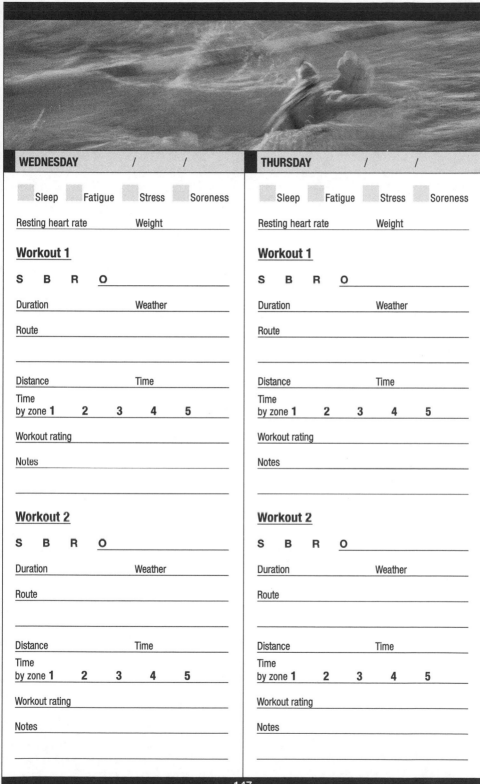

WEDNESDAY   /   /

Sleep   Fatigue   Stress   Soreness

Resting heart rate _____ Weight _____

Workout 1

S   B   R   O _____

Duration _____ Weather _____

Route _____

_____

Distance _____ Time _____

Time
by zone **1**   **2**   **3**   **4**   **5**

Workout rating _____

Notes _____

_____

Workout 2

S   B   R   O _____

Duration _____ Weather _____

Route _____

_____

Distance _____ Time _____

Time
by zone **1**   **2**   **3**   **4**   **5**

Workout rating _____

Notes _____

_____

THURSDAY   /   /

Sleep   Fatigue   Stress   Soreness

Resting heart rate _____ Weight _____

Workout 1

S   B   R   O _____

Duration _____ Weather _____

Route _____

_____

Distance _____ Time _____

Time
by zone **1**   **2**   **3**   **4**   **5**

Workout rating _____

Notes _____

_____

Workout 2

S   B   R   O _____

Duration _____ Weather _____

Route _____

_____

Distance _____ Time _____

Time
by zone **1**   **2**   **3**   **4**   **5**

Workout rating _____

Notes _____

_____

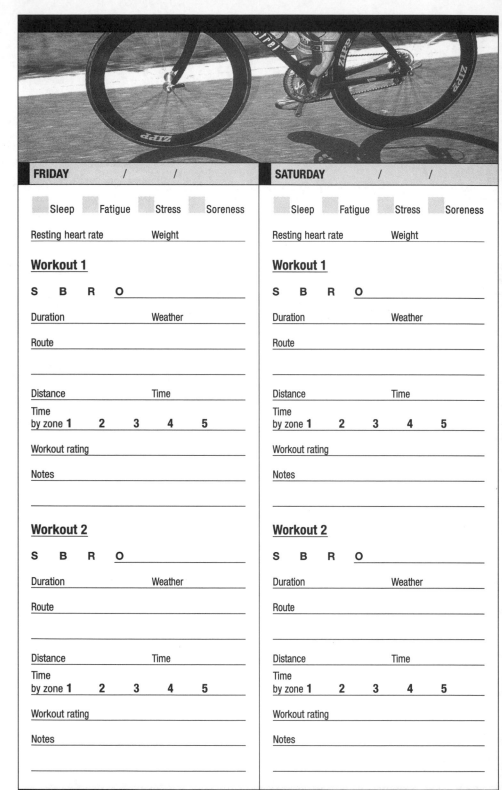

FRIDAY / /

Sleep Fatigue Stress Soreness

Resting heart rate _____ Weight _____

Workout 1

S   B   R   O _____

Duration _____ Weather _____

Route _____

_____

Distance _____ Time _____

Time
by zone **1   2   3   4   5**

Workout rating _____

Notes _____

_____

Workout 2

S   B   R   O _____

Duration _____ Weather _____

Route _____

_____

Distance _____ Time _____

Time
by zone **1   2   3   4   5**

Workout rating _____

Notes _____

_____

SATURDAY / /

Sleep Fatigue Stress Soreness

Resting heart rate _____ Weight _____

Workout 1

S   B   R   O _____

Duration _____ Weather _____

Route _____

_____

Distance _____ Time _____

Time
by zone **1   2   3   4   5**

Workout rating _____

Notes _____

_____

Workout 2

S   B   R   O _____

Duration _____ Weather _____

Route _____

_____

Distance _____ Time _____

Time
by zone **1   2   3   4   5**

Workout rating _____

Notes _____

_____

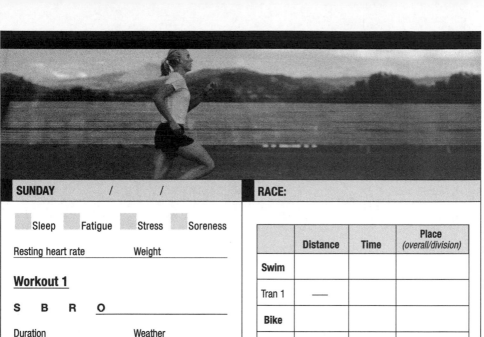

SUNDAY   /   /

Sleep **Fatigue** **Stress** **Soreness**

Resting heart rate _____ Weight _____

Workout 1

S   B   R   O _____

Duration _____ Weather _____

Route _____

_____

Distance _____ Time _____

Time
by zone **1**   **2**   **3**   **4**   **5** _____

Workout rating _____

Notes _____

_____

Workout 2

S   B   R   O _____

Duration _____ Weather _____

Route _____

_____

Distance _____ Time _____

Time
by zone **1**   **2**   **3**   **4**   **5** _____

Workout rating _____

Notes _____

_____

RACE:

	Distance	Time	Place *(overall/division)*
Swim			
Tran 1	—		
Bike			
Tran 2	—		
Run			
Finish	—		

Notes _____

_____

WEEKLY SUMMARY

	Time/dist.	Year to date
Swim		
Bike		
Run		
Strength		

Weekly   Year-to-date
total   total

Soreness _____

Notes _____

_____

WEEK BEGINNING: **PLANNED WEEKLY HOURS:**

Week's goals (check off as achieved)

▢ _____

▢ _____

▢ _____

MONDAY / /	**TUESDAY** / /

▢ Sleep ▢ Fatigue ▢ Stress ▢ Soreness

Resting heart rate _____ Weight _____

Workout 1

S   B   R   O _____

Duration _____ Weather _____

Route _____

_____

Distance _____ Time _____

Time
by zone **1**   **2**   **3**   **4**   **5**

Workout rating _____

Notes _____

_____

Workout 2

S   B   R   O _____

Duration _____ Weather _____

Route _____

_____

Distance _____ Time _____

Time
by zone **1**   **2**   **3**   **4**   **5**

Workout rating _____

Notes _____

_____

▢ Sleep ▢ Fatigue ▢ Stress ▢ Soreness

Resting heart rate _____ Weight _____

Workout 1

S   B   R   O _____

Duration _____ Weather _____

Route _____

_____

Distance _____ Time _____

Time
by zone **1**   **2**   **3**   **4**   **5**

Workout rating _____

Notes _____

_____

Workout 2

S   B   R   O _____

Duration _____ Weather _____

Route _____

_____

Distance _____ Time _____

Time
by zone **1**   **2**   **3**   **4**   **5**

Workout rating _____

Notes _____

_____

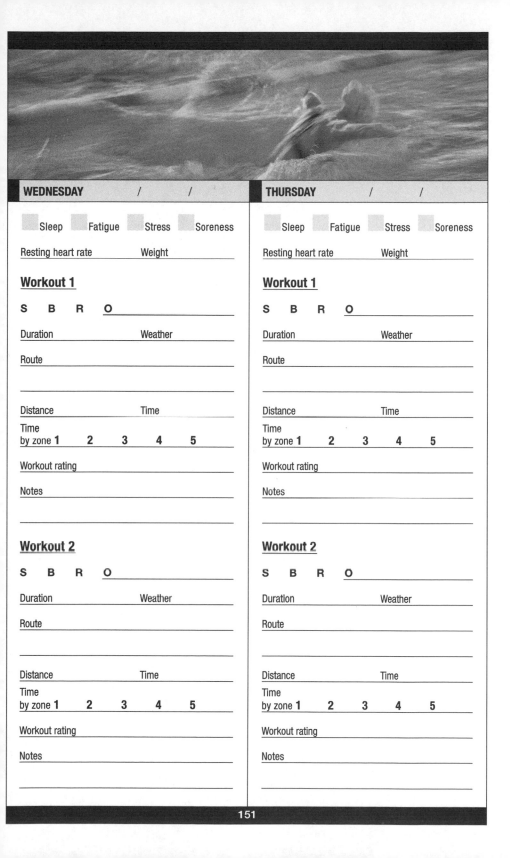

WEDNESDAY / /

Sleep Fatigue Stress Soreness

Resting heart rate _____ Weight _____

Workout 1

S   B   R   O _____

Duration _____ Weather _____

Route _____

_____

Distance _____ Time _____

Time
by zone **1   2   3   4   5**

Workout rating _____

Notes _____

_____

Workout 2

S   B   R   O _____

Duration _____ Weather _____

Route _____

_____

Distance _____ Time _____

Time
by zone **1   2   3   4   5**

Workout rating _____

Notes _____

_____

THURSDAY / /

Sleep Fatigue Stress Soreness

Resting heart rate _____ Weight _____

Workout 1

S   B   R   O _____

Duration _____ Weather _____

Route _____

_____

Distance _____ Time _____

Time
by zone **1   2   3   4   5**

Workout rating _____

Notes _____

_____

Workout 2

S   B   R   O _____

Duration _____ Weather _____

Route _____

_____

Distance _____ Time _____

Time
by zone **1   2   3   4   5**

Workout rating _____

Notes _____

_____

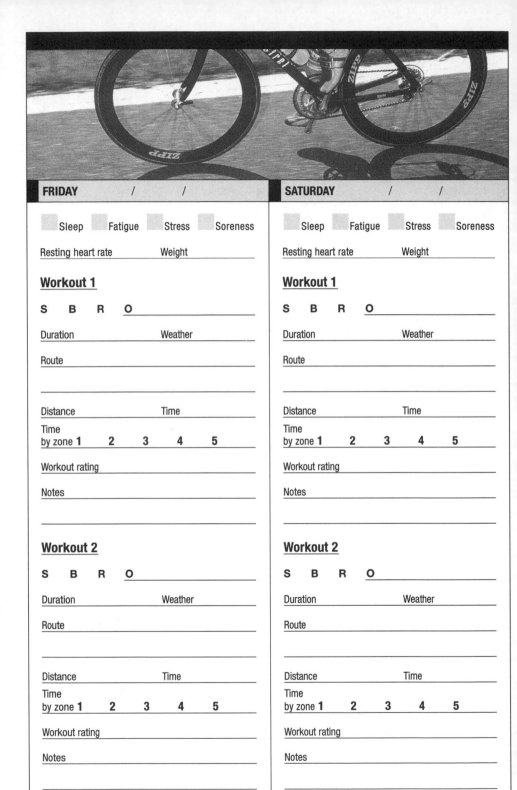

FRIDAY   /   /

Sleep   Fatigue   Stress   Soreness

Resting heart rate _____ Weight _____

Workout 1

S   B   R   O _____

Duration _____ Weather _____

Route _____

_____

Distance _____ Time _____

Time
by zone 1   2   3   4   5

Workout rating _____

Notes _____

_____

Workout 2

S   B   R   O _____

Duration _____ Weather _____

Route _____

_____

Distance _____ Time _____

Time
by zone 1   2   3   4   5

Workout rating _____

Notes _____

_____

SATURDAY   /   /

Sleep   Fatigue   Stress   Soreness

Resting heart rate _____ Weight _____

Workout 1

S   B   R   O _____

Duration _____ Weather _____

Route _____

_____

Distance _____ Time _____

Time
by zone 1   2   3   4   5

Workout rating _____

Notes _____

_____

Workout 2

S   B   R   O _____

Duration _____ Weather _____

Route _____

_____

Distance _____ Time _____

Time
by zone 1   2   3   4   5

Workout rating _____

Notes _____

_____

Sleep   Fatigue   Stress   Soreness

Resting heart rate _____ Weight _____

Workout 1

S   B   R   O _____

Duration _____ Weather _____

Route _____

_____

Distance _____ Time _____

Time
by zone **1   2   3   4   5**

Workout rating _____

Notes _____

_____

Workout 2

S   B   R   O _____

Duration _____ Weather _____

Route _____

_____

Distance _____ Time _____

Time
by zone **1   2   3   4   5**

Workout rating _____

Notes _____

_____

RACE: _____

	Distance	Time	Place *(overall/division)*
Swim			
Tran 1	—		
Bike			
Tran 2	—		
Run			
Finish	—		

Notes _____

_____

WEEKLY SUMMARY

	Time/dist.	Year to date
Swim		
Bike		
Run		
Strength		

Weekly   Year-to-date
total   total

Soreness _____

Notes _____

_____

WEEK BEGINNING: **PLANNED WEEKLY HOURS:**

Week's goals (check off as achieved)

▢ _____

▢ _____

▢ _____

| MONDAY | / | / | | TUESDAY | / | / |

▢ Sleep ▢ Fatigue ▢ Stress ▢ Soreness

Resting heart rate _____ Weight _____

Workout 1

S   B   R   O _____

Duration _____ Weather _____

Route _____

_____

Distance _____ Time _____

Time
by zone **1   2   3   4   5**

Workout rating _____

Notes _____

_____

Workout 2

S   B   R   O _____

Duration _____ Weather _____

Route _____

_____

Distance _____ Time _____

Time
by zone **1   2   3   4   5**

Workout rating _____

Notes _____

_____

▢ Sleep ▢ Fatigue ▢ Stress ▢ Soreness

Resting heart rate _____ Weight _____

Workout 1

S   B   R   O _____

Duration _____ Weather _____

Route _____

_____

Distance _____ Time _____

Time
by zone **1   2   3   4   5**

Workout rating _____

Notes _____

_____

Workout 2

S   B   R   O _____

Duration _____ Weather _____

Route _____

_____

Distance _____ Time _____

Time
by zone **1   2   3   4   5**

Workout rating _____

Notes _____

_____

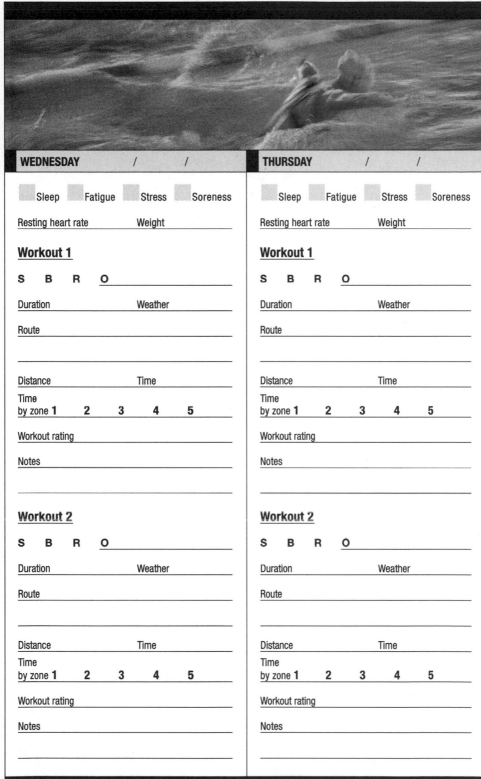

WEDNESDAY	/	/

Sleep Fatigue Stress Soreness

Resting heart rate _____ Weight _____

Workout 1

S   B   R   O _____

Duration _____ Weather _____

Route _____

_____

Distance _____ Time _____

Time
by zone **1   2   3   4   5**

Workout rating _____

Notes _____

_____

Workout 2

S   B   R   O _____

Duration _____ Weather _____

Route _____

_____

Distance _____ Time _____

Time
by zone **1   2   3   4   5**

Workout rating _____

Notes _____

_____

THURSDAY	/	/

Sleep Fatigue Stress Soreness

Resting heart rate _____ Weight _____

Workout 1

S   B   R   O _____

Duration _____ Weather _____

Route _____

_____

Distance _____ Time _____

Time
by zone **1   2   3   4   5**

Workout rating _____

Notes _____

_____

Workout 2

S   B   R   O _____

Duration _____ Weather _____

Route _____

_____

Distance _____ Time _____

Time
by zone **1   2   3   4   5**

Workout rating _____

Notes _____

_____

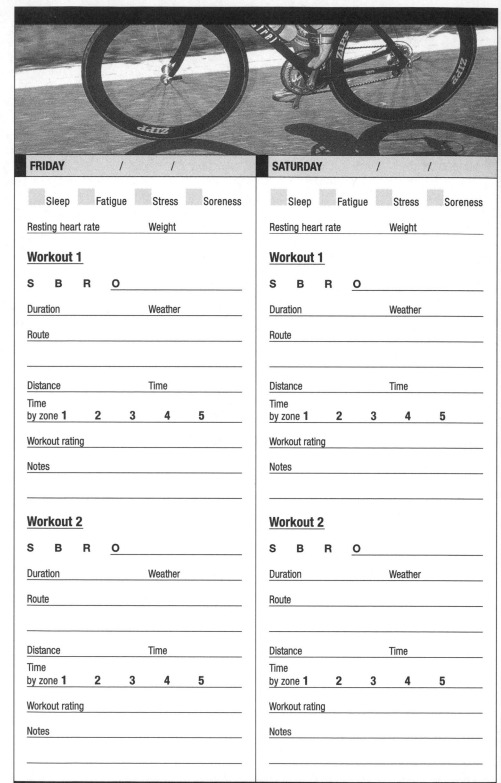

FRIDAY   /   /

Sleep   Fatigue   Stress   Soreness

Resting heart rate   Weight

Workout 1

S   B   R   O

Duration   Weather

Route

Distance   Time

Time
by zone **1   2   3   4   5**

Workout rating

Notes

Workout 2

S   B   R   O

Duration   Weather

Route

Distance   Time

Time
by zone **1   2   3   4   5**

Workout rating

Notes

SATURDAY   /   /

Sleep   Fatigue   Stress   Soreness

Resting heart rate   Weight

Workout 1

S   B   R   O

Duration   Weather

Route

Distance   Time

Time
by zone **1   2   3   4   5**

Workout rating

Notes

Workout 2

S   B   R   O

Duration   Weather

Route

Distance   Time

Time
by zone **1   2   3   4   5**

Workout rating

Notes

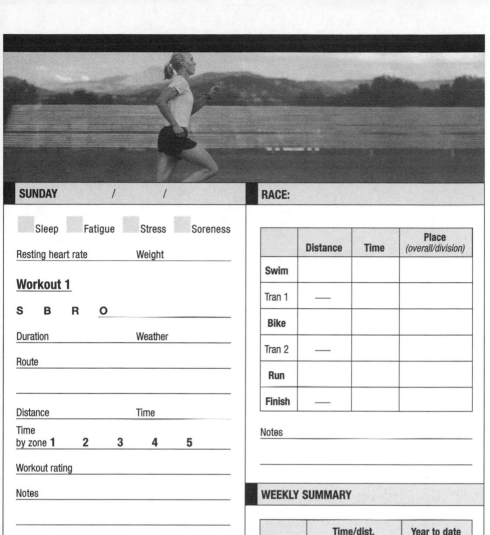

SUNDAY / /

Sleep   Fatigue   Stress   Soreness

Resting heart rate   Weight

Workout 1

S   B   R   O

Duration   Weather

Route

Distance   Time

Time
by zone **1   2   3   4   5**

Workout rating

Notes

Workout 2

S   B   R   O

Duration   Weather

Route

Distance   Time

Time
by zone **1   2   3   4   5**

Workout rating

Notes

RACE:

	Distance	Time	Place (overall/division)
Swim			
Tran 1	—		
Bike			
Tran 2	—		
Run			
Finish	—		

Notes

WEEKLY SUMMARY

	Time/dist.	Year to date
Swim		
Bike		
Run		
Strength		

Weekly   Year-to-date
total   total

Soreness

Notes

157

WEEK BEGINNING: **PLANNED WEEKLY HOURS:**

Week's goals (check off as achieved)

☐ _____

☐ _____

☐ _____

MONDAY / /	**TUESDAY** / /

☐ Sleep ☐ Fatigue ☐ Stress ☐ Soreness

Resting heart rate _____ Weight _____

Workout 1

S   B   R   O _____

Duration _____ Weather _____

Route _____

_____

Distance _____ Time _____

Time
by zone **1   2   3   4   5**

Workout rating _____

Notes _____

_____

Workout 2

S   B   R   O _____

Duration _____ Weather _____

Route _____

_____

Distance _____ Time _____

Time
by zone **1   2   3   4   5**

Workout rating _____

Notes _____

_____

☐ Sleep ☐ Fatigue ☐ Stress ☐ Soreness

Resting heart rate _____ Weight _____

Workout 1

S   B   R   O _____

Duration _____ Weather _____

Route _____

_____

Distance _____ Time _____

Time
by zone **1   2   3   4   5**

Workout rating _____

Notes _____

_____

Workout 2

S   B   R   O _____

Duration _____ Weather _____

Route _____

_____

Distance _____ Time _____

Time
by zone **1   2   3   4   5**

Workout rating _____

Notes _____

_____

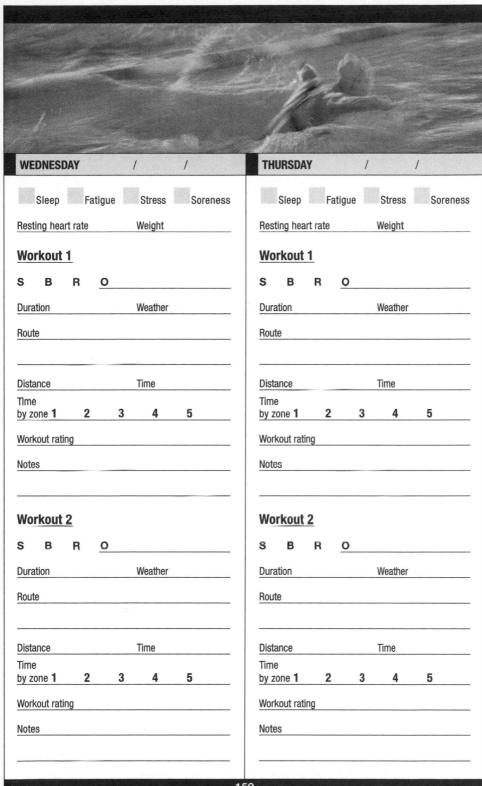

WEDNESDAY	/	/

Sleep Fatigue Stress Soreness

Resting heart rate _____ Weight _____

Workout 1

S   B   R   O _____

Duration _____ Weather _____

Route _____

_____

Distance _____ Time _____

Time
by zone **1   2   3   4   5**

Workout rating _____

Notes _____

_____

Workout 2

S   B   R   O _____

Duration _____ Weather _____

Route _____

_____

Distance _____ Time _____

Time
by zone **1   2   3   4   5**

Workout rating _____

Notes _____

_____

THURSDAY	/	/

Sleep Fatigue Stress Soreness

Resting heart rate _____ Weight _____

Workout 1

S   B   R   O _____

Duration _____ Weather _____

Route _____

_____

Distance _____ Time _____

Time
by zone **1   2   3   4   5**

Workout rating _____

Notes _____

_____

Workout 2

S   B   R   O _____

Duration _____ Weather _____

Route _____

_____

Distance _____ Time _____

Time
by zone **1   2   3   4   5**

Workout rating _____

Notes _____

_____

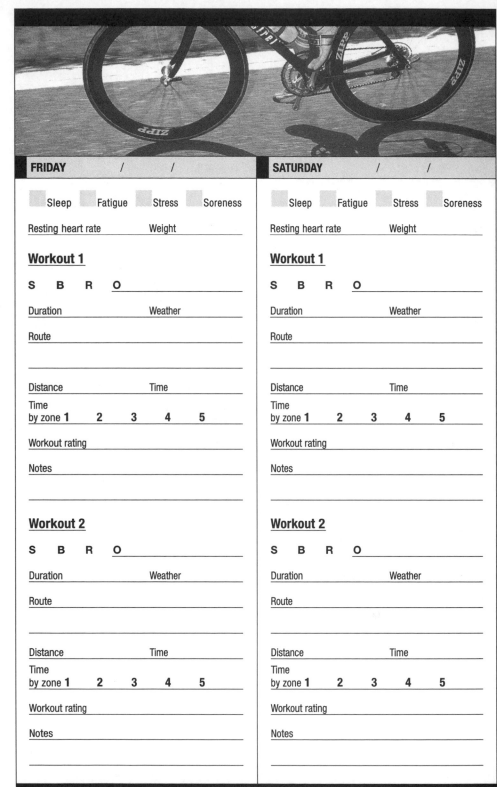

FRIDAY   /   /

Sleep   Fatigue   Stress   Soreness

Resting heart rate _____ Weight _____

Workout 1

S   B   R   O _____

Duration _____ Weather _____

Route _____

_____

Distance _____ Time _____

Time
by zone **1   2   3   4   5**

Workout rating _____

Notes _____

_____

Workout 2

S   B   R   O _____

Duration _____ Weather _____

Route _____

_____

Distance _____ Time _____

Time
by zone **1   2   3   4   5**

Workout rating _____

Notes _____

_____

SATURDAY   /   /

Sleep   Fatigue   Stress   Soreness

Resting heart rate _____ Weight _____

Workout 1

S   B   R   O _____

Duration _____ Weather _____

Route _____

_____

Distance _____ Time _____

Time
by zone **1   2   3   4   5**

Workout rating _____

Notes _____

_____

Workout 2

S   B   R   O _____

Duration _____ Weather _____

Route _____

_____

Distance _____ Time _____

Time
by zone **1   2   3   4   5**

Workout rating _____

Notes _____

_____

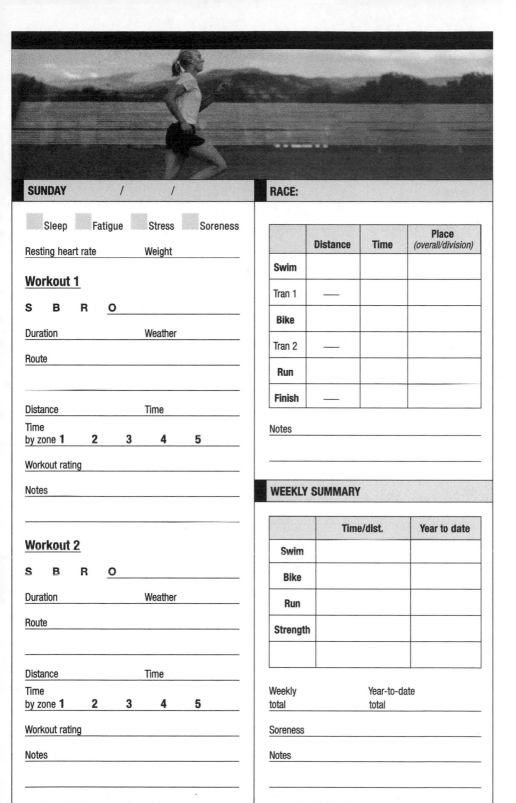

SUNDAY / /

Sleep Fatigue Stress Soreness

Resting heart rate _____ Weight _____

Workout 1

S   B   R   O _____

Duration _____ Weather _____

Route _____

_____

Distance _____ Time _____

Time
by zone **1   2   3   4   5**

Workout rating _____

Notes _____

_____

Workout 2

S   B   R   O _____

Duration _____ Weather _____

Route _____

_____

Distance _____ Time _____

Time
by zone **1   2   3   4   5**

Workout rating _____

Notes _____

_____

RACE: _____

	Distance	Time	Place *(overall/division)*
Swim			
Tran 1	—		
Bike			
Tran 2	—		
Run			
Finish	—		

Notes _____

_____

WEEKLY SUMMARY

	Time/dist.	Year to date
Swim		
Bike		
Run		
Strength		

Weekly
total _____   Year-to-date
total _____

Soreness _____

Notes _____

_____

WEEK BEGINNING:　　　　　　**PLANNED WEEKLY HOURS:**

Week's goals (check off as achieved)

- ☐ _____
- ☐ _____
- ☐ _____

MONDAY / /	**TUESDAY** / /

☐ Sleep ☐ Fatigue ☐ Stress ☐ Soreness　　　☐ Sleep ☐ Fatigue ☐ Stress ☐ Soreness

Resting heart rate _____ Weight _____　　　Resting heart rate _____ Weight _____

Workout 1　　　　　　　　　　　### Workout 1

S　**B**　**R**　**O** _____　　　**S**　**B**　**R**　**O** _____

Duration _____ Weather _____　　Duration _____ Weather _____

Route _____　Route _____

Distance _____ Time _____　　　Distance _____ Time _____

Time
by zone **1**　**2**　**3**　**4**　**5**　　Time
by zone **1**　**2**　**3**　**4**　**5**

Workout rating _____　Workout rating _____

Notes _____　Notes _____

Workout 2　　　　　　　　　　　### Workout 2

S　**B**　**R**　**O** _____　　　**S**　**B**　**R**　**O** _____

Duration _____ Weather _____　　Duration _____ Weather _____

Route _____　Route _____

Distance _____ Time _____　　　Distance _____ Time _____

Time
by zone **1**　**2**　**3**　**4**　**5**　　Time
by zone **1**　**2**　**3**　**4**　**5**

Workout rating _____　Workout rating _____

Notes _____　Notes _____

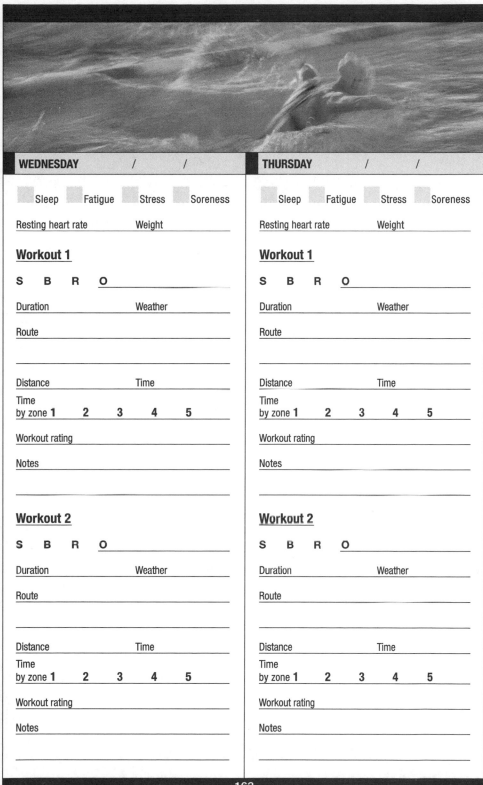

WEDNESDAY /   /

■ Sleep   ■ Fatigue   ■ Stress   ■ Soreness

Resting heart rate _____   Weight _____

Workout 1

S   B   R   O _____

Duration _____   Weather _____

Route _____

_____

Distance _____   Time _____

Time
by zone **1   2   3   4   5**

Workout rating _____

Notes _____

_____

Workout 2

S   B   R   O _____

Duration _____   Weather _____

Route _____

_____

Distance _____   Time _____

Time
by zone **1   2   3   4   5**

Workout rating _____

Notes _____

_____

THURSDAY /   /

■ Sleep   ■ Fatigue   ■ Stress   ■ Soreness

Resting heart rate _____   Weight _____

Workout 1

S   B   R   O _____

Duration _____   Weather _____

Route _____

_____

Distance _____   Time _____

Time
by zone **1   2   3   4   5**

Workout rating _____

Notes _____

_____

Workout 2

S   B   R   O _____

Duration _____   Weather _____

Route _____

_____

Distance _____   Time _____

Time
by zone **1   2   3   4   5**

Workout rating _____

Notes _____

_____

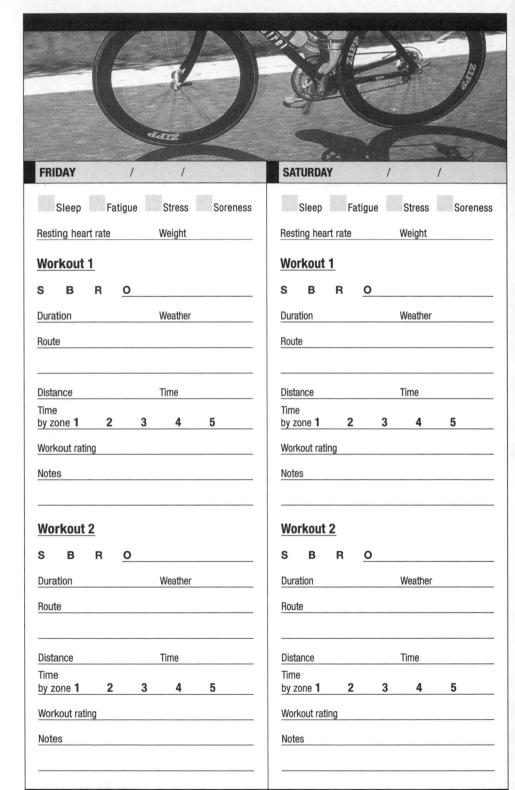

FRIDAY   /   /

Sleep   Fatigue   Stress   Soreness

Resting heart rate _____ Weight _____

Workout 1

S   B   R   O _____

Duration _____ Weather _____

Route _____

_____

Distance _____ Time _____

Time
by zone 1   2   3   4   5

Workout rating _____

Notes _____

_____

Workout 2

S   B   R   O _____

Duration _____ Weather _____

Route _____

_____

Distance _____ Time _____

Time
by zone 1   2   3   4   5

Workout rating _____

Notes _____

_____

SATURDAY   /   /

Sleep   Fatigue   Stress   Soreness

Resting heart rate _____ Weight _____

Workout 1

S   B   R   O _____

Duration _____ Weather _____

Route _____

_____

Distance _____ Time _____

Time
by zone 1   2   3   4   5

Workout rating _____

Notes _____

_____

Workout 2

S   B   R   O _____

Duration _____ Weather _____

Route _____

_____

Distance _____ Time _____

Time
by zone 1   2   3   4   5

Workout rating _____

Notes _____

_____

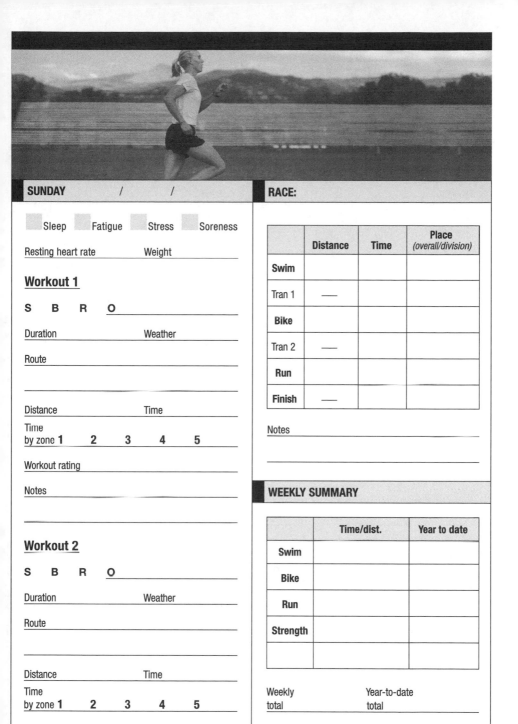

SUNDAY   /   /

☐ Sleep   ☐ Fatigue   ☐ Stress   ☐ Soreness

Resting heart rate   Weight

Workout 1

S   B   R   O

Duration   Weather

Route

Distance   Time

Time
by zone **1**   **2**   **3**   **4**   **5**

Workout rating

Notes

Workout 2

S   B   R   O

Duration   Weather

Route

Distance   Time

Time
by zone **1**   **2**   **3**   **4**   **5**

Workout rating

Notes

	Distance	Time	Place *(overall/division)*
Swim			
Tran 1	—		
Bike			
Tran 2	—		
Run			
Finish	—		

Notes

WEEKLY SUMMARY

	Time/dist.	Year to date
Swim		
Bike		
Run		
Strength		

Weekly total   Year-to-date total

Soreness

Notes

WEEK BEGINNING: _____   **PLANNED WEEKLY HOURS:** _____

Week's goals (check off as achieved)

☐ _____

☐ _____

☐ _____

MONDAY / /	**TUESDAY** / /

☐ Sleep ☐ Fatigue ☐ Stress ☐ Soreness

Resting heart rate _____ Weight _____

Workout 1

S   B   R   O _____

Duration _____ Weather _____

Route _____

_____

Distance _____ Time _____

Time by zone **1**   **2**   **3**   **4**   **5**

Workout rating _____

Notes _____

_____

Workout 2

S   B   R   O _____

Duration _____ Weather _____

Route _____

_____

Distance _____ Time _____

Time by zone **1**   **2**   **3**   **4**   **5**

Workout rating _____

Notes _____

_____

☐ Sleep ☐ Fatigue ☐ Stress ☐ Soreness

Resting heart rate _____ Weight _____

Workout 1

S   B   R   O _____

Duration _____ Weather _____

Route _____

_____

Distance _____ Time _____

Time by zone **1**   **2**   **3**   **4**   **5**

Workout rating _____

Notes _____

_____

Workout 2

S   B   R   O _____

Duration _____ Weather _____

Route _____

_____

Distance _____ Time _____

Time by zone **1**   **2**   **3**   **4**   **5**

Workout rating _____

Notes _____

_____

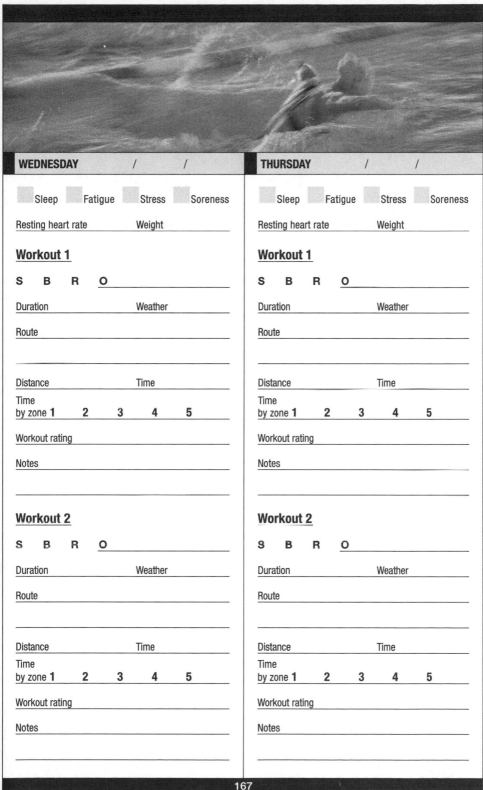

| WEDNESDAY | / | / |

Sleep   Fatigue   Stress   Soreness

Resting heart rate   Weight

Workout 1

S   B   R   O

Duration   Weather

Route

Distance   Time

Time
by zone 1   2   3   4   5

Workout rating

Notes

Workout 2

S   B   R   O

Duration   Weather

Route

Distance   Time

Time
by zone 1   2   3   4   5

Workout rating

Notes

| THURSDAY | / | / |

Sleep   Fatigue   Stress   Soreness

Resting heart rate   Weight

Workout 1

S   B   R   O

Duration   Weather

Route

Distance   Time

Time
by zone 1   2   3   4   5

Workout rating

Notes

Workout 2

S   B   R   O

Duration   Weather

Route

Distance   Time

Time
by zone 1   2   3   4   5

Workout rating

Notes

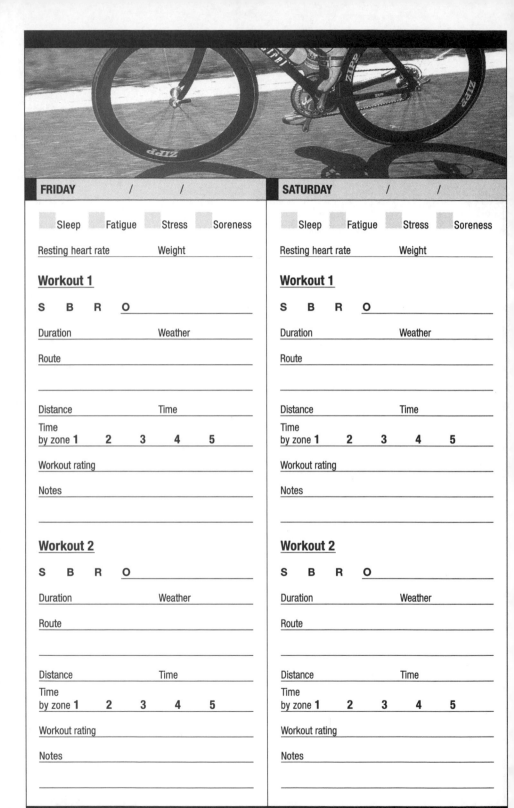

FRIDAY / /

Sleep   Fatigue   Stress   Soreness

Resting heart rate _____   Weight _____

Workout 1

S   B   R   O _____

Duration _____   Weather _____

Route _____
_____

Distance _____   Time _____

Time
by zone **1**   **2**   **3**   **4**   **5** _____

Workout rating _____

Notes _____
_____

Workout 2

S   B   R   O _____

Duration _____   Weather _____

Route _____
_____

Distance _____   Time _____

Time
by zone **1**   **2**   **3**   **4**   **5** _____

Workout rating _____

Notes _____
_____

SATURDAY / /

Sleep   Fatigue   Stress   Soreness

Resting heart rate _____   Weight _____

Workout 1

S   B   R   O _____

Duration _____   Weather _____

Route _____
_____

Distance _____   Time _____

Time
by zone **1**   **2**   **3**   **4**   **5** _____

Workout rating _____

Notes _____
_____

Workout 2

S   B   R   O _____

Duration _____   Weather _____

Route _____
_____

Distance _____   Time _____

Time
by zone **1**   **2**   **3**   **4**   **5** _____

Workout rating _____

Notes _____
_____

SUNDAY	/	/

Sleep ▢ Fatigue ▢ Stress ▢ Soreness ▢

Resting heart rate _____ Weight _____

Workout 1

S   B   R   O _____

Duration _____   Weather _____

Route _____

_____

Distance _____   Time _____

Time
by zone **1**   **2**   **3**   **4**   **5**

Workout rating _____

Notes _____

_____

Workout 2

S   B   R   O _____

Duration _____   Weather _____

Route _____

_____

Distance _____   Time _____

Time
by zone **1**   **2**   **3**   **4**   **5**

Workout rating _____

Notes _____

_____

RACE: _____

	Distance	Time	Place *(overall/division)*
Swim			
Tran 1	—		
Bike			
Tran 2	—		
Run			
Finish	—		

Notes _____

_____

WEEKLY SUMMARY

	Time/dist.	Year to date
Swim		
Bike		
Run		
Strength		

Weekly total _____   Year-to-date total _____

Soreness _____

Notes _____

_____

WEEK BEGINNING: **PLANNED WEEKLY HOURS:**

Week's goals (check off as achieved)

☐ _____

☐ _____

☐ _____

MONDAY / /	**TUESDAY** / /

☐ Sleep ☐ Fatigue ☐ Stress ☐ Soreness

Resting heart rate _____ Weight _____

Workout 1

S   B   R   O _____

Duration _____ Weather _____

Route _____

_____

Distance _____ Time _____

Time
by zone **1**   **2**   **3**   **4**   **5**

Workout rating _____

Notes _____

_____

Workout 2

S   B   R   O _____

Duration _____ Weather _____

Route _____

_____

Distance _____ Time _____

Time
by zone **1**   **2**   **3**   **4**   **5**

Workout rating _____

Notes _____

_____

☐ Sleep ☐ Fatigue ☐ Stress ☐ Soreness

Resting heart rate _____ Weight _____

Workout 1

S   B   R   O _____

Duration _____ Weather _____

Route _____

_____

Distance _____ Time _____

Time
by zone **1**   **2**   **3**   **4**   **5**

Workout rating _____

Notes _____

_____

Workout 2

S   B   R   O _____

Duration _____ Weather _____

Route _____

_____

Distance _____ Time _____

Time
by zone **1**   **2**   **3**   **4**   **5**

Workout rating _____

Notes _____

_____

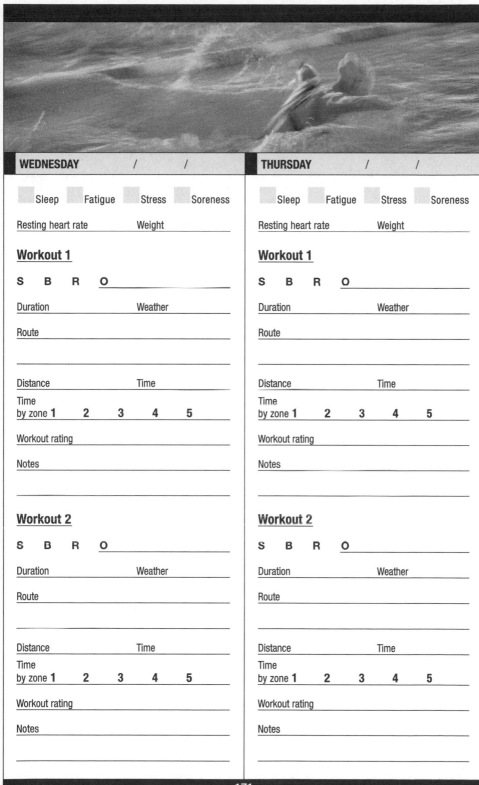

Sleep ☐ Fatigue ☐ Stress ☐ Soreness

Resting heart rate _____ Weight _____

Workout 1

S   B   R   O _____

Duration _____ Weather _____

Route _____

_____

Distance _____ Time _____

Time
by zone **1   2   3   4   5**

Workout rating _____

Notes _____

_____

Workout 2

S   B   R   O _____

Duration _____ Weather _____

Route _____

_____

Distance _____ Time _____

Time
by zone **1   2   3   4   5**

Workout rating _____

Notes _____

_____

Sleep ☐ Fatigue ☐ Stress ☐ Soreness

Resting heart rate _____ Weight _____

Workout 1

S   B   R   O _____

Duration _____ Weather _____

Route _____

_____

Distance _____ Time _____

Time
by zone **1   2   3   4   5**

Workout rating _____

Notes _____

_____

Workout 2

S   B   R   O _____

Duration _____ Weather _____

Route _____

_____

Distance _____ Time _____

Time
by zone **1   2   3   4   5**

Workout rating _____

Notes _____

_____

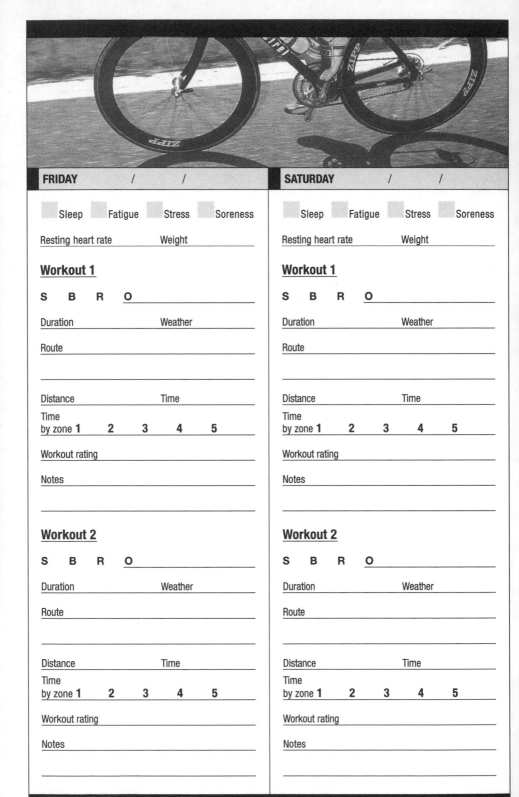

FRIDAY / /

Sleep Fatigue Stress Soreness

Resting heart rate _____ Weight _____

Workout 1

S   B   R   O _____

Duration _____ Weather _____

Route _____

_____

Distance _____ Time _____

Time
by zone **1   2   3   4   5**

Workout rating _____

Notes _____

_____

Workout 2

S   B   R   O _____

Duration _____ Weather _____

Route _____

_____

Distance _____ Time _____

Time
by zone **1   2   3   4   5**

Workout rating _____

Notes _____

_____

SATURDAY / /

Sleep Fatigue Stress Soreness

Resting heart rate _____ Weight _____

Workout 1

S   B   R   O _____

Duration _____ Weather _____

Route _____

_____

Distance _____ Time _____

Time
by zone **1   2   3   4   5**

Workout rating _____

Notes _____

_____

Workout 2

S   B   R   O _____

Duration _____ Weather _____

Route _____

_____

Distance _____ Time _____

Time
by zone **1   2   3   4   5**

Workout rating _____

Notes _____

_____

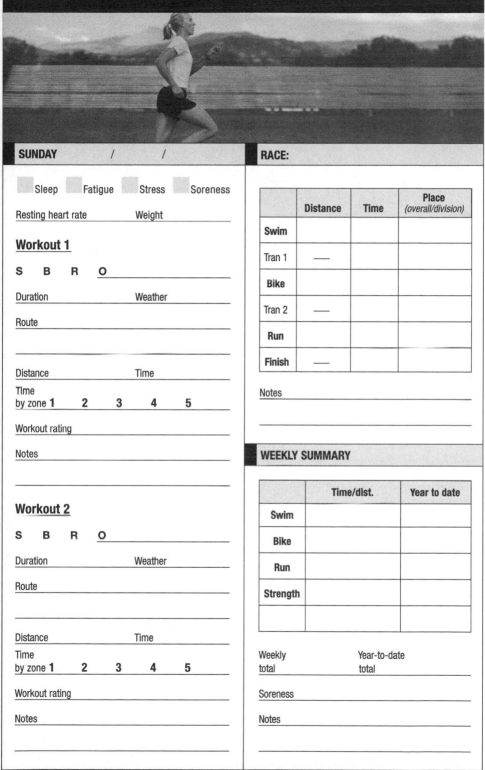

SUNDAY / /

Sleep Fatigue Stress Soreness

Resting heart rate _____ Weight _____

Workout 1

S   B   R   O _____

Duration _____ Weather _____

Route _____

_____

Distance _____ Time _____

Time
by zone **1   2   3   4   5** _____

Workout rating _____

Notes _____

_____

Workout 2

S   B   R   O _____

Duration _____ Weather _____

Route _____

_____

Distance _____ Time _____

Time
by zone **1   2   3   4   5** _____

Workout rating _____

Notes _____

_____

RACE: _____

	Distance	Time	Place *(overall/division)*
Swim			
Tran 1	—		
Bike			
Tran 2	—		
Run			
Finish	—		

Notes _____

_____

WEEKLY SUMMARY

	Time/dist.	Year to date
Swim		
Bike		
Run		
Strength		

Weekly total _____ Year-to-date total _____

Soreness _____

Notes _____

_____

WEEK BEGINNING: **PLANNED WEEKLY HOURS:**

Week's goals (check off as achieved)

☐ _____

☐ _____

☐ _____

MONDAY / /	TUESDAY / /

☐ Sleep ☐ Fatigue ☐ Stress ☐ Soreness

Resting heart rate _____ Weight _____

Workout 1

S   B   R   O _____

Duration _____ Weather _____

Route _____

_____

Distance _____ Time _____

Time
by zone **1   2   3   4   5**

Workout rating _____

Notes _____

_____

Workout 2

S   B   R   O _____

Duration _____ Weather _____

Route _____

_____

Distance _____ Time _____

Time
by zone **1   2   3   4   5**

Workout rating _____

Notes _____

_____

☐ Sleep ☐ Fatigue ☐ Stress ☐ Soreness

Resting heart rate _____ Weight _____

Workout 1

S   B   R   O _____

Duration _____ Weather _____

Route _____

_____

Distance _____ Time _____

Time
by zone **1   2   3   4   5**

Workout rating _____

Notes _____

_____

Workout 2

S   B   R   O _____

Duration _____ Weather _____

Route _____

_____

Distance _____ Time _____

Time
by zone **1   2   3   4   5**

Workout rating _____

Notes _____

_____

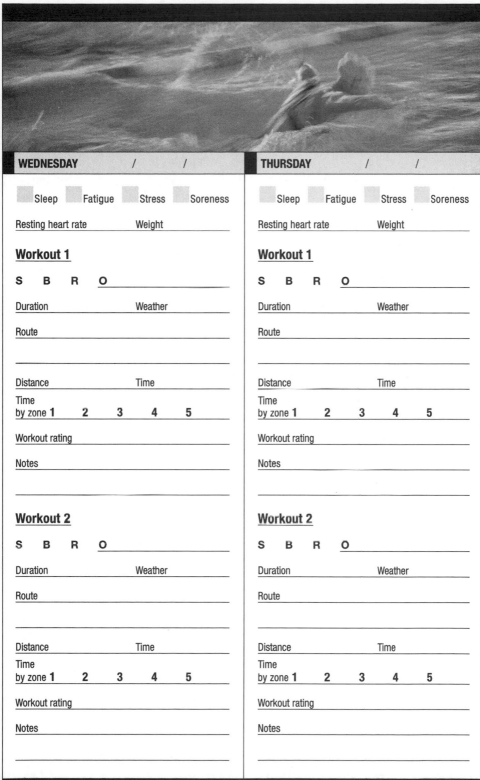

WEDNESDAY   /   /

■ Sleep ■ Fatigue ■ Stress ■ Soreness

Resting heart rate _____ Weight _____

Workout 1

S   B   R   O _____

Duration _____ Weather _____

Route _____

_____

Distance _____ Time _____

Time
by zone **1**   **2**   **3**   **4**   **5**

Workout rating _____

Notes _____

_____

Workout 2

S   B   R   O _____

Duration _____ Weather _____

Route _____

_____

Distance _____ Time _____

Time
by zone **1**   **2**   **3**   **4**   **5**

Workout rating _____

Notes _____

_____

THURSDAY   /   /

■ Sleep ■ Fatigue ■ Stress ■ Soreness

Resting heart rate _____ Weight _____

Workout 1

S   B   R   O _____

Duration _____ Weather _____

Route _____

_____

Distance _____ Time _____

Time
by zone **1**   **2**   **3**   **4**   **5**

Workout rating _____

Notes _____

_____

Workout 2

S   B   R   O _____

Duration _____ Weather _____

Route _____

_____

Distance _____ Time _____

Time
by zone **1**   **2**   **3**   **4**   **5**

Workout rating _____

Notes _____

_____

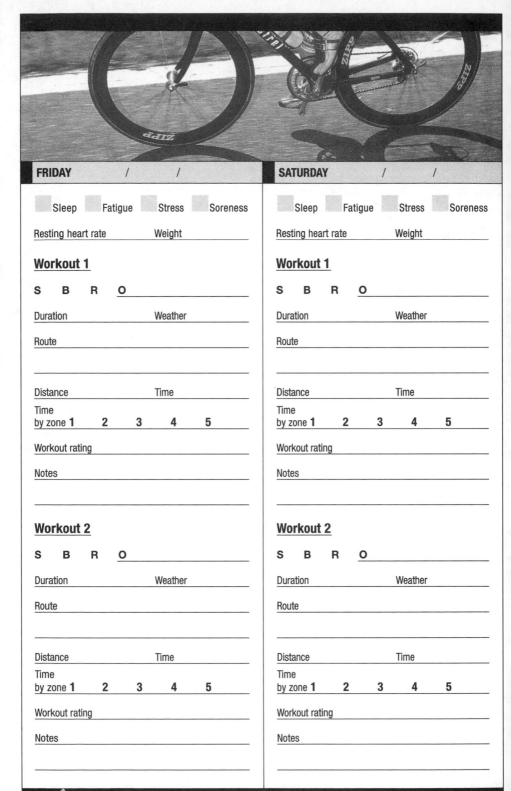

FRIDAY / /

Sleep Fatigue Stress Soreness

Resting heart rate _____ Weight _____

Workout 1

S   B   R   O _____

Duration _____ Weather _____

Route _____

_____

Distance _____ Time _____

Time
by zone **1   2   3   4   5**

Workout rating _____

Notes _____

_____

Workout 2

S   B   R   O _____

Duration _____ Weather _____

Route _____

_____

Distance _____ Time _____

Time
by zone **1   2   3   4   5**

Workout rating _____

Notes _____

_____

SATURDAY / /

Sleep Fatigue Stress Soreness

Resting heart rate _____ Weight _____

Workout 1

S   B   R   O _____

Duration _____ Weather _____

Route _____

_____

Distance _____ Time _____

Time
by zone **1   2   3   4   5**

Workout rating _____

Notes _____

_____

Workout 2

S   B   R   O _____

Duration _____ Weather _____

Route _____

_____

Distance _____ Time _____

Time
by zone **1   2   3   4   5**

Workout rating _____

Notes _____

_____

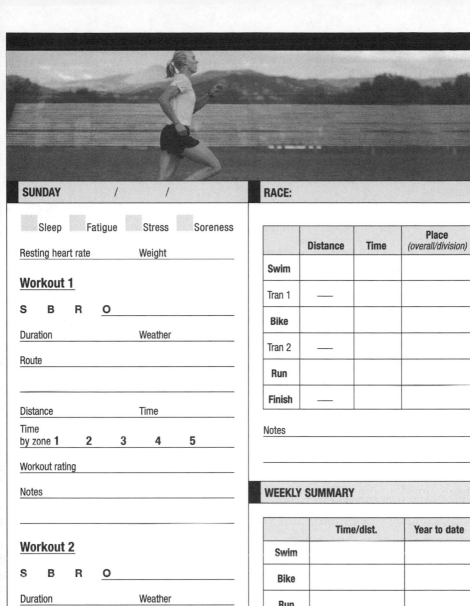

SUNDAY / /

Sleep Fatigue Stress Soreness

Resting heart rate _____ Weight _____

Workout 1

S   B   R   O _____

Duration _____ Weather _____

Route _____

_____

Distance _____ Time _____

Time
by zone **1**   **2**   **3**   **4**   **5** _____

Workout rating _____

Notes _____

_____

Workout 2

S   B   R   O _____

Duration _____ Weather _____

Route _____

_____

Distance _____ Time _____

Time
by zone **1**   **2**   **3**   **4**   **5** _____

Workout rating _____

Notes _____

_____

RACE: _____

	Distance	Time	Place *(overall/division)*
Swim			
Tran 1	—		
Bike			
Tran 2	—		
Run			
Finish	—		

Notes _____

_____

WEEKLY SUMMARY

	Time/dist.	Year to date
Swim		
Bike		
Run		
Strength		

Weekly total _____ Year-to-date total _____

Soreness _____

Notes _____

WEEK BEGINNING:　　　　　**PLANNED WEEKLY HOURS:**

Week's goals (check off as achieved)

☐ _____

☐ _____

☐ _____

MONDAY / /	**TUESDAY** / /

☐ Sleep ☐ Fatigue ☐ Stress ☐ Soreness

Resting heart rate _____ Weight _____

Workout 1

S　　B　　R　　O _____

Duration _____ Weather _____

Route _____

_____

Distance _____ Time _____

Time
by zone **1　　2　　3　　4　　5**

Workout rating _____

Notes _____

_____

Workout 2

S　　B　　R　　O _____

Duration _____ Weather _____

Route _____

_____

Distance _____ Time _____

Time
by zone **1　　2　　3　　4　　5**

Workout rating _____

Notes _____

_____

☐ Sleep ☐ Fatigue ☐ Stress ☐ Soreness

Resting heart rate _____ Weight _____

Workout 1

S　　B　　R　　O _____

Duration _____ Weather _____

Route _____

_____

Distance _____ Time _____

Time
by zone **1　　2　　3　　4　　5**

Workout rating _____

Notes _____

_____

Workout 2

S　　B　　R　　O _____

Duration _____ Weather _____

Route _____

_____

Distance _____ Time _____

Time
by zone **1　　2　　3　　4　　5**

Workout rating _____

Notes _____

_____

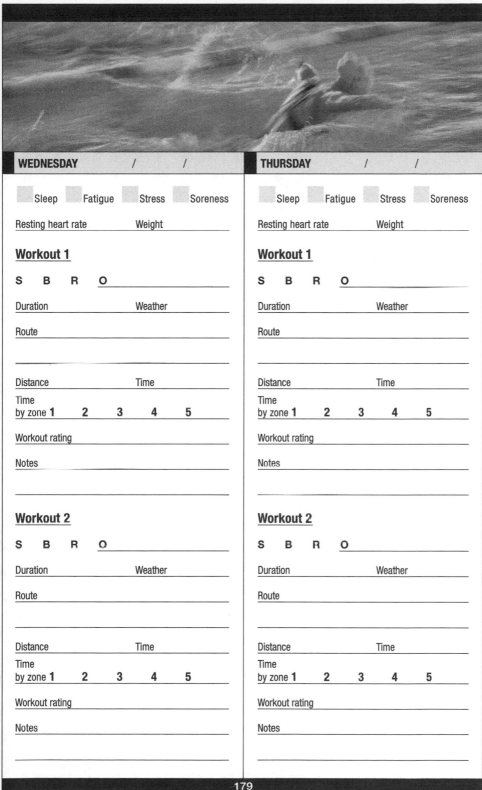

| WEDNESDAY | / | / |

☐ Sleep ☐ Fatigue ☐ Stress ☐ Soreness

Resting heart rate _____ Weight _____

Workout 1

S   B   R   O _____

Duration _____ Weather _____

Route _____

_____

Distance _____ Time _____

Time
by zone **1**   **2**   **3**   **4**   **5**

Workout rating _____

Notes _____

_____

Workout 2

S   B   R   O _____

Duration _____ Weather _____

Route _____

_____

Distance _____ Time _____

Time
by zone **1**   **2**   **3**   **4**   **5**

Workout rating _____

Notes _____

_____

| THURSDAY | / | / |

☐ Sleep ☐ Fatigue ☐ Stress ☐ Soreness

Resting heart rate _____ Weight _____

Workout 1

S   B   R   O _____

Duration _____ Weather _____

Route _____

_____

Distance _____ Time _____

Time
by zone **1**   **2**   **3**   **4**   **5**

Workout rating _____

Notes _____

_____

Workout 2

S   B   R   O _____

Duration _____ Weather _____

Route _____

_____

Distance _____ Time _____

Time
by zone **1**   **2**   **3**   **4**   **5**

Workout rating _____

Notes _____

_____

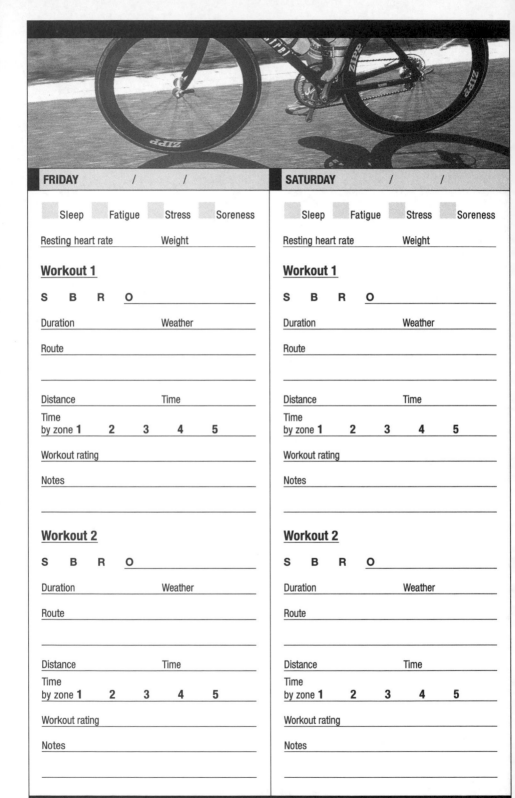

FRIDAY   /   /

Sleep   Fatigue   Stress   Soreness

Resting heart rate _____   Weight _____

Workout 1

S   B   R   O _____

Duration _____   Weather _____

Route _____

_____

Distance _____   Time _____

Time
by zone **1   2   3   4   5**

Workout rating _____

Notes _____

_____

Workout 2

S   B   R   O _____

Duration _____   Weather _____

Route _____

_____

Distance _____   Time _____

Time
by zone **1   2   3   4   5**

Workout rating _____

Notes _____

_____

SATURDAY   /   /

Sleep   Fatigue   Stress   Soreness

Resting heart rate _____   Weight _____

Workout 1

S   B   R   O _____

Duration _____   Weather _____

Route _____

_____

Distance _____   Time _____

Time
by zone **1   2   3   4   5**

Workout rating _____

Notes _____

_____

Workout 2

S   B   R   O _____

Duration _____   Weather _____

Route _____

_____

Distance _____   Time _____

Time
by zone **1   2   3   4   5**

Workout rating _____

Notes _____

_____

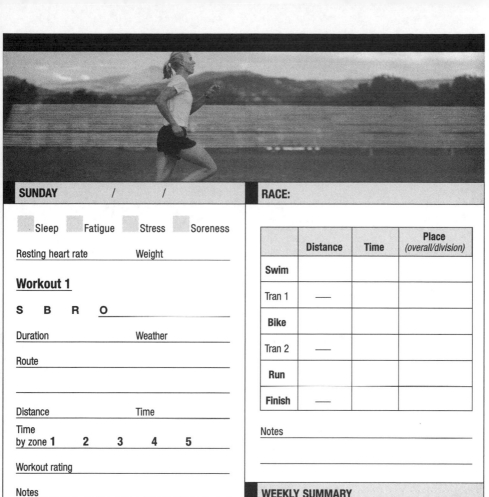

SUNDAY   /   /

RACE:

■ Sleep   ■ Fatigue   ■ Stress   ■ Soreness

Resting heart rate _____ Weight _____

Workout 1

S   B   R   O _____

Duration _____ Weather _____

Route _____

_____

Distance _____ Time _____

Time
by zone **1   2   3   4   5**

Workout rating _____

Notes _____

_____

Workout 2

S   B   R   O _____

Duration _____ Weather _____

Route _____

_____

Distance _____ Time _____

Time
by zone **1   2   3   4   5**

Workout rating _____

Notes _____

_____

	Distance	Time	Place *(overall/division)*
Swim			
Tran 1	—		
Bike			
Tran 2	—		
Run			
Finish	—		

Notes _____

_____

WEEKLY SUMMARY

	Time/dist.	Year to date
Swim		
Bike		
Run		
Strength		

Weekly total _____ Year-to-date total _____

Soreness _____

Notes _____

_____

WEEK BEGINNING: _____ **PLANNED WEEKLY HOURS:** _____

Week's goals (check off as achieved)

▪ _____

▪ _____

▪ _____

MONDAY / /	TUESDAY / /

▪ Sleep ▪ Fatigue ▪ Stress ▪ Soreness

Resting heart rate _____ Weight _____

Workout 1

S   B   R   O _____

Duration _____ Weather _____

Route _____

_____

Distance _____ Time _____

Time
by zone **1   2   3   4   5** _____

Workout rating _____

Notes _____

_____

Workout 2

S   B   R   O _____

Duration _____ Weather _____

Route _____

_____

Distance _____ Time _____

Time
by zone **1   2   3   4   5** _____

Workout rating _____

Notes _____

_____

▪ Sleep ▪ Fatigue ▪ Stress ▪ Soreness

Resting heart rate _____ Weight _____

Workout 1

S   B   R   O _____

Duration _____ Weather _____

Route _____

_____

Distance _____ Time _____

Time
by zone **1   2   3   4   5** _____

Workout rating _____

Notes _____

_____

Workout 2

S   B   R   O _____

Duration _____ Weather _____

Route _____

_____

Distance _____ Time _____

Time
by zone **1   2   3   4   5** _____

Workout rating _____

Notes _____

_____

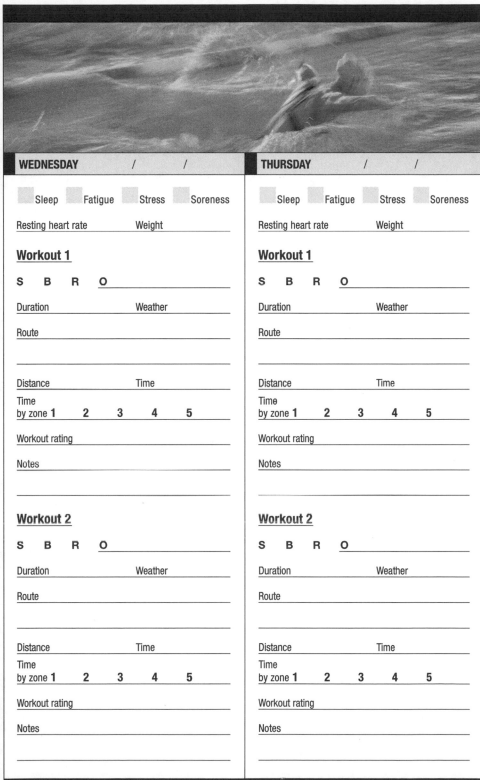

WEDNESDAY	/	/

Sleep Fatigue Stress Soreness

Resting heart rate _____ Weight _____

Workout 1

S   B   R   O _____

Duration _____ Weather _____

Route _____

_____

Distance _____ Time _____

Time
by zone **1   2   3   4   5**

Workout rating _____

Notes _____

_____

Workout 2

S   B   R   O _____

Duration _____ Weather _____

Route _____

_____

Distance _____ Time _____

Time
by zone **1   2   3   4   5**

Workout rating _____

Notes _____

_____

THURSDAY	/	/

Sleep Fatigue Stress Soreness

Resting heart rate _____ Weight _____

Workout 1

S   B   R   O _____

Duration _____ Weather _____

Route _____

_____

Distance _____ Time _____

Time
by zone **1   2   3   4   5**

Workout rating _____

Notes _____

_____

Workout 2

S   B   R   O _____

Duration _____ Weather _____

Route _____

_____

Distance _____ Time _____

Time
by zone **1   2   3   4   5**

Workout rating _____

Notes _____

_____

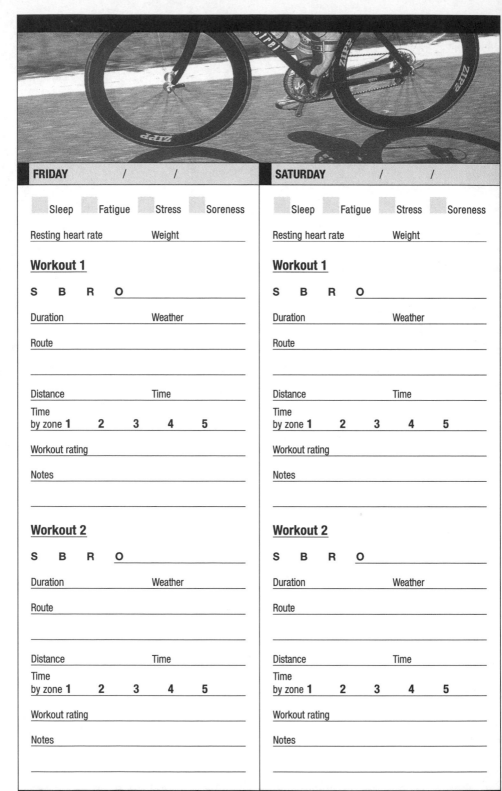

FRIDAY   /   /

Sleep   Fatigue   Stress   Soreness

Resting heart rate _____   Weight _____

Workout 1

S   B   R   O _____

Duration _____   Weather _____

Route _____

_____

Distance _____   Time _____

Time
by zone **1   2   3   4   5**

Workout rating _____

Notes _____

_____

Workout 2

S   B   R   O _____

Duration _____   Weather _____

Route _____

_____

Distance _____   Time _____

Time
by zone **1   2   3   4   5**

Workout rating _____

Notes _____

_____

SATURDAY   /   /

Sleep   Fatigue   Stress   Soreness

Resting heart rate _____   Weight _____

Workout 1

S   B   R   O _____

Duration _____   Weather _____

Route _____

_____

Distance _____   Time _____

Time
by zone **1   2   3   4   5**

Workout rating _____

Notes _____

_____

Workout 2

S   B   R   O _____

Duration _____   Weather _____

Route _____

_____

Distance _____   Time _____

Time
by zone **1   2   3   4   5**

Workout rating _____

Notes _____

_____

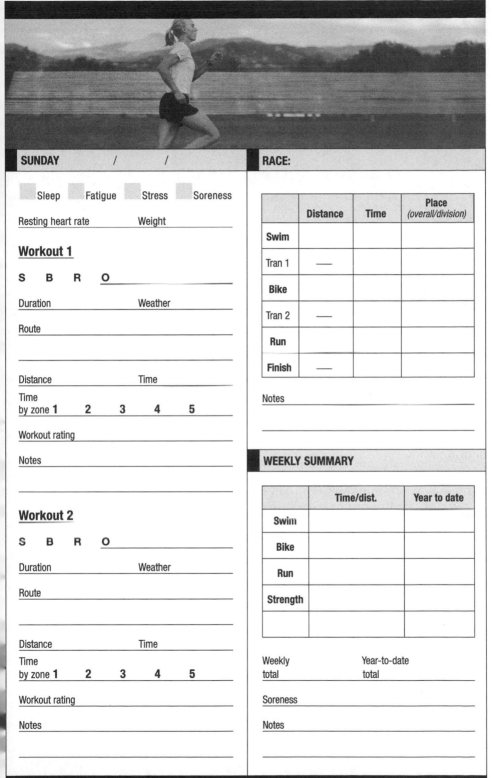

SUNDAY / /

Sleep Fatigue Stress Soreness

Resting heart rate _____ Weight _____

Workout 1

S B R O _____

Duration _____ Weather _____

Route _____

_____

Distance _____ Time _____

Time
by zone **1   2   3   4   5**

Workout rating _____

Notes _____

_____

Workout 2

S B R O _____

Duration _____ Weather _____

Route _____

_____

Distance _____ Time _____

Time
by zone **1   2   3   4   5**

Workout rating _____

Notes _____

_____

RACE:

	Distance	Time	Place *(overall/division)*
Swim			
Tran 1	—		
Bike			
Tran 2	—		
Run			
Finish	—		

Notes _____

_____

WEEKLY SUMMARY

	Time/dist.	Year to date
Swim		
Bike		
Run		
Strength		

Weekly _____ Year-to-date
total _____ total

Soreness _____

Notes _____

_____

WEEK BEGINNING:　　　　　　　**PLANNED WEEKLY HOURS:**

Week's goals (check off as achieved)

☐ _____

☐ _____

☐ _____

MONDAY　　　/　　　/	TUESDAY　　　/　　　/

☐ Sleep　☐ Fatigue　☐ Stress　☐ Soreness

Resting heart rate _____ Weight _____

Workout 1

S　　B　　R　　O _____

Duration _____ Weather _____

Route _____

_____

Distance _____ Time _____

Time
by zone **1**　　**2**　　**3**　　**4**　　**5**

Workout rating _____

Notes _____

_____

Workout 2

S　　B　　R　　O _____

Duration _____ Weather _____

Route _____

_____

Distance _____ Time _____

Time
by zone **1**　　**2**　　**3**　　**4**　　**5**

Workout rating _____

Notes _____

_____

☐ Sleep　☐ Fatigue　☐ Stress　☐ Soreness

Resting heart rate _____ Weight _____

Workout 1

S　　B　　R　　O _____

Duration _____ Weather _____

Route _____

_____

Distance _____ Time _____

Time
by zone **1**　　**2**　　**3**　　**4**　　**5**

Workout rating _____

Notes _____

_____

Workout 2

S　　B　　R　　O _____

Duration _____ Weather _____

Route _____

_____

Distance _____ Time _____

Time
by zone **1**　　**2**　　**3**　　**4**　　**5**

Workout rating _____

Notes _____

_____

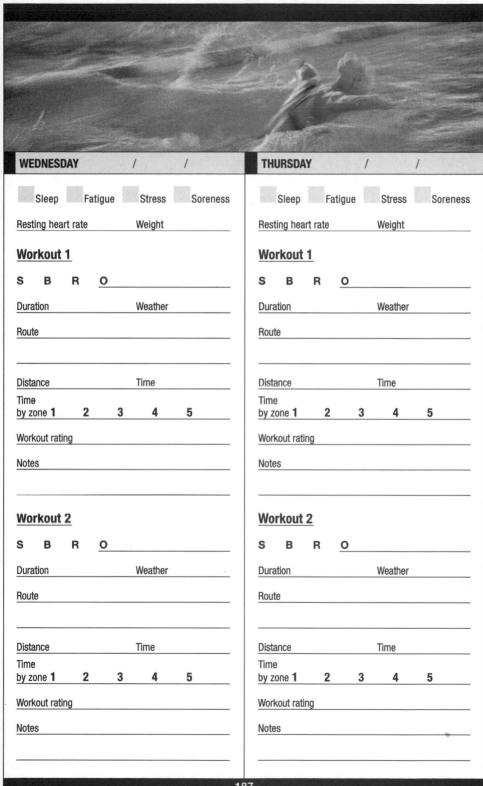

WEDNESDAY	/	/

Sleep   Fatigue   Stress   Soreness

Resting heart rate   Weight

Workout 1

S   **B**   **R**   **O**

Duration   Weather

Route

Distance   Time

Time
by zone **1**   **2**   **3**   **4**   **5**

Workout rating

Notes

Workout 2

S   **B**   **R**   **O**

Duration   Weather

Route

Distance   Time

Time
by zone **1**   **2**   **3**   **4**   **5**

Workout rating

Notes

THURSDAY	/	/

Sleep   Fatigue   Stress   Soreness

Resting heart rate   Weight

Workout 1

S   **B**   **R**   **O**

Duration   Weather

Route

Distance   Time

Time
by zone **1**   **2**   **3**   **4**   **5**

Workout rating

Notes

Workout 2

S   **B**   **R**   **O**

Duration   Weather

Route

Distance   Time

Time
by zone **1**   **2**   **3**   **4**   **5**

Workout rating

Notes

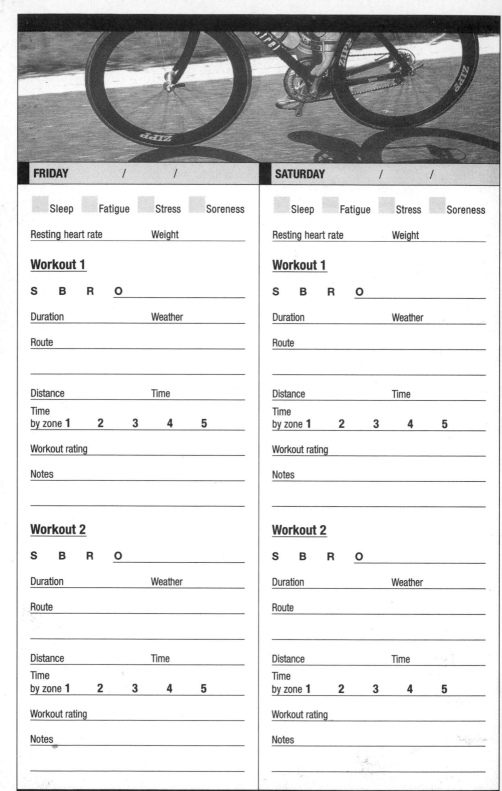

FRIDAY / /

Sleep　Fatigue　Stress　Soreness

Resting heart rate _____ Weight _____

Workout 1

S　B　R　O _____

Duration _____ Weather _____

Route _____

_____

Distance _____ Time _____

Time
by zone **1　2　3　4　5**

Workout rating _____

Notes _____

_____

Workout 2

S　B　R　O _____

Duration _____ Weather _____

Route _____

_____

Distance _____ Time _____

Time
by zone **1　2　3　4　5**

Workout rating _____

Notes _____

_____

SATURDAY / /

Sleep　Fatigue　Stress　Soreness

Resting heart rate _____ Weight _____

Workout 1

S　B　R　O _____

Duration _____ Weather _____

Route _____

_____

Distance _____ Time _____

Time
by zone **1　2　3　4　5**

Workout rating _____

Notes _____

_____

Workout 2

S　B　R　O _____

Duration _____ Weather _____

Route _____

_____

Distance _____ Time _____

Time
by zone **1　2　3　4　5**

Workout rating _____

Notes _____

_____

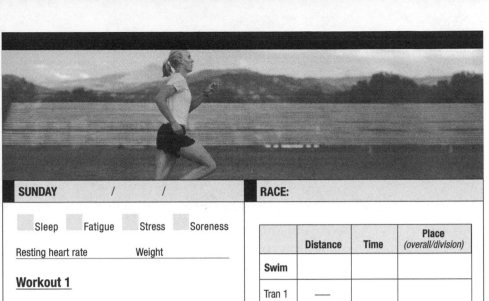

SUNDAY / /

Sleep ▮ Fatigue ▮ Stress ▮ Soreness

Resting heart rate _____ Weight _____

Workout 1

S   B   R   O _____

Duration _____ Weather _____

Route _____

_____

Distance _____ Time _____

Time
by zone **1   2   3   4   5**

Workout rating _____

Notes _____

_____

Workout 2

S   B   R   O _____

Duration _____ Weather _____

Route _____

_____

Distance _____ Time _____

Time
by zone **1   2   3   4   5**

Workout rating _____

Notes _____

_____

RACE: _____

	Distance	Time	Place *(overall/division)*
Swim			
Tran 1	—		
Bike			
Tran 2	—		
Run			
Finish	—		

Notes _____

_____

WEEKLY SUMMARY

	Time/dist.	Year to date
Swim		
Bike		
Run		
Strength		

Weekly   Year-to-date
total   total

Soreness _____

Notes _____

Week's goals (check off as achieved)

▨ _____

▨ _____

▨ _____

MONDAY / /	**TUESDAY** / /

▨ Sleep ▨ Fatigue ▨ Stress ▨ Soreness

Resting heart rate _____ Weight _____

Workout 1

S   B   R   O _____

Duration _____ Weather _____

Route _____

_____

Distance _____ Time _____

Time
by zone **1   2   3   4   5**

Workout rating _____

Notes _____

_____

Workout 2

S   B   R   O _____

Duration _____ Weather _____

Route _____

_____

Distance _____ Time _____

Time
by zone **1   2   3   4   5**

Workout rating _____

Notes _____

_____

▨ Sleep ▨ Fatigue ▨ Stress ▨ Soreness

Resting heart rate _____ Weight _____

Workout 1

S   B   R   O _____

Duration _____ Weather _____

Route _____

_____

Distance _____ Time _____

Time
by zone **1   2   3   4   5**

Workout rating _____

Notes _____

_____

Workout 2

S   B   R   O _____

Duration _____ Weather _____

Route _____

_____

Distance _____ Time _____

Time
by zone **1   2   3   4   5**

Workout rating _____

Notes _____

_____

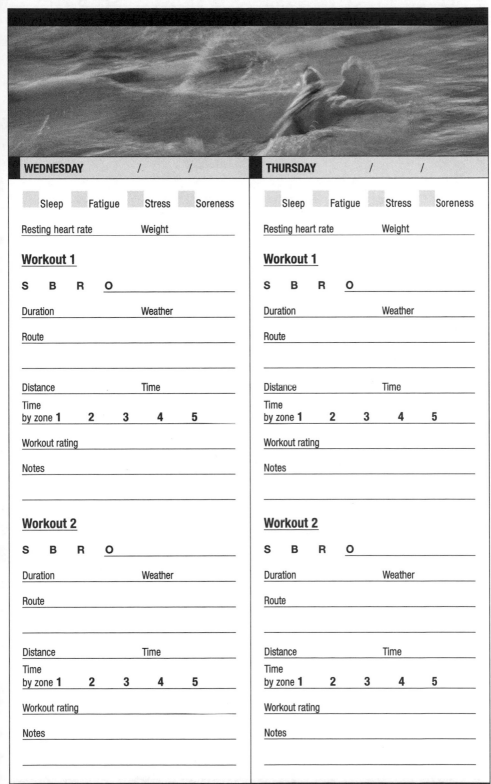

WEDNESDAY	/	/

Sleep Fatigue Stress Soreness

Resting heart rate _____ Weight _____

Workout 1

S   B   R   O _____

Duration _____ Weather _____

Route _____

_____

Distance _____ Time _____

Time
by zone 1   2   3   4   5

Workout rating _____

Notes _____

_____

Workout 2

S   B   R   O _____

Duration _____ Weather _____

Route _____

_____

Distance _____ Time _____

Time
by zone 1   2   3   4   5

Workout rating _____

Notes _____

_____

THURSDAY	/	/

Sleep Fatigue Stress Soreness

Resting heart rate _____ Weight _____

Workout 1

S   B   R   O _____

Duration _____ Weather _____

Route _____

_____

Distance _____ Time _____

Time
by zone 1   2   3   4   5

Workout rating _____

Notes _____

_____

Workout 2

S   B   R   O _____

Duration _____ Weather _____

Route _____

_____

Distance _____ Time _____

Time
by zone 1   2   3   4   5

Workout rating _____

Notes _____

_____

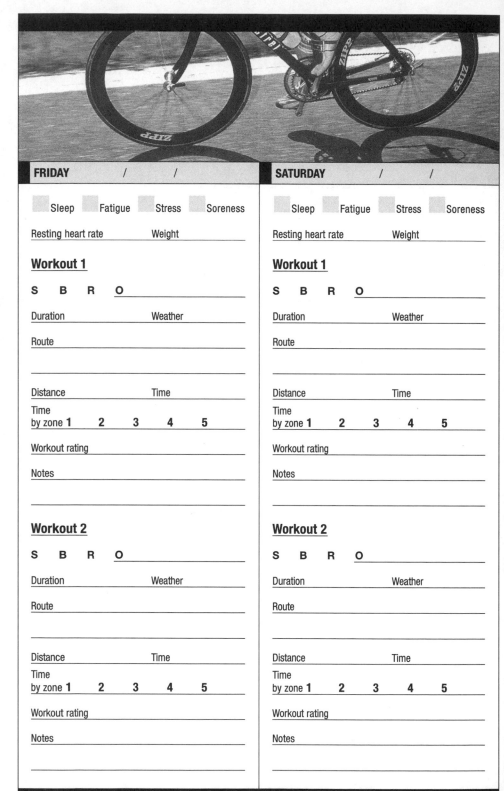

FRIDAY / /

Sleep Fatigue Stress Soreness

Resting heart rate _____ Weight _____

Workout 1

S   B   R   O _____

Duration _____ Weather _____

Route _____

_____

Distance _____ Time _____

Time
by zone **1   2   3   4   5**

Workout rating _____

Notes _____

_____

Workout 2

S   B   R   O _____

Duration _____ Weather _____

Route _____

_____

Distance _____ Time _____

Time
by zone **1   2   3   4   5**

Workout rating _____

Notes _____

_____

SATURDAY / /

Sleep Fatigue Stress Soreness

Resting heart rate _____ Weight _____

Workout 1

S   B   R   O _____

Duration _____ Weather _____

Route _____

_____

Distance _____ Time _____

Time
by zone **1   2   3   4   5**

Workout rating _____

Notes _____

_____

Workout 2

S   B   R   O _____

Duration _____ Weather _____

Route _____

_____

Distance _____ Time _____

Time
by zone **1   2   3   4   5**

Workout rating _____

Notes _____

_____

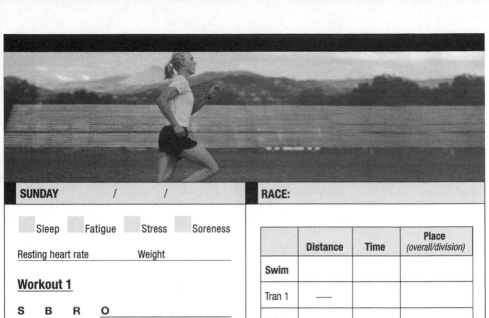

SUNDAY / /

Sleep Fatigue Stress Soreness

Resting heart rate _____ Weight _____

Workout 1

S   B   R   O _____

Duration _____ Weather _____

Route _____

_____

Distance _____ Time _____

Time
by zone **1   2   3   4   5**

Workout rating _____

Notes _____

_____

Workout 2

S   B   R   O _____

Duration _____ Weather _____

Route _____

_____

Distance _____ Time _____

Time
by zone **1   2   3   4   5**

Workout rating _____

Notes _____

_____

RACE: _____

	Distance	Time	Place *(overall/division)*
Swim			
Tran 1	—		
Bike			
Tran 2	—		
Run			
Finish	—		

Notes _____

_____

WEEKLY SUMMARY

	Time/dist.	Year to date
Swim		
Bike		
Run		
Strength		

Weekly total _____ Year-to-date total _____

Soreness _____

Notes _____

_____

WEEK BEGINNING: **PLANNED WEEKLY HOURS:**

Week's goals (check off as achieved)

☐ _____

☐ _____

☐ _____

| MONDAY   /   / | TUESDAY   /   / |

☐ Sleep ☐ Fatigue ☐ Stress ☐ Soreness

Resting heart rate _____ Weight _____

Workout 1

S   B   R   O _____

Duration _____ Weather _____

Route _____

_____

Distance _____ Time _____

Time
by zone **1   2   3   4   5**

Workout rating _____

Notes _____

_____

Workout 2

S   B   R   O _____

Duration _____ Weather _____

Route _____

_____

Distance _____ Time _____

Time
by zone **1   2   3   4   5**

Workout rating _____

Notes _____

_____

☐ Sleep ☐ Fatigue ☐ Stress ☐ Soreness

Resting heart rate _____ Weight _____

Workout 1

S   B   R   O _____

Duration _____ Weather _____

Route _____

_____

Distance _____ Time _____

Time
by zone **1   2   3   4   5**

Workout rating _____

Notes _____

_____

Workout 2

S   B   R   O _____

Duration _____ Weather _____

Route _____

_____

Distance _____ Time _____

Time
by zone **1   2   3   4   5**

Workout rating _____

Notes _____

_____

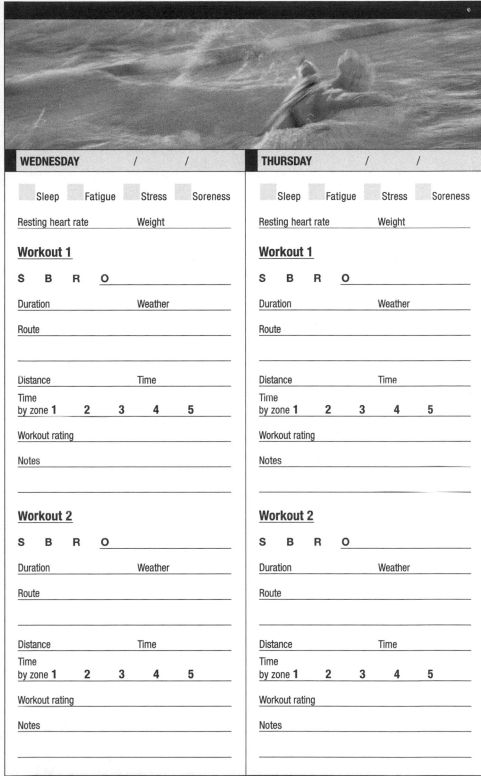

WEDNESDAY   /   /

Sleep   Fatigue   Stress   Soreness

Resting heart rate   Weight

Workout 1

S   B   R   O

Duration   Weather

Route

Distance   Time

Time
by zone **1   2   3   4   5**

Workout rating

Notes

Workout 2

S   B   R   O

Duration   Weather

Route

Distance   Time

Time
by zone **1   2   3   4   5**

Workout rating

Notes

THURSDAY   /   /

Sleep   Fatigue   Stress   Soreness

Resting heart rate   Weight

Workout 1

S   B   R   O

Duration   Weather

Route

Distance   Time

Time
by zone **1   2   3   4   5**

Workout rating

Notes

Workout 2

S   B   R   O

Duration   Weather

Route

Distance   Time

Time
by zone **1   2   3   4   5**

Workout rating

Notes

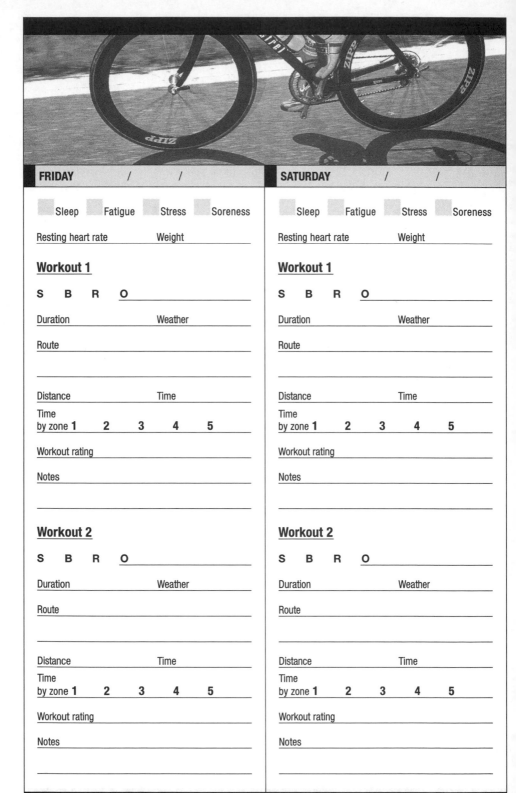

FRIDAY   /   /

Sleep   Fatigue   Stress   Soreness

Resting heart rate _____   Weight _____

Workout 1

S   B   R   O _____

Duration _____   Weather _____

Route _____

_____

Distance _____   Time _____

Time
by zone 1   2   3   4   5

Workout rating _____

Notes _____

_____

Workout 2

S   B   R   O _____

Duration _____   Weather _____

Route _____

_____

Distance _____   Time _____

Time
by zone 1   2   3   4   5

Workout rating _____

Notes _____

_____

SATURDAY   /   /

Sleep   Fatigue   Stress   Soreness

Resting heart rate _____   Weight _____

Workout 1

S   B   R   O _____

Duration _____   Weather _____

Route _____

_____

Distance _____   Time _____

Time
by zone 1   2   3   4   5

Workout rating _____

Notes _____

_____

Workout 2

S   B   R   O _____

Duration _____   Weather _____

Route _____

_____

Distance _____   Time _____

Time
by zone 1   2   3   4   5

Workout rating _____

Notes _____

_____

SUNDAY / /

Sleep   Fatigue   Stress   Soreness

Resting heart rate _____   Weight _____

Workout 1

S   B   R   O _____

Duration _____   Weather _____

Route _____

_____

Distance _____   Time _____

Time
by zone **1**   **2**   **3**   **4**   **5**

Workout rating _____

Notes _____

_____

Workout 2

S   B   R   O _____

Duration _____   Weather _____

Route _____

_____

Distance _____   Time _____

Time
by zone **1**   **2**   **3**   **4**   **5**

Workout rating _____

Notes _____

_____

RACE:

	Distance	Time	Place *(overall/division)*
Swim			
Tran 1	—		
Bike			
Tran 2	—		
Run			
Finish	—		

Notes _____

_____

WEEKLY SUMMARY

	Time/dist.	Year to date
Swim		
Bike		
Run		
Strength		

Weekly
total _____   Year-to-date
total _____

Soreness _____

Notes _____

_____

197

WEEK BEGINNING: _____ **PLANNED WEEKLY HOURS:** _____

Week's goals (check off as achieved)

▨ _____

▨ _____

▨ _____

MONDAY	/	/

▨ Sleep ▨ Fatigue ▨ Stress ▨ Soreness

Resting heart rate _____ Weight _____

Workout 1

S   B   R   O _____

Duration _____ Weather _____

Route _____

_____

Distance _____ Time _____

Time
by zone **1   2   3   4   5**

Workout rating _____

Notes _____

_____

Workout 2

S   B   R   O _____

Duration _____ Weather _____

Route _____

_____

Distance _____ Time _____

Time
by zone **1   2   3   4   5**

Workout rating _____

Notes _____

_____

TUESDAY	/	/

▨ Sleep ▨ Fatigue ▨ Stress ▨ Soreness

Resting heart rate _____ Weight _____

Workout 1

S   B   R   O _____

Duration _____ Weather _____

Route _____

_____

Distance _____ Time _____

Time
by zone **1   2   3   4   5**

Workout rating _____

Notes _____

_____

Workout 2

S   B   R   O _____

Duration _____ Weather _____

Route _____

_____

Distance _____ Time _____

Time
by zone **1   2   3   4   5**

Workout rating _____

Notes _____

_____

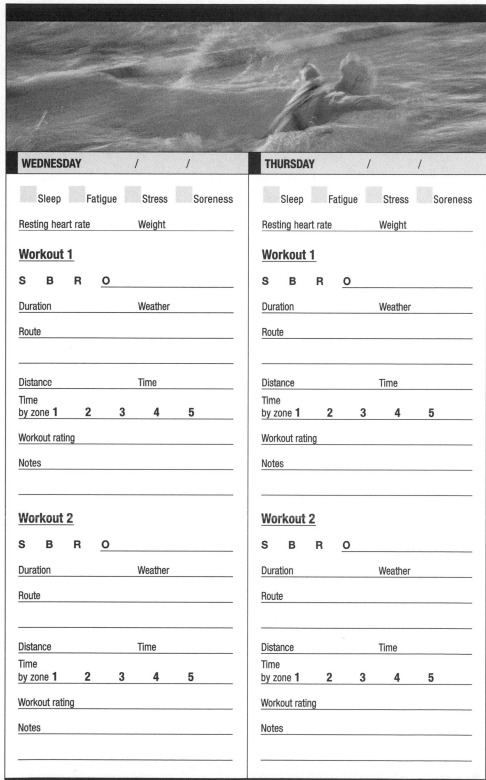

WEDNESDAY   /   /

■ Sleep   ■ Fatigue   ■ Stress   ■ Soreness

Resting heart rate _____ Weight _____

Workout 1

S   B   R   O _____

Duration _____ Weather _____

Route _____

_____

Distance _____ Time _____

Time
by zone 1   2   3   4   5

Workout rating _____

Notes _____

_____

Workout 2

S   B   R   O _____

Duration _____ Weather _____

Route _____

_____

Distance _____ Time _____

Time
by zone 1   2   3   4   5

Workout rating _____

Notes _____

_____

THURSDAY   /   /

■ Sleep   ■ Fatigue   ■ Stress   ■ Soreness

Resting heart rate _____ Weight _____

Workout 1

S   B   R   O _____

Duration _____ Weather _____

Route _____

_____

Distance _____ Time _____

Time
by zone 1   2   3   4   5

Workout rating _____

Notes _____

_____

Workout 2

S   B   R   O _____

Duration _____ Weather _____

Route _____

_____

Distance _____ Time _____

Time
by zone 1   2   3   4   5

Workout rating _____

Notes _____

_____

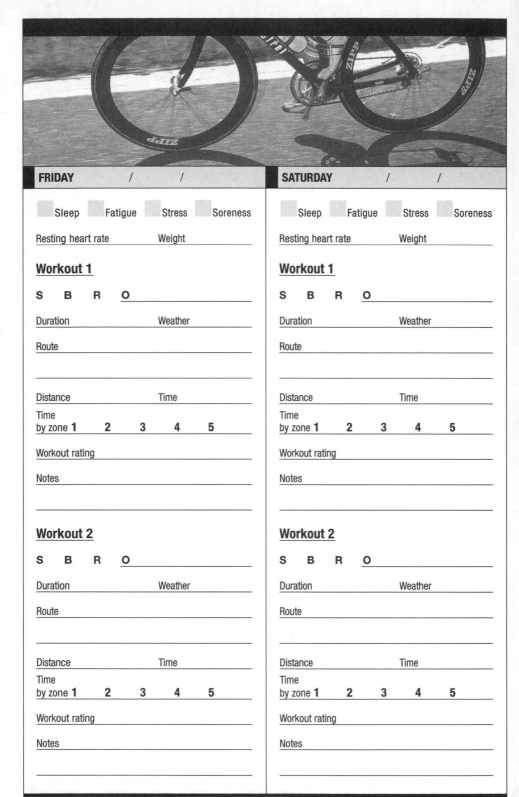

FRIDAY / /

Sleep Fatigue Stress Soreness

Resting heart rate   Weight

Workout 1

S   B   R   O

Duration   Weather

Route

Distance   Time

Time
by zone 1   2   3   4   5

Workout rating

Notes

Workout 2

S   B   R   O

Duration   Weather

Route

Distance   Time

Time
by zone 1   2   3   4   5

Workout rating

Notes

SATURDAY / /

Sleep Fatigue Stress Soreness

Resting heart rate   Weight

Workout 1

S   B   R   O

Duration   Weather

Route

Distance   Time

Time
by zone 1   2   3   4   5

Workout rating

Notes

Workout 2

S   B   R   O

Duration   Weather

Route

Distance   Time

Time
by zone 1   2   3   4   5

Workout rating

Notes

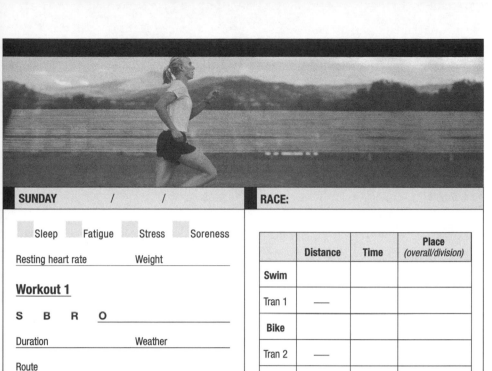

SUNDAY / /

Sleep   Fatigue   Stress   Soreness

Resting heart rate _____ Weight _____

Workout 1

S   B   R   O _____

Duration _____ Weather _____

Route _____

_____

Distance _____ Time _____

Time
by zone **1**   **2**   **3**   **4**   **5**

Workout rating _____

Notes _____

_____

Workout 2

S   B   R   O _____

Duration _____ Weather _____

Route _____

_____

Distance _____ Time _____

Time
by zone **1**   **2**   **3**   **4**   **5**

Workout rating _____

Notes _____

_____

RACE: _____

	Distance	Time	Place (overall/division)
Swim			
Tran 1	—		
Bike			
Tran 2	—		
Run			
Finish	—		

Notes _____

_____

WEEKLY SUMMARY

	Time/dist.	Year to date
Swim		
Bike		
Run		
Strength		

Weekly total _____   Year-to-date total _____

Soreness _____

Notes _____

_____

WEEK BEGINNING: **PLANNED WEEKLY HOURS:**

Week's goals (check off as achieved)

☐ _____

☐ _____

☐ _____

MONDAY / /	**TUESDAY** / /

☐ Sleep ☐ Fatigue ☐ Stress ☐ Soreness   ☐ Sleep ☐ Fatigue ☐ Stress ☐ Soreness

Resting heart rate _____ Weight _____   Resting heart rate _____ Weight _____

Workout 1

S   B   R   O _____

Duration _____ Weather _____

Route _____

_____

Distance _____ Time _____

Time by zone **1**   **2**   **3**   **4**   **5**

Workout rating _____

Notes _____

_____

Workout 2

S   B   R   O _____

Duration _____ Weather _____

Route _____

_____

Distance _____ Time _____

Time by zone **1**   **2**   **3**   **4**   **5**

Workout rating _____

Notes _____

_____

Workout 1

S   B   R   O _____

Duration _____ Weather _____

Route _____

_____

Distance _____ Time _____

Time by zone **1**   **2**   **3**   **4**   **5**

Workout rating _____

Notes _____

_____

Workout 2

S   B   R   O _____

Duration _____ Weather _____

Route _____

_____

Distance _____ Time _____

Time by zone **1**   **2**   **3**   **4**   **5**

Workout rating _____

Notes _____

_____

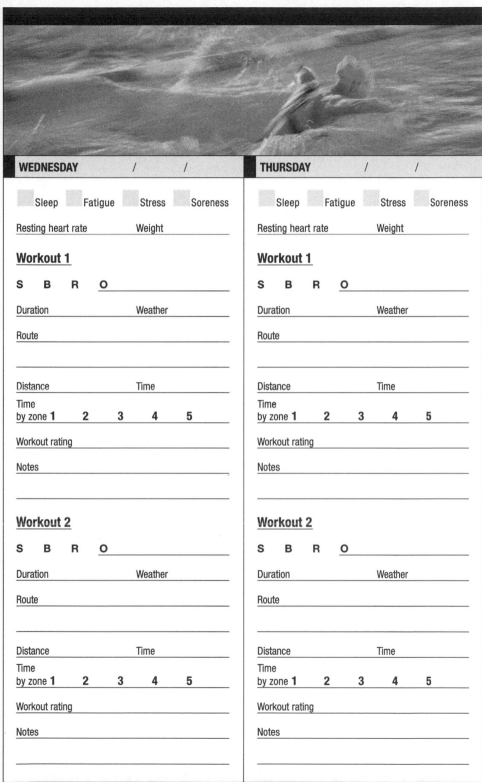

WEDNESDAY	/	/

Sleep Fatigue Stress Soreness

Resting heart rate _____ Weight _____

Workout 1

S   B   R   O _____

Duration _____ Weather _____

Route _____

_____

Distance _____ Time _____

Time
by zone **1   2   3   4   5**

Workout rating _____

Notes _____

_____

Workout 2

S   B   R   O _____

Duration _____ Weather _____

Route _____

_____

Distance _____ Time _____

Time
by zone **1   2   3   4   5**

Workout rating _____

Notes _____

_____

THURSDAY	/	/

Sleep Fatigue Stress Soreness

Resting heart rate _____ Weight _____

Workout 1

S   B   R   O _____

Duration _____ Weather _____

Route _____

_____

Distance _____ Time _____

Time
by zone **1   2   3   4   5**

Workout rating _____

Notes _____

_____

Workout 2

S   B   R   O _____

Duration _____ Weather _____

Route _____

_____

Distance _____ Time _____

Time
by zone **1   2   3   4   5**

Workout rating _____

Notes _____

_____

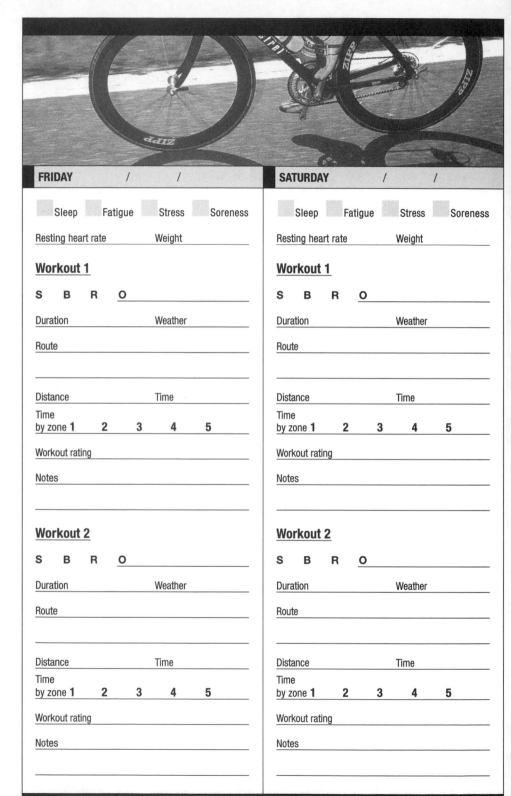

FRIDAY   /   /

Sleep   Fatigue   Stress   Soreness

Resting heart rate _____ Weight _____

Workout 1

S   B   R   O _____

Duration _____ Weather _____

Route _____

_____

Distance _____ Time _____

Time
by zone **1   2   3   4   5**

Workout rating _____

Notes _____

_____

Workout 2

S   B   R   O _____

Duration _____ Weather _____

Route _____

_____

Distance _____ Time _____

Time
by zone **1   2   3   4   5**

Workout rating _____

Notes _____

_____

SATURDAY   /   /

Sleep   Fatigue   Stress   Soreness

Resting heart rate _____ Weight _____

Workout 1

S   B   R   O _____

Duration _____ Weather _____

Route _____

_____

Distance _____ Time _____

Time
by zone **1   2   3   4   5**

Workout rating _____

Notes _____

_____

Workout 2

S   B   R   O _____

Duration _____ Weather _____

Route _____

_____

Distance _____ Time _____

Time
by zone **1   2   3   4   5**

Workout rating _____

Notes _____

_____

SUNDAY   /   /

■ Sleep   ■ Fatigue   ■ Stress   ■ Soreness

Resting heart rate _____   Weight _____

Workout 1

S   B   R   O _____

Duration _____   Weather _____

Route _____

_____

Distance _____   Time _____

Time
by zone **1   2   3   4   5**

Workout rating _____

Notes _____

_____

Workout 2

S   B   R   O _____

Duration _____   Weather _____

Route _____

_____

Distance _____   Time _____

Time
by zone **1   2   3   4   5**

Workout rating _____

Notes _____

_____

RACE: _____

	Distance	Time	Place *(overall/division)*
Swim			
Tran 1	—		
Bike			
Tran 2	—		
Run			
Finish	—		

Notes _____

_____

WEEKLY SUMMARY

	Time/dist.	Year to date
Swim		
Bike		
Run		
Strength		

Weekly
total _____   Year-to-date
total _____

Soreness _____

Notes _____

_____

WEEK BEGINNING:　　　　　　　　**PLANNED WEEKLY HOURS:**

Week's goals (check off as achieved)

☐ _____

☐ _____

☐ _____

MONDAY / /	**TUESDAY** / /

☐ Sleep　☐ Fatigue　☐ Stress　☐ Soreness

Resting heart rate _____ Weight _____

Workout 1

S　　B　　R　　O _____

Duration _____ Weather _____

Route _____

_____

Distance _____ Time _____

Time
by zone **1**　**2**　**3**　**4**　**5**

Workout rating _____

Notes _____

_____

Workout 2

S　　B　　R　　O _____

Duration _____ Weather _____

Route _____

_____

Distance _____ Time _____

Time
by zone **1**　**2**　**3**　**4**　**5**

Workout rating _____

Notes _____

_____

☐ Sleep　☐ Fatigue　☐ Stress　☐ Soreness

Resting heart rate _____ Weight _____

Workout 1

S　　B　　R　　O _____

Duration _____ Weather _____

Route _____

_____

Distance _____ Time _____

Time
by zone **1**　**2**　**3**　**4**　**5**

Workout rating _____

Notes _____

_____

Workout 2

S　　B　　R　　O _____

Duration _____ Weather _____

Route _____

_____

Distance _____ Time _____

Time
by zone **1**　**2**　**3**　**4**　**5**

Workout rating _____

Notes _____

_____

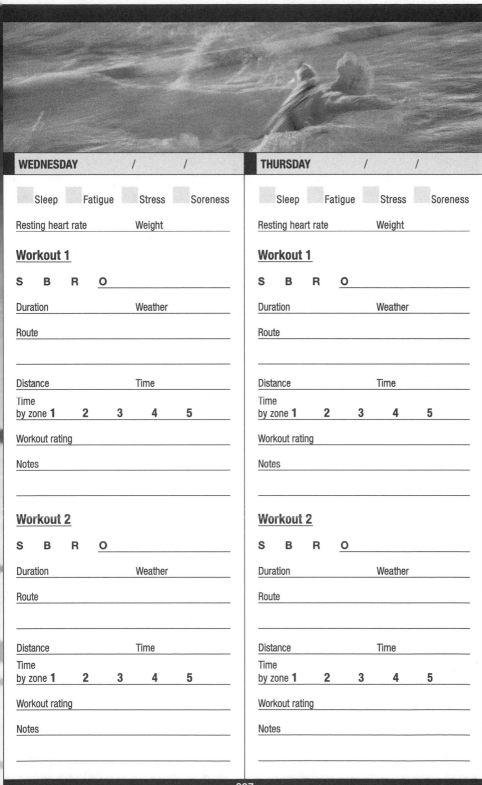

WEDNESDAY	/	/

▢ Sleep ▢ Fatigue ▢ Stress ▢ Soreness

Resting heart rate _____ Weight _____

Workout 1

S   B   R   O _____

Duration _____ Weather _____

Route _____

_____

Distance _____ Time _____

Time
by zone **1   2   3   4   5**

Workout rating _____

Notes _____

_____

Workout 2

S   B   R   O _____

Duration _____ Weather _____

Route _____

_____

Distance _____ Time _____

Time
by zone **1   2   3   4   5**

Workout rating _____

Notes _____

_____

THURSDAY	/	/

▢ Sleep ▢ Fatigue ▢ Stress ▢ Soreness

Resting heart rate _____ Weight _____

Workout 1

S   B   R   O _____

Duration _____ Weather _____

Route _____

_____

Distance _____ Time _____

Time
by zone **1   2   3   4   5**

Workout rating _____

Notes _____

_____

Workout 2

S   B   R   O _____

Duration _____ Weather _____

Route _____

_____

Distance _____ Time _____

Time
by zone **1   2   3   4   5**

Workout rating _____

Notes _____

_____

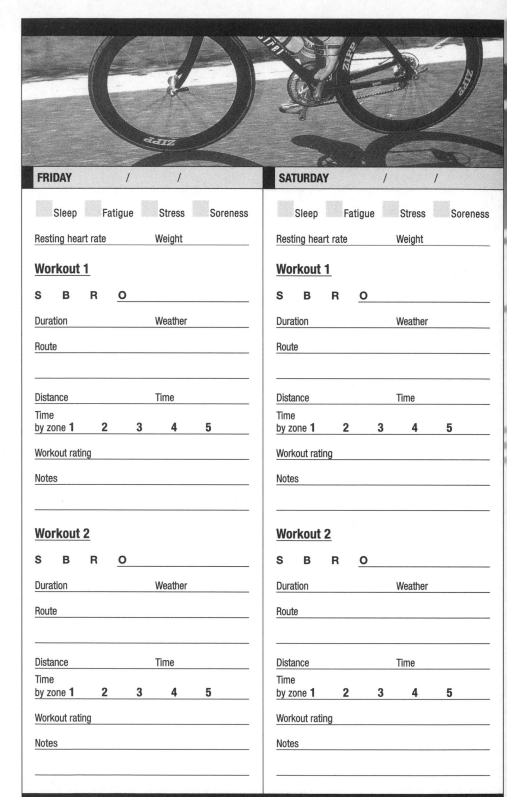

FRIDAY	/	/

Sleep　Fatigue　Stress　Soreness

Resting heart rate _____ Weight _____

Workout 1

S　B　R　O _____

Duration _____ Weather _____

Route _____

_____

Distance _____ Time _____

Time
by zone **1　2　3　4　5** _____

Workout rating _____

Notes _____

_____

Workout 2

S　B　R　O _____

Duration _____ Weather _____

Route _____

_____

Distance _____ Time _____

Time
by zone **1　2　3　4　5** _____

Workout rating _____

Notes _____

_____

SATURDAY	/	/

Sleep　Fatigue　Stress　Soreness

Resting heart rate _____ Weight _____

Workout 1

S　B　R　O _____

Duration _____ Weather _____

Route _____

_____

Distance _____ Time _____

Time
by zone **1　2　3　4　5** _____

Workout rating _____

Notes _____

_____

Workout 2

S　B　R　O _____

Duration _____ Weather _____

Route _____

_____

Distance _____ Time _____

Time
by zone **1　2　3　4　5** _____

Workout rating _____

Notes _____

_____

SUNDAY / /

Resting heart rate _____ Weight _____

Workout 1

S   B   R   O _____

Duration _____ Weather _____

Route _____

Distance _____ Time _____

Time
by zone **1   2   3   4   5**

Workout rating _____

Notes _____

Workout 2

S   B   R   O _____

Duration _____ Weather _____

Route _____

Distance _____ Time _____

Time
by zone **1   2   3   4   5**

Workout rating _____

Notes _____

RACE:

	Distance	Time	Place (overall/division)
Swim			
Tran 1	—		
Bike			
Tran 2	—		
Run			
Finish	—		

Notes _____

WEEKLY SUMMARY

	Time/dist.	Year to date
Swim		
Bike		
Run		
Strength		

Weekly total _____ Year-to-date total _____

Soreness _____

Notes _____

WEEK BEGINNING: **PLANNED WEEKLY HOURS:**

Week's goals (check off as achieved)

☐ _____

☐ _____

☐ _____

MONDAY / /	TUESDAY / /

☐ Sleep ☐ Fatigue ☐ Stress ☐ Soreness

Resting heart rate _____ Weight _____

Workout 1

S   B   R   O _____

Duration _____ Weather _____

Route _____

_____

Distance _____ Time _____

Time
by zone **1**   **2**   **3**   **4**   **5**

Workout rating _____

Notes _____

_____

Workout 2

S   B   R   O _____

Duration _____ Weather _____

Route _____

_____

Distance _____ Time _____

Time
by zone **1**   **2**   **3**   **4**   **5**

Workout rating _____

Notes _____

_____

☐ Sleep ☐ Fatigue ☐ Stress ☐ Soreness

Resting heart rate _____ Weight _____

Workout 1

S   B   R   O _____

Duration _____ Weather _____

Route _____

_____

Distance _____ Time _____

Time
by zone **1**   **2**   **3**   **4**   **5**

Workout rating _____

Notes _____

_____

Workout 2

S   B   R   O _____

Duration _____ Weather _____

Route _____

_____

Distance _____ Time _____

Time
by zone **1**   **2**   **3**   **4**   **5**

Workout rating _____

Notes _____

_____

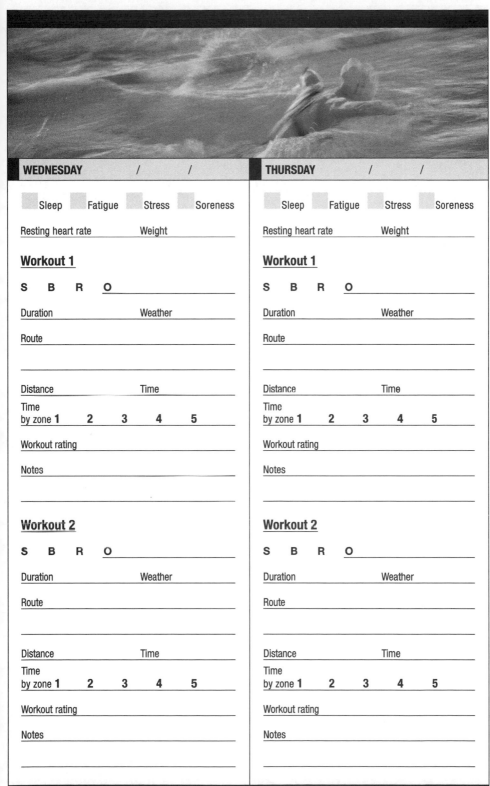

WEDNESDAY	/	/

Sleep Fatigue Stress Soreness

Resting heart rate _____ Weight _____

Workout 1

S   B   R   O _____

Duration _____ Weather _____

Route _____

_____

Distance _____ Time _____

Time
by zone **1   2   3   4   5**

Workout rating _____

Notes _____

_____

Workout 2

S   B   R   O _____

Duration _____ Weather _____

Route _____

_____

Distance _____ Time _____

Time
by zone **1   2   3   4   5**

Workout rating _____

Notes _____

_____

THURSDAY	/	/

Sleep Fatigue Stress Soreness

Resting heart rate _____ Weight _____

Workout 1

S   B   R   O _____

Duration _____ Weather _____

Route _____

_____

Distance _____ Time _____

Time
by zone **1   2   3   4   5**

Workout rating _____

Notes _____

_____

Workout 2

S   B   R   O _____

Duration _____ Weather _____

Route _____

_____

Distance _____ Time _____

Time
by zone **1   2   3   4   5**

Workout rating _____

Notes _____

_____

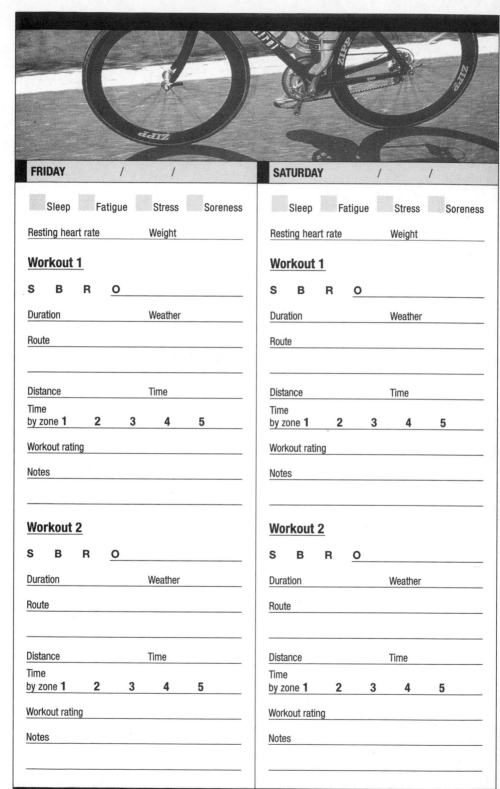

Sleep   Fatigue   Stress   Soreness

Resting heart rate   Weight

Workout 1

S   B   R   O

Duration   Weather

Route

Distance   Time

Time
by zone 1   2   3   4   5

Workout rating

Notes

Workout 2

S   B   R   O

Duration   Weather

Route

Distance   Time

Time
by zone 1   2   3   4   5

Workout rating

Notes

Sleep   Fatigue   Stress   Soreness

Resting heart rate   Weight

Workout 1

S   B   R   O

Duration   Weather

Route

Distance   Time

Time
by zone 1   2   3   4   5

Workout rating

Notes

Workout 2

S   B   R   O

Duration   Weather

Route

Distance   Time

Time
by zone 1   2   3   4   5

Workout rating

Notes

SUNDAY / /

◻ Sleep ◻ Fatigue ◻ Stress ◻ Soreness

Resting heart rate _____ Weight _____

Workout 1

S   B   R   O   _____

Duration _____   Weather _____

Route _____

_____

Distance _____   Time _____

Time
by zone **1**   **2**   **3**   **4**   **5**

Workout rating _____

Notes _____

_____

Workout 2

S   B   R   O   _____

Duration _____   Weather _____

Route _____

_____

Distance _____   Time _____

Time
by zone **1**   **2**   **3**   **4**   **5**

Workout rating _____

Notes _____

_____

RACE: _____

	Distance	Time	Place *(overall/division)*
Swim			
Tran 1	—		
Bike			
Tran 2	—		
Run			
Finish	—		

Notes _____

_____

WEEKLY SUMMARY

	Time/dist.	Year to date
Swim		
Bike		
Run		
Strength		

Weekly total _____   Year-to-date total _____

Soreness _____

Notes _____

_____

WEEK BEGINNING: **PLANNED WEEKLY HOURS:**

Week's goals (check off as achieved)

☐ _____

☐ _____

☐ _____

| **MONDAY**   /   / | **TUESDAY**   /   / |

☐ Sleep ☐ Fatigue ☐ Stress ☐ Soreness   ☐ Sleep ☐ Fatigue ☐ Stress ☐ Soreness

Resting heart rate _____ Weight _____   Resting heart rate _____ Weight _____

Workout 1

S   B   R   O _____

Duration _____ Weather _____

Route _____

_____

Distance _____ Time _____

Time
by zone **1   2   3   4   5**

Workout rating _____

Notes _____

_____

Workout 2

S   B   R   O _____

Duration _____ Weather _____

Route _____

_____

Distance _____ Time _____

Time
by zone **1   2   3   4   5**

Workout rating _____

Notes _____

_____

Workout 1

S   B   R   O _____

Duration _____ Weather _____

Route _____

_____

Distance _____ Time _____

Time
by zone **1   2   3   4   5**

Workout rating _____

Notes _____

_____

Workout 2

S   B   R   O _____

Duration _____ Weather _____

Route _____

_____

Distance _____ Time _____

Time
by zone **1   2   3   4   5**

Workout rating _____

Notes _____

_____

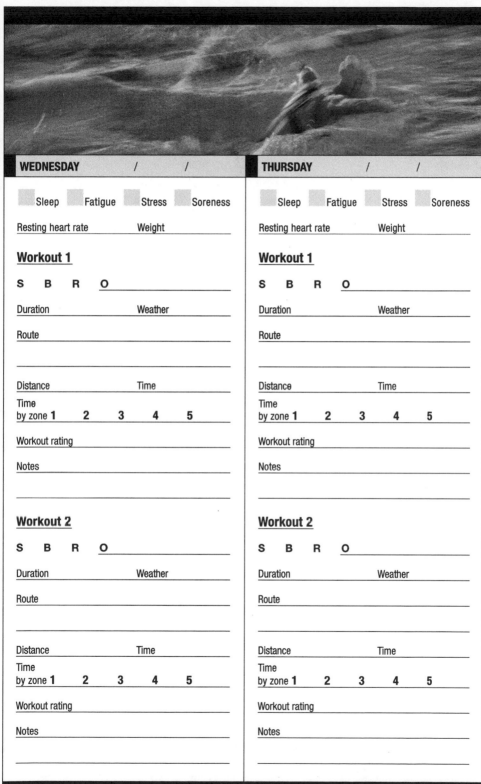

WEDNESDAY   /   /

Sleep   Fatigue   Stress   Soreness

Resting heart rate _____   Weight _____

Workout 1

S   B   R   O _____

Duration _____   Weather _____

Route _____

_____

Distance _____   Time _____

Time
by zone **1   2   3   4   5**

Workout rating _____

Notes _____

_____

Workout 2

S   B   R   O _____

Duration _____   Weather _____

Route _____

_____

Distance _____   Time _____

Time
by zone **1   2   3   4   5**

Workout rating _____

Notes _____

_____

THURSDAY   /   /

Sleep   Fatigue   Stress   Soreness

Resting heart rate _____   Weight _____

Workout 1

S   B   R   O _____

Duration _____   Weather _____

Route _____

_____

Distance _____   Time _____

Time
by zone **1   2   3   4   5**

Workout rating _____

Notes _____

_____

Workout 2

S   B   R   O _____

Duration _____   Weather _____

Route _____

_____

Distance _____   Time _____

Time
by zone **1   2   3   4   5**

Workout rating _____

Notes _____

_____

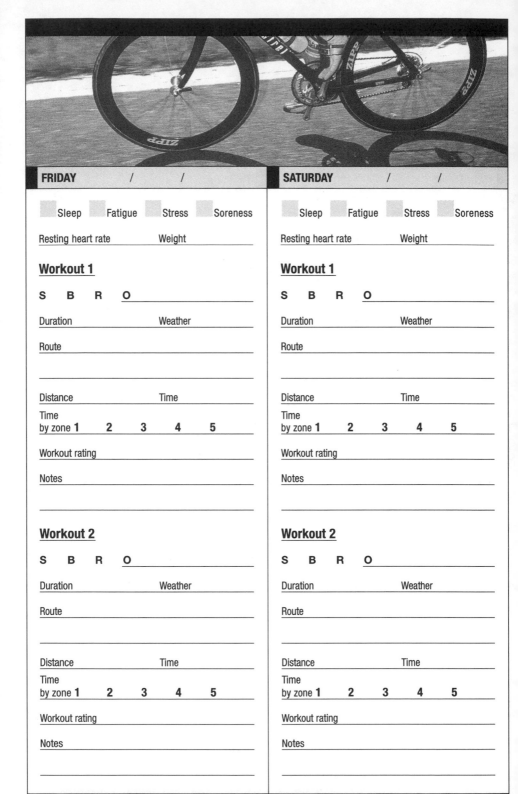

FRIDAY   /   /

Sleep   Fatigue   Stress   Soreness

Resting heart rate _____   Weight _____

Workout 1

S   B   R   O _____

Duration _____   Weather _____

Route _____
_____

Distance _____   Time _____

Time
by zone 1   2   3   4   5

Workout rating _____

Notes _____
_____

Workout 2

S   B   R   O _____

Duration _____   Weather _____

Route _____
_____

Distance _____   Time _____

Time
by zone 1   2   3   4   5

Workout rating _____

Notes _____
_____

SATURDAY   /   /

Sleep   Fatigue   Stress   Soreness

Resting heart rate _____   Weight _____

Workout 1

S   B   R   O _____

Duration _____   Weather _____

Route _____
_____

Distance _____   Time _____

Time
by zone 1   2   3   4   5

Workout rating _____

Notes _____
_____

Workout 2

S   B   R   O _____

Duration _____   Weather _____

Route _____
_____

Distance _____   Time _____

Time
by zone 1   2   3   4   5

Workout rating _____

Notes _____
_____

Sleep   Fatigue   Stress   Soreness

Resting heart rate   Weight

Workout 1

S   B   R   O

Duration   Weather

Route

Distance   Time

Time
by zone 1   2   3   4   5

Workout rating

Notes

Workout 2

S   B   R   O

Duration   Weather

Route

Distance   Time

Time
by zone 1   2   3   4   5

Workout rating

Notes

RACE:

	Distance	Time	Place *(overall/division)*
Swim			
Tran 1	—		
Bike			
Tran 2	—		
Run			
Finish	—		

Notes

WEEKLY SUMMARY

	Time/dist.	Year to date
Swim		
Bike		
Run		
Strength		

Weekly   Year-to-date
total   total

Soreness

Notes

WEEK BEGINNING: **PLANNED WEEKLY HOURS:**

Week's goals (check off as achieved)

☐ _____

☐ _____

☐ _____

| MONDAY   /   / | TUESDAY   /   / |

☐ Sleep ☐ Fatigue ☐ Stress ☐ Soreness

Resting heart rate _____ Weight _____

Workout 1

S   B   R   O _____

Duration _____ Weather _____

Route _____

_____

Distance _____ Time _____

Time
by zone **1   2   3   4   5**

Workout rating _____

Notes _____

_____

Workout 2

S   B   R   O _____

Duration _____ Weather _____

Route _____

_____

Distance _____ Time _____

Time
by zone **1   2   3   4   5**

Workout rating _____

Notes _____

_____

☐ Sleep ☐ Fatigue ☐ Stress ☐ Soreness

Resting heart rate _____ Weight _____

Workout 1

S   B   R   O _____

Duration _____ Weather _____

Route _____

_____

Distance _____ Time _____

Time
by zone **1   2   3   4   5**

Workout rating _____

Notes _____

_____

Workout 2

S   B   R   O _____

Duration _____ Weather _____

Route _____

_____

Distance _____ Time _____

Time
by zone **1   2   3   4   5**

Workout rating _____

Notes _____

_____

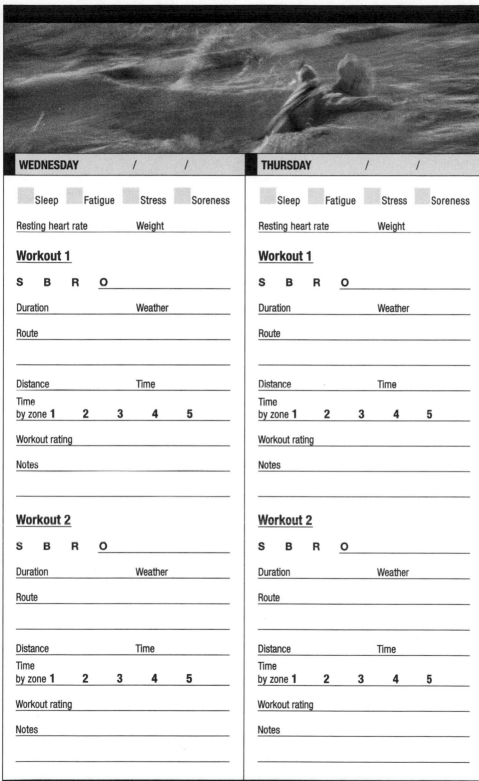

WEDNESDAY	/	/

Sleep   Fatigue   Stress   Soreness

Resting heart rate _____   Weight _____

Workout 1

S   B   R   O _____

Duration _____   Weather _____

Route _____

_____

Distance _____   Time _____

Time
by zone **1   2   3   4   5**

Workout rating _____

Notes _____

Workout 2

S   B   R   O _____

Duration _____   Weather _____

Route _____

_____

Distance _____   Time _____

Time
by zone **1   2   3   4   5**

Workout rating _____

Notes _____

THURSDAY	/	/

Sleep   Fatigue   Stress   Soreness

Resting heart rate _____   Weight _____

Workout 1

S   B   R   O _____

Duration _____   Weather _____

Route _____

_____

Distance _____   Time _____

Time
by zone **1   2   3   4   5**

Workout rating _____

Notes _____

Workout 2

S   B   R   O _____

Duration _____   Weather _____

Route _____

_____

Distance _____   Time _____

Time
by zone **1   2   3   4   5**

Workout rating _____

Notes _____

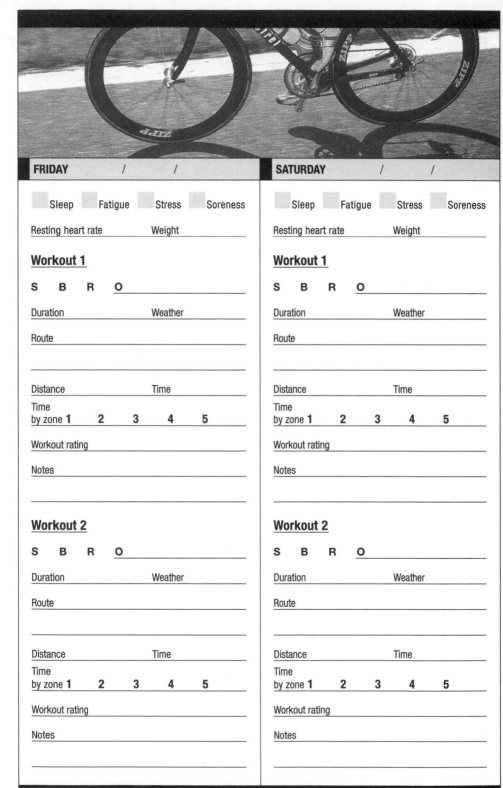

FRIDAY   /   /

Sleep   Fatigue   Stress   Soreness

Resting heart rate _____ Weight _____

Workout 1

S   B   R   O _____

Duration _____ Weather _____

Route _____

_____

Distance _____ Time _____

Time
by zone **1   2   3   4   5**

Workout rating _____

Notes _____

_____

Workout 2

S   B   R   O _____

Duration _____ Weather _____

Route _____

_____

Distance _____ Time _____

Time
by zone **1   2   3   4   5**

Workout rating _____

Notes _____

_____

SATURDAY   /   /

Sleep   Fatigue   Stress   Soreness

Resting heart rate _____ Weight _____

Workout 1

S   B   R   O _____

Duration _____ Weather _____

Route _____

_____

Distance _____ Time _____

Time
by zone **1   2   3   4   5**

Workout rating _____

Notes _____

_____

Workout 2

S   B   R   O _____

Duration _____ Weather _____

Route _____

_____

Distance _____ Time _____

Time
by zone **1   2   3   4   5**

Workout rating _____

Notes _____

_____

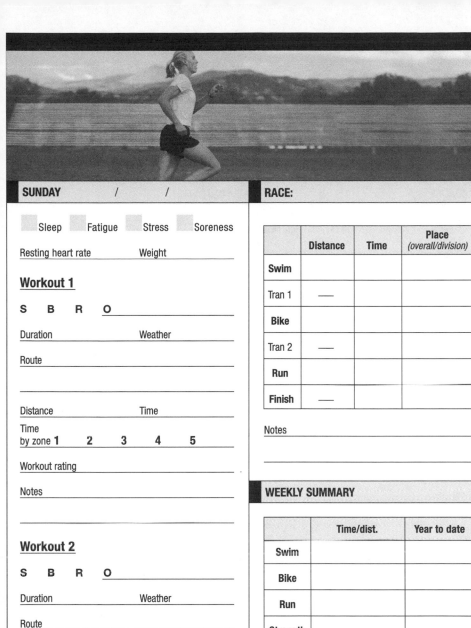

Sleep   Fatigue   Stress   Soreness

Resting heart rate _____ Weight _____

Workout 1

S   B   R   O _____

Duration _____ Weather _____

Route _____

_____

Distance _____ Time _____

Time
by zone **1   2   3   4   5**

Workout rating _____

Notes _____

_____

Workout 2

S   B   R   O _____

Duration _____ Weather _____

Route _____

_____

Distance _____ Time _____

Time
by zone **1   2   3   4   5**

Workout rating _____

Notes _____

_____

RACE:

	Distance	Time	Place *(overall/division)*
Swim			
Tran 1	—		
Bike			
Tran 2	—		
Run			
Finish	—		

Notes _____

_____

WEEKLY SUMMARY

	Time/dist.	Year to date
Swim		
Bike		
Run		
Strength		

Weekly   Year-to-date
total   total
_____

Soreness _____

Notes _____

_____

WEEK BEGINNING: **PLANNED WEEKLY HOURS:**

Week's goals (check off as achieved)

☐ _____

☐ _____

☐ _____

MONDAY   /   /

☐ Sleep ☐ Fatigue ☐ Stress ☐ Soreness

Resting heart rate _____ Weight _____

Workout 1

S   B   R   O _____

Duration _____ Weather _____

Route _____

_____

Distance _____ Time _____

Time
by zone **1   2   3   4   5**

Workout rating _____

Notes _____

_____

Workout 2

S   B   R   O _____

Duration _____ Weather _____

Route _____

_____

Distance _____ Time _____

Time
by zone **1   2   3   4   5**

Workout rating _____

Notes _____

_____

TUESDAY   /   /

☐ Sleep ☐ Fatigue ☐ Stress ☐ Soreness

Resting heart rate _____ Weight _____

Workout 1

S   B   R   O _____

Duration _____ Weather _____

Route _____

_____

Distance _____ Time _____

Time
by zone **1   2   3   4   5**

Workout rating _____

Notes _____

_____

Workout 2

S   B   R   O _____

Duration _____ Weather _____

Route _____

_____

Distance _____ Time _____

Time
by zone **1   2   3   4   5**

Workout rating _____

Notes _____

_____

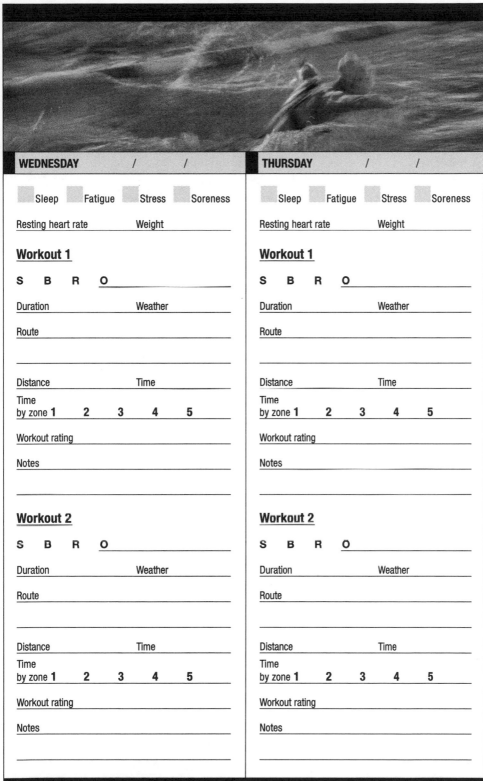

| WEDNESDAY | / | / |

☐ Sleep   ☐ Fatigue   ☐ Stress   ☐ Soreness

Resting heart rate _____   Weight _____

Workout 1

S   B   R   O _____

Duration _____   Weather _____

Route _____

_____

Distance _____   Time _____

Time
by zone **1   2   3   4   5**

Workout rating _____

Notes _____

_____

Workout 2

S   B   R   O _____

Duration _____   Weather _____

Route _____

_____

Distance _____   Time _____

Time
by zone **1   2   3   4   5**

Workout rating _____

Notes _____

_____

| THURSDAY | / | / |

☐ Sleep   ☐ Fatigue   ☐ Stress   ☐ Soreness

Resting heart rate _____   Weight _____

Workout 1

S   B   R   O _____

Duration _____   Weather _____

Route _____

_____

Distance _____   Time _____

Time
by zone **1   2   3   4   5**

Workout rating _____

Notes _____

_____

Workout 2

S   B   R   O _____

Duration _____   Weather _____

Route _____

_____

Distance _____   Time _____

Time
by zone **1   2   3   4   5**

Workout rating _____

Notes _____

_____

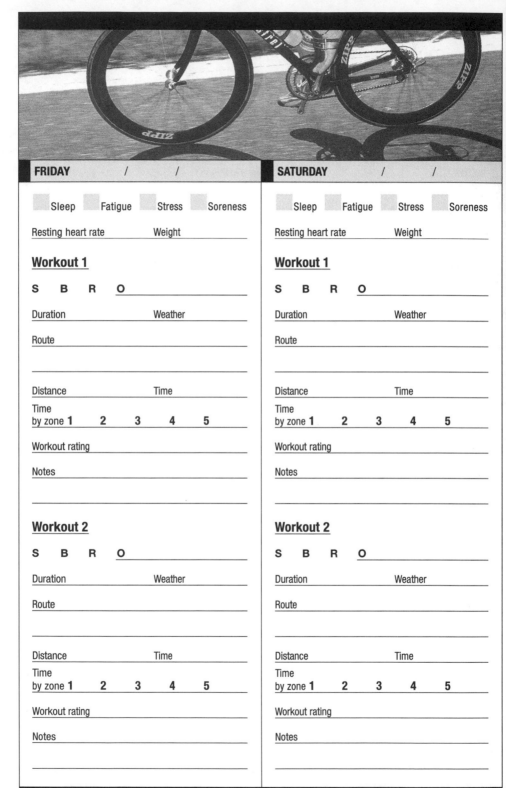

| FRIDAY | / | / | | SATURDAY | / | / |

Sleep   Fatigue   Stress   Soreness

Resting heart rate   Weight

Workout 1

S   B   R   O

Duration   Weather

Route

Distance   Time

Time
by zone **1   2   3   4   5**

Workout rating

Notes

Workout 2

S   B   R   O

Duration   Weather

Route

Distance   Time

Time
by zone **1   2   3   4   5**

Workout rating

Notes

Sleep   Fatigue   Stress   Soreness

Resting heart rate   Weight

Workout 1

S   B   R   O

Duration   Weather

Route

Distance   Time

Time
by zone **1   2   3   4   5**

Workout rating

Notes

Workout 2

S   B   R   O

Duration   Weather

Route

Distance   Time

Time
by zone **1   2   3   4   5**

Workout rating

Notes

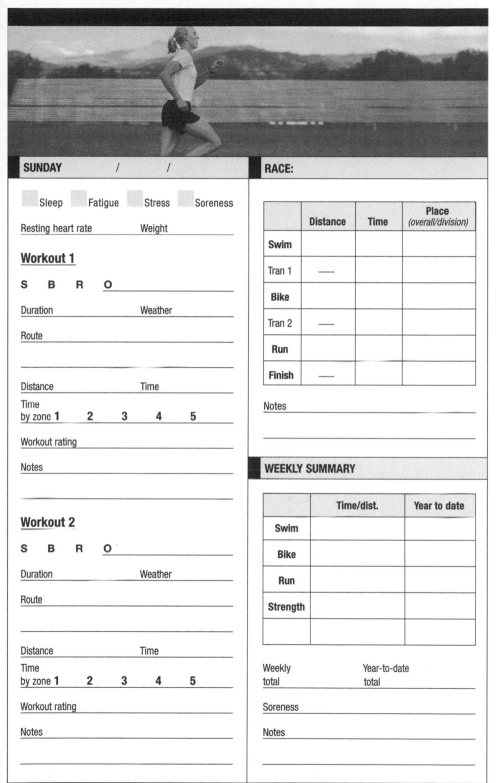

Sleep   Fatigue   Stress   Soreness

Resting heart rate   Weight

Workout 1

S   B   R   O

Duration   Weather

Route

Distance   Time

Time
by zone 1   2   3   4   5

Workout rating

Notes

Workout 2

S   B   R   O

Duration   Weather

Route

Distance   Time

Time
by zone 1   2   3   4   5

Workout rating

Notes

RACE:

	Distance	Time	Place *(overall/division)*
Swim			
Tran 1	—		
Bike			
Tran 2	—		
Run			
Finish	—		

Notes

WEEKLY SUMMARY

	Time/dist.	Year to date
Swim		
Bike		
Run		
Strength		

Weekly   Year-to-date
total   total

Soreness

Notes

MONTH

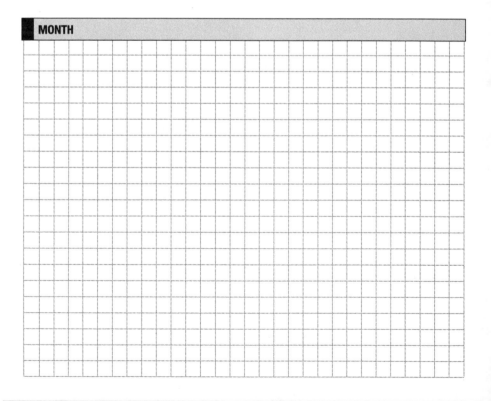

MONTH

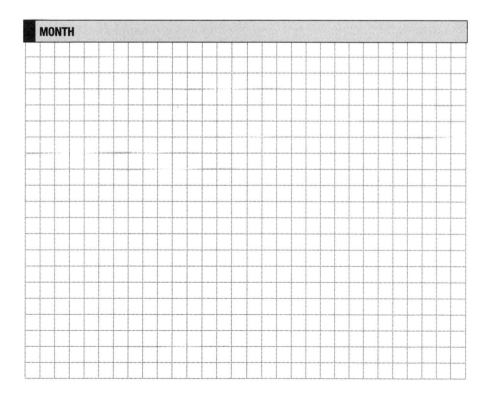

MONTH

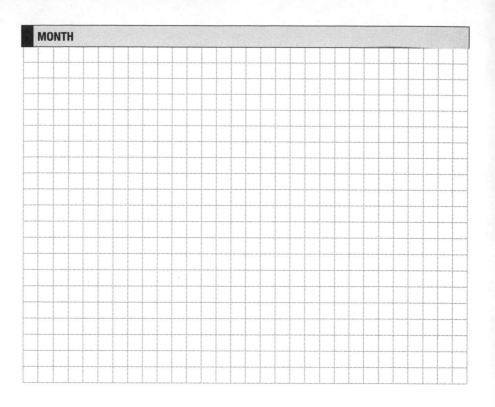

MONTH

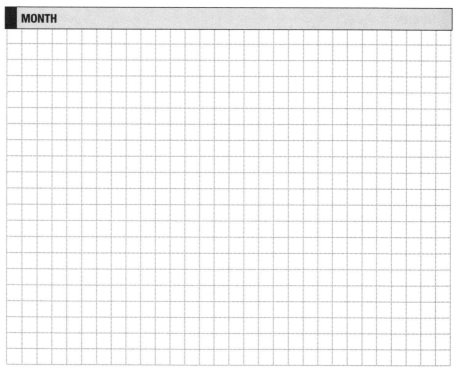

MONTH

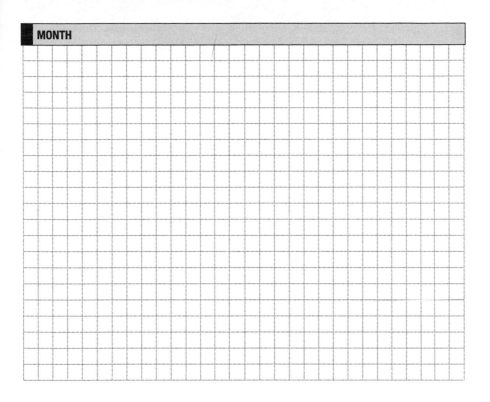

MONTH

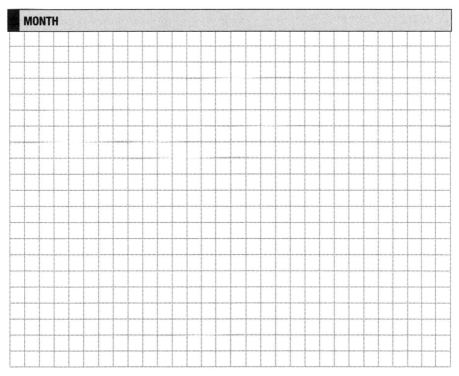

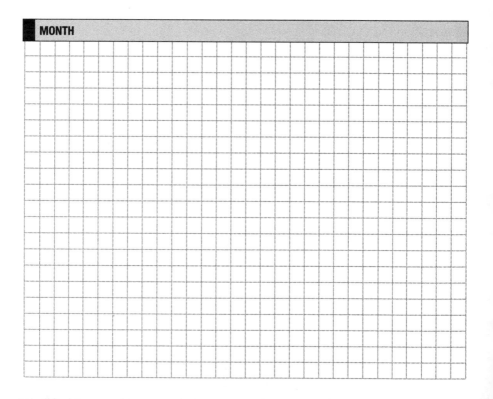

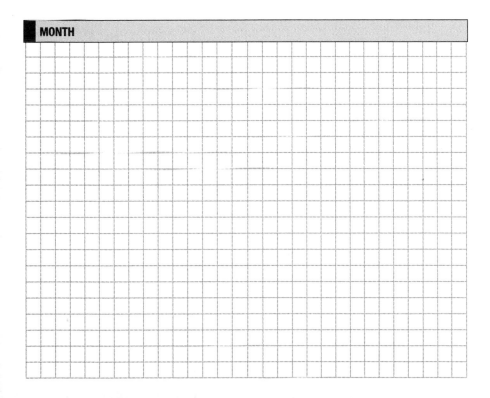

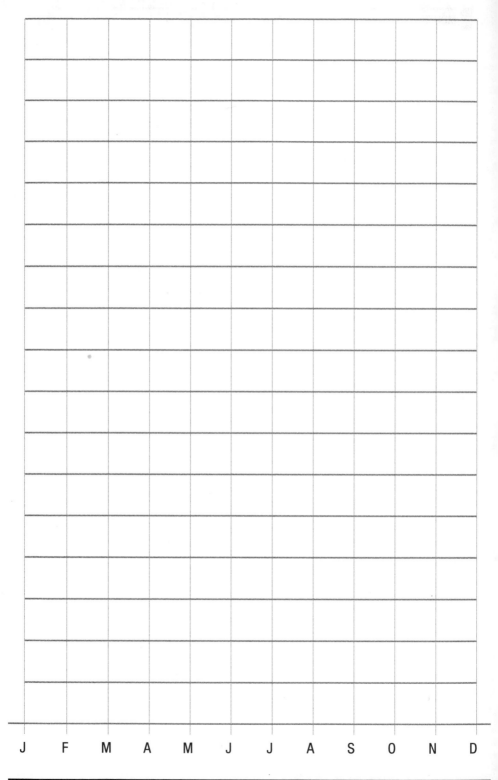

J   F   M   A   M   J   J   A   S   O   N   D

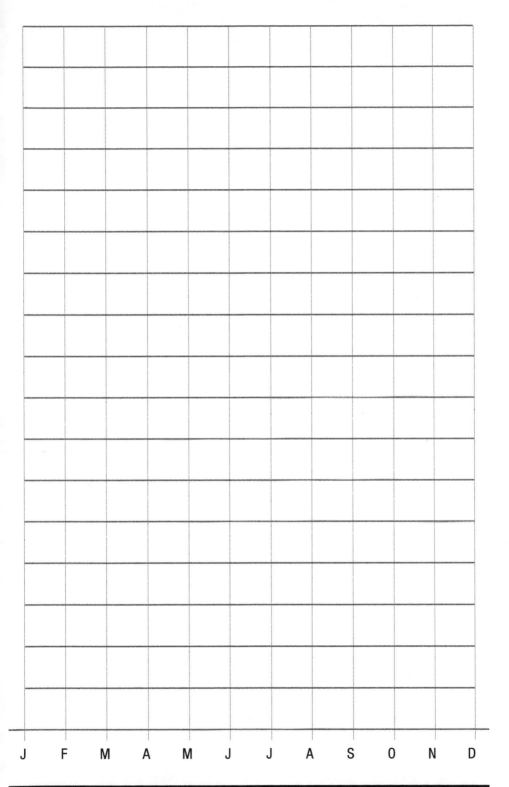

J F M A M J J A S O N D

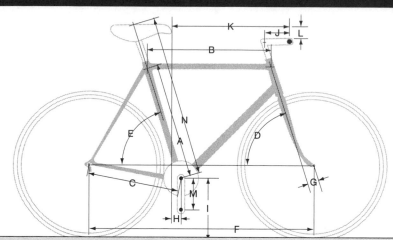

ROAD/TRACK BIKE MEASUREMENTS

A. Seat tube length

B. Top tube length

C. Chainstay length

D. Head angle

E. Seat angle

F. Wheelbase

G. Fork offset

H. Sear setback

I. Bottom bracket height

J. Stem length

K. Reach

L. Seat-to handlebar drop

M. Crank length

N. Seat height

Rear wheel spacing

Head tube diameter

Steering tube stack height

Seat tube diameter

Serial number

Date of purchase

• *Seat height is measured from the center of the bottom bracket to the top of the saddle. The distance from the rails to the top of the saddle is not the same for all seats, so if you change saddles, this dimension may change.*

• *Reach is measured from the nose of the saddle to the center of the bars. If you change saddles, remember that you may sit in a different position on the new saddle, and that may affect this dimension.*

• *Crank length is measured from the center of the bottom bracket to the center of the pedal spindle.*

• *Drop a weighted plumb line from the nose of the saddle to determine seat setback from the center of the bottom bracket.*

EQUIPMENT CHANGES

Date	Component	What was changed

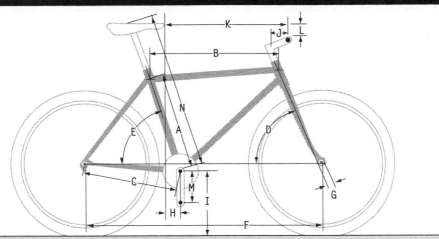

MOUNTAIN BIKE MEASUREMENTS

A. Seat tube length

B. Top tube length

C. Chainstay length

D. Head angle

E. Seat angle

F. Wheelbase

G. Fork offset

H. Sear setback

I. Bottom bracket height

J. Stem length

K. Reach

L. Seat-to handlebar drop

M. Crank length

N. Seat height

    Rear wheel spacing

    Head tube diameter

    Steering tube stack height

    Seat tube diameter

    Serial number

    Date of purchase

- *Seat height is measured from the center of the bottom bracket to the top of the saddle. The distance from the rails to the top of the saddle is not the same for all seats, so if you change saddles, this dimension may change.*

- *Reach is measured from the nose of the saddle to the center of the bars. If you change saddles, remember that you may sit in a different position on the new saddle, and that may affect this dimension.*

- *Crank length is measured from the center of the bottom bracket to the center of the pedal spindle.*

- *Drop a weighted plumb line from the nose of the saddle to determine seat setback from the center of the bottom bracket.*

EQUIPMENT CHANGES

Date	Component	What was changed

ROUTES AND BEST TIMES

Route	Date	Time

Date	Race	Distance	Place	Comments

RACE DAY CHECKLIST

To reduce pre-race stress and the possibility of forgetting an important item of clothing or equipment, please use this checklist before leaving the house for your race. Better yet, use it the night before. You may not need everything, but you'll be sure to have it if the need arises.

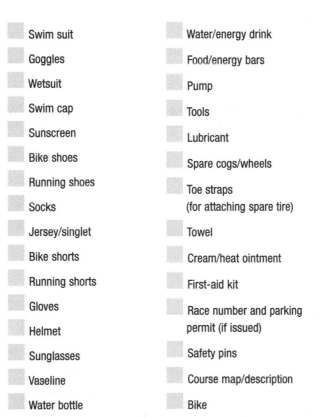

- Swim suit
- Goggles
- Wetsuit
- Swim cap
- Sunscreen
- Bike shoes
- Running shoes
- Socks
- Jersey/singlet
- Bike shorts
- Running shorts
- Gloves
- Helmet
- Sunglasses
- Vaseline
- Water bottle

- Water/energy drink
- Food/energy bars
- Pump
- Tools
- Lubricant
- Spare cogs/wheels
- Toe straps (for attaching spare tire)
- Towel
- Cream/heat ointment
- First-aid kit
- Race number and parking permit (if issued)
- Safety pins
- Course map/description
- Bike

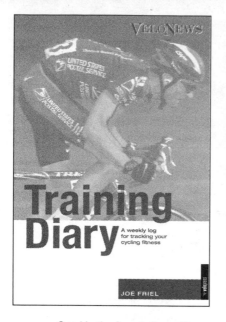

Send in the form below with your check or money order to receive your next training diary.

For faster service or to order with your VISA or MasterCard, call our toll-free number **800-234-8356**. You may fax your order to **303-444-6788** or email your order to Velo@insideinc.com. Check out our Web site for specials at www.velogear.com.

Name _____

Address _____

City _____ State _____ Zip _____

Daytime phone (____) _____

E-mail _____

QTY	ITEM	
	VeloNews Training Diary VP-DIN2 @ $12.95 each	$
	Inside Triathlon Training Diary VP-IDN2 @ $12.95 each	$
	Subtotal	$
	Sales Tax (Colorado residents add 2.9% sales tax)	$
	add $4.25 shipping and handling per item	$
	Total order	$

_____ Please send me a free Velo catalog